MARY SHELLEY'S EARLY NOVELS

Mary Shelley's Early Novels

'This Child of Imagination and Misery'

Jane Blumberg

University of Iowa Press, Iowa City

823
S54 zbLu Copyright © 1993 by Jane Blumberg

University of Iowa Press, Iowa City 52242

International Standard Book Number 0–87745–397–7

Library of Congress Catalog Card Number 92–61803

97 96 95 94 93 C 5 4 3 2 1

AL

Printed in Hong Kong

For my mother and father
Baruch and Jean Blumberg
with love and thanks

Contents

Preface

In its attempt to provide a thorough-going examination and evaluation of Mary Shelley's literary achievement, this book employs a range of different critical methods. I have used biography to shape the book and to illustrate the multifarious influences that impinged on Shelley's life as a writer. When discussing her contribution as an editor, and especially the work she did for Lord Byron, I have combined biographical context with selective textual criticism, paying particular attention to those extant manuscripts of *Don Juan* and other poems which she fair-copied for the poet. Finally, I have considered her central literary achievements – the three major novels *Frankenstein, Valperga* and *The Last Man* – from both a biographical and a critical standpoint; with the obvious exception of *Frankenstein*, the novels have attracted scant critical attention until now. I have tried to address this lack both in the case of *Valperga* and of *The Last Man*, by offering more detailed and wide-ranging interpretive criticism than either novel has received before.

Although I have stressed the biographical basis of much of this book, I must also make it clear that this is not a psychological study of Mary Shelley. This critical approach lies at the heart of many of the analyses of *Frankenstein* that have appeared in recent years, and has often led to what in my view is the central fallacy in contemporary Mary Shelley studies; namely the suggestion, whether stated or implied, that *Frankenstein* was a psychological fluke, produced under the influence of the powerful male creative forces around her (her husband Percy Shelley and father William Godwin). This study will seek to argue that the evidence, both biographical and critical, points in a quite different direction; to an independent artist of complexity and depth, whose intellectual development took place in contradistinction to those male forces, and whose own philosophy is clearly and triumphantly expressed in her three central novels.

Finally, a word about Mary and her attitude to her husband. A significant part of this book is about the intellectual break Mary made with Percy Shelley's radical ideas; a break which was to bring her much pain, both from her own sense of guilt, and from the disappointment of his former friends and colleagues. Recognizing the significance of that break is essential to an understanding of Mary's artistic development, but it should not be assumed that Mary's *intellectual* rejection of Percy's manifesto ever affected her *feelings* for the poet. Far from it: Mary was, and forever remained, utterly devoted to her husband and his memory. It is probably also true that Mary's chief source for what she took to be his beliefs and ideology was Percy's poem *Queen Mab*, which he gave her as his first token of love. Though Percy's thinking unquestionably went through modifications and sophistications over the years, Mary perceived it, rightly or wrongly, as being fundamentally unchanged from its earliest and most vehement expression in that poem. It is important to note that Kelvin Everest, in the first volume of his new edition of PBS's poetry, has established a later date for the composition of *Queen Mab* – if it was written when he was nearly twenty, as Everest has established, the work cannot really be considered juvenilia after all. Perhaps PBS's early beliefs were retained in adulthood with greater tenacity than has been maintained. Shelley almost certainly believed this to be the case. She did not so readily register the changes in PBS's philosophy (as contemporary critics do) though in 1839 she did try to highlight "Christian" elements in his work. Nevertheless, her understanding of his ideology remains rooted in PBS's early radicalism.

Editorial symbols used:

1. <   > – Words appearing between <   > are those which Shelley crossed out.
2. [?   ] – Words appearing between brackets and preceded by "?" are uncertain readings.

Acknowledgements

I would like to thank Virginia Murray and John Murray Publishers Ltd., for their assistance and great generosity in allowing me to use their Byron manuscript collection. Lord Abinger very kindly granted permission for the publication of Mary Shelley's MS essay. Michael Rossington was a particularly thorough and expert reader and he receives profoundest thanks and gratitude.

I thank Mark Thompson for many years of support, encouragement and wise critical reading. Special thanks are also due to Professor Marilyn Butler for her generous help and guidance.

Author's Note

In the interests of clarity, I shall call Mary Wollstonecraft Godwin Shelley "Shelley" throughout. I shall refer to Percy Bysshe Shelley as "PBS". Though the latter is perhaps a little inelegant, it seems appropriate to refer to my subject rather than to her husband in the standard manner.

1
Introduction

Greatness was expected of Mary Wollstonecraft Godwin Shelley; she stood to inherit the passionate literary ambitions of her radical, idealistic parents William Godwin and Mary Wollstonecraft, and later her marriage to the poet Percy Bysshe Shelley seemed part of a momentous destiny. Almost until her death in 1851, she pursued a literary career with discipline, dedicated scholarship, and often desperation when her pen provided a meagre income for her tiny, nomadic household. Her first novel, *Frankenstein*, was begun shortly after her teenage elopement with Percy and was ready for publication before her twentieth birthday. She went on to write a novella,[1] five novels, travelogues, poetry, two dramas, many popular short stories, and a large collection of biographical and critical notes for *Lardner's Cabinet Cyclopaedia*, contributing the best part of five volumes to the distinguished series. She witnessed the transformation of her first and best book into international cultural myth with a number of popular stage productions, translations and appropriations of *Frankenstein*. The combined effort of her edition of PBS's *Posthumous Poems* and *Collected Works* with essays, letters and fragments, established the poet's reputation. Shelley lived up to expectations of great achievement but apart from *Frankenstein*, arguably the best known product of the Romantic period in English literature, and a 1985 edition of *The Last Man*, her work, until very recently, has been out of print.[2]

As far as the later novels are concerned, this neglect may be understandable. *The Fortunes of Perkin Warbeck* (1830) is a straightforward historical tale of the pretender to the throne of Henry VII in the style of Walter Scott. Despite Shelley's very original theory about the fate of the youngest prince in the Tower, the book is of limited interest. In her 1886 biography of Shelley, Helen Moore says of *Lodore* (1835), Shelley's novel of fashionable London life and sensibility, "this poor book has no excuse for being".[3] *Falkner* (1837), her last novel, is strikingly similar to its predecessor.

1

Yet, the two novels which followed *Frankenstein* are fascinating, ambitious and innovative in their imagery and themes. *Valperga: or, the Life and Adventures of Castruccio, Prince of Lucca* (1823) is a meticulously researched historical romance that is as difficult to place accurately in an existing novel genre as Shelley's so-called "socio-philosophical novel"[4] *The Last Man* (1826). In his introduction to her letters, Frederick Jones asserts that *Valperga* is Shelley's best novel,[5] and Muriel Spark, Elizabeth Nitchie and Lee Sterrenburg maintain that *The Last Man* is superior to or at least as important as *Frankenstein*. Hugh Luke, editor of a 1965 edition of *The Last Man*,[6] has demonstrated its bold experimental handling of the narrative-fictional form. All critics, in discussing Shelley's work either favourably or disparagingly, agree that the novel's theme at least is remarkably ambitious and monumental, detailing as it does the relentless and painful demise of the world's population.

Yet, through a predisposition to regard Shelley's work principally as a means of further illuminating that of her husband, the independent strengths of *Valperga* and *The Last Man* have been sadly ignored. Indeed, in his introduction to his 1945 edition of her letters Jones writes, " . . . a collection of the present size could not be justified by the general quality of the letters or by Mary Shelley's importance as a writer. It is as the wife of [PBS] that she excites our interest . . . ".[7] Furthermore, Shelley's novels have been passed off as the product of idealized autobiography. (Many of her characters are indeed sketches or conglomerates of friends and relatives).

Even *Frankenstein* has been traditionally regarded as a creative accident and its analysis limited to the psychological and unconscious motivations behind its story. As early as 1921, in her survey of the gothic novel, Edith Birkhead claimed that *Frankenstein* is "obviously the work of an immature writer who has no experience in shaping a plot . . . but . . . Mrs. Shelley is so engrossed in her theme that she impels her readers onward".[8] This attitude had changed little by 1978. Brendan Hennessey maintains that " . . . the power and vitality of *Frankenstein* derive partly from the fact that Mary Shelley did not quite know what she was doing, and when she became more mature and had to understand what she wrote, her imagination lost its force."[9]

Critics have read *Frankenstein* in isolation from the other novels, as Robert Kiely does in his 1972 study. And plainly loathe to give Shelley credit for her own creation, they attribute to PBS not just editorial input, but total responsibility for its success. Don Locke places great weight on the Godwinian element and says, " . . . in a real sense, it was Godwin who created *Frankenstein*".[10] Kiely remarks that "in places the narrative seems chiefly to provide the occasion for Mary to write a tribute to her father's idealism and a love poem to her husband."[11]

It is perhaps only specialists in science fiction who have always appreciated Shelley as completely independent from her husband and recognized the innovation and impact of her work. In the 1979 *Reader's Guide to Science Fiction* she is lauded, "Hail, Mary, Mother of Science Fiction".[12] More seriously, in a 1951 article for *The Listener* Muriel Spark says of Shelley, in regard to *Frankenstein* and *The Last Man*, that

> in these novels she did something in English Fiction which had not been done before; and that was to combine rational and natural (as distinct from supernatural) themes with the imaginative elements of Gothic fiction. She initiated, in these books, that fictional species which H. G. Wells made popular in his early novels, and which he called 'fantasias of possibility'.[13]

It is perhaps significant that it was the science fiction novelist Brian Aldiss who wrote the introduction to Hogarth's new edition of *The Last Man* (1985), a reprint of Luke's 1965 edition.

Several recent critics have begun to consider Shelley the novelist and to examine her work beyond *Frankenstein*. Mary Poovey's *The Proper Lady and the Woman Writer* (1984) considers *The Last Man* and *Frankenstein*, contrasting the two daring novels to Shelley's later, more obviously conventional work. Anne Mellor's *Mary Shelley: Her Life, Her Fictions, Her Monsters* (1988) also looks at *The Last Man* and *Lodore*, but it too neglects a proper discussion of *Valperga*. Jean de Palacio's *Mary Shelley dans son oeuvre* (1969) remains the most comprehensive and detailed study, though it has never been translated. William Walling's biography (1972) also provides insightful readings of all the novels. This study will place *Frankenstein* in relationship to Shelley's other important novels, all within the context of her life, her philosophical and artistic development.

The recent publication of the new edition of Shelley's journals by Paula Feldman and Diana Scott-Kilvert and the now completed three-volume edition of her letters by Betty Bennett will undoubtedly facilitate a burgeoning of Mary Shelley studies.

The most recent biography, by Emily Sunstein, makes the most of this new material.

Sandra Gilbert and Susan Gubar have attempted to explain in general the contemporary reader's resentment towards the nineteenth-century woman writer and to some extent modern neglect as well: "If she refused to be modest, self-deprecating, subservient, refused to present her artistic productions as mere trifles designed to divert and distract readers in moments of idleness, she could expect to be ignored or (sometimes scurrilously) attacked".[14]

This suggests something of, though by no means provides the full explanation for Shelley's plight. All her best novels are disturbing and demand concentration and perseverance and they often out-raged their original public; Shelley's femininity was not solely to blame. One can see, particularly in the light of the kind of novel that Jane Austen – always popular – was writing, just how great an affront Shelley and her aggressive, demanding work must have seemed.

The real reason for Shelley's neglect may lie in the genuine moral horror that her novels instill. The theme of an uncontrollable creation that threatens the whole of humankind is one that she develops in *Frankenstein*, portrays as a spiritual emptiness in *Valperga*, and reanimates as the all-destructive plague of *The Last Man* that depopulates the entire earth. The ultimate horror intimated in the first novel is realized in the third. *Valperga* is not at first an obvious development of the idea of annihilation but it nonetheless carries the seed of Shelley's blasphemous notion. Castruccio, the ambitious soldier-prince of *Valperga*, begins life as a guileless and warm-hearted youth. He first betrays then rejects the love of Euthanasia, Countess of Valperga – whom he loves in return – then deceives the innocent prophetess Beatrice; ultimately destroying both women. Shelley leaves us the moral nothingness of the complete devaluation of human love. At the conclusion of *The Last Man*, with only the terrifying presence of a single soul to experience the empty world for the reader, Shelley pictures the end of humanity without salvation or reward for earthly suffering. These novels offer no consolation, and indeed outstrip *Frankenstein* in despair. The reader experiences a moral void much like that of Lionel Verney, the last man left on earth after the relentless devastation of the plague. One is shocked by the sudden loss of humanity's value, the obliteration of the notion of redemption, and by the proof of love's ineffectualness. Nature and time lay low the idea of the Promethean man, the god-like mortal (so perverted in *Frankenstein*), and wipe him from the face of the earth. Thus Shelley's posthumous reputation was not hampered solely by her femininity, but by the sheer ambition – and pessimism – of the important themes that she addressed. To read her best novels requires the additional understanding that no obvious balm or consolation is offered.

But more disturbing still for the modern reader content to admire PBS for his crusading idealism and Shelley for her devotion to and support of his image, is what this study aims to establish: Shelley's "disloyalty" to the idealistic radicalism of PBS and his circle. Shelley came to reject many of her husband's tenets; at a very early stage in their relationship she began to question many of the ideals that he championed and expected her to embrace as well. In fact, *Frankenstein* is the starting point for the development of her reactive philosophy, one that violently opposes her husband's optimism and mocks its apparent simplicity to a degree that suggests intellectual antagonism as one reason behind the couple's much-discussed disharmony immediately before the poet's death. *Frankenstein*, which, as I will show, satirizes and rejects Godwinian and Shelleyan perfectibility, is anything but "her homage to her father", as Locke would have it.[15]

Shelley's imagination was honed by wide reading and strong intellect. It was also assaulted by physical hardship and emotional crises and, perhaps more significantly, by the isolation and frustration that she no doubt felt as a woman intellectual among male intellectuals without an autonomous role to play. Although vocal advocates for the alteration of women's traditional, subservient role in society, her male role models nevertheless depended on her femininity in a traditional way. Her husband's writing came first (though it brought in no money) and Shelley herself was responsible for children, housekeeping, the purchase of paper and writing materials and for the endless moves across England and Italy that the dunned and restless PBS required. Shelley had the education that her mother advocated for women – despite her father's haphazard approach – but once equipped for an intellectual life she became burdened with life's banalities. The sheer amount of her literary production is a testimony to her determination, strength of character and intelligence.

Shelley was no doubt troubled by her conflicting roles of successful author (eventually a widely celebrated one and, unlike her husband, during her own lifetime) and wife-mother-daughter. And it should not be forgotten that her love for and devotion to her husband, both before and after his death, was an overriding focus of Shelley's life. Though she desperately wanted children, motherhood was a source of tremendous mental and physical anguish. Shelley's first child died after a few days, her second after three years, her third after one. She miscarried once and nearly died as a result. Only one child, Percy Florence, survived into adulthood to ease her old age.[16]

Yet, what actually drove Shelley's fiction seems to have been a fundamental intellectual conflict with the men in her life, men that she loved deeply. By the time PBS met Godwin the latter had long since revised considerably his political views. Indeed, he had done so by the time that he began to educate his daughter. Shelley's challenge to PBS developed over the years, but even by the time of their first meetings she was unlikely to have shared his singled-minded commitment and uncompromising views; he was dedicated to the doctrinaire Godwin, the Godwin of the first edition of *Political Justice*. K. N. Cameron has pointed out, "Godwin's book is . . . the most important single influence among the many works that molded (PBS's) political thinking".[17] Because of his adoration for a long-defunct Godwin, PBS became her most profound intellectual antagonist.

The powerful Whig ascendency had long since passed, and sympathy for the Revolution in France, and many of the ideas of reform that followed from it were, by 1812, in profound disfavour. But PBS was still immersed in such outdated ideology. He went to visit another of his idols, Southey, still enraptured with the now mellowed older poet's early republican contributions to the literary battles that had surrounded the French Revolution in England. PBS still carried a torch for pantisocracy:

> . . . Southey was amazed. Here on his doorstep was a perfect example of the spirit of 1793. The species had never been common, and after fourteen years of anti-Jacobinism, it was generally assumed to be extinct. But Shelley was genuine, pure and uncompromising.[18]

PBS had imbibed not just the early Godwin, but the unmodified Godwin of the first edition of *Political Justice*. He did not bother with the later, more moderate editions. Indeed, as Cameron has pointed

out, PBS's eventual intellectual break with Godwin came when he
found that the political philosopher did not and would not posit a
system for active political organization. In the end, Godwin was not
radical enough for PBS:

> While Paine's revolutionary tactics could – as the American and
> French examples showed – produce results, Godwin's genteel
> propaganda campaign would have produced precisely nothing.
> In this opposition to political organization [PBS] and Godwin
> parted ways.[19]

Shelley's relationship with her lover was passionate and physical,
but it was also overweighted with her father's intellectual authority
and influence. Thus, through PBS, Shelley was still dominated
by the pervasive ideology of her father; her eventual intellectual
conflict with PBS actually incorporated a painful rebellion against
Godwin. She venerated her father whom she believed had shared a
perfect intellectual and emotional accord with her martyred mother,
and she remained devoted to him, despite his intermittent cruelty and selfishness.[20] It is also difficult to overstate her love
and admiration for PBS. Shelley rebelled against the unsocializing
ideological education that they gave her, but her rebellion was
profoundly fraught; she loved and worshipped both men yet still
felt compelled to disagree with them. This paradox, this tension
between the autonomy of her own intellect and her emotional ties,
informs Shelley's art.

Shelley recognized that both Godwin and PBS motivated and
encouraged her to write. They had great faith in her abilities. As
well as handling her business with publishers, PBS in particular
pushed her to challenge herself and was to some extent responsible
for the self-confidence that characterized her career. But Shelley also
had confidence in and respect for her own independence of thought,
inspired no doubt by her remarkably courageous mother.

Shelley's intellectual and emotional struggle is realized in her
most powerful writing; her concept of imagination reflects this
internal conflict. For her the creative, artistic imagination is in
many ways a malevolent and irksome force, anything but benign. It
has more in common with Byron's Romanticism than her husband's
and, as I shall show, she felt a great affinity for the other poet.
Shelley's artistic imagination is not consoling like Wordsworth's;
it conveys no panacea, like her father's Reason or her husband's

Truth. Rather, it is a potentially vicious and destructive agent whose persistent denial of some ultimate ascendancy of good is uncommonly tenacious. We see a model for it, perhaps, in the delirious poet of Coleridge's *Kubla Khan*. Indeed, the release of Shelley's own creative powers seems to bring forth a flood of agonized destruction; like the relentless plague in *The Last Man*. Beatrice, the self-deluded prophetess of *Valperga*, driven to madness by the revelation of her fallibility and the impotence of human love is, in her ravings, much like her agonized creator, a "child of imagination and misery".[21]

For Shelley, misery and imagination go hand in hand, and the visions of her malevolent imagination are vivified – in a sense *literally* brought to life – in *Frankenstein, Valperga* and *The Last Man*.

Shelley was not actively involved in any struggle for the rights of women, yet her frustration was keen and her conflicted reaction against her male milieu resulted in often powerful fiction. Her best works are aggressive reactions to the often high-minded principles of human improvement, the programmatic willed optimism that characterized the male, Romantic ideals that she was brought up on. They constitute an intellectual critique just as surely as they are an emotional response to the miseries of her own life. Shelley subverts particulars of the Romantic lessons taught by her revolutionary father, husband and friends, and creates a new voice. Its accents of turmoil and moral horror express quite as legitimately as Romanticism the authentic post-revolutionary malaise. This study seeks then to isolate more effectively than has yet been done the distinctive character of her imagination, and above all to reopen the issue of the nature of her subtle revolt against her circle, so often misconstrued as an unfortunate slide into early Victorian conventionality.

This study begins, in Chapters 2 and 3, by examining Mary Shelley's intellectual and emotional struggle from her earliest writing under the exclusive influence of her father and PBS, through the first developments of her growing reaction in *Frankenstein*. Chapter 4 explores her relationship with Byron, and her affinity for the other poet which corresponded to her dawning intellectual disaffection from PBS. Chapters 5 and 6 chart the progress of her reaction against the influence of her husband and examine its ultimate and complete realization in *Valperga* and *The Last Man*, that extreme reach of her dark vision. In the light of these discussions, the vexed question of Shelley's editing of PBS's poetry and prose can be re-examined. Through a selection of her editorial notes I will show, in Chapter 8, that her role was not simply one of censorious master or deifying acolyte. Shelley became another kind of literary professional, of a type familiar in modern times: an editor whose mission to represent PBS's oeuvre as whole and justified, to exhalt and disseminate his reputation, was subtly at odds with her private estimation of some of the poetry and its associated ideology.

2

Early Influences: "A History of the Jews"

When Shelley fell in love with the twenty-two year old Percy Bysshe, she was no doubt partly drawn by his identification with the ideas of her mother and father. She also knew that like her parents, the new lodestar in her life would encourage and promote her potential. She believed that she had much to offer – her mind was open and at the age of sixteen she was already very widely read. She was exhilarated by PBS's intellect – of all the young men who sought out her father, the poet very quickly came to be the most favoured – and by his admiration for her talents.

In *Valperga* Shelley describes the emotional turmoil of first love, that of the young and wildly impressionable prophetess Beatrice for the soldier Castruccio. The lines read as a retrospective analysis by Shelley of her own early love:

> There is so much life in love! Beatrice was hardly seventeen, and she loved for the first time; and all the exquisite pleasures of that passion were consecrated to her, by a mysteriousness and delusive sanctity that gave them tenfold zest. It is said, that in love we idolize the object; and, placing him apart and selecting him from his fellows, look on him as superior in nature to all others. We do so; but, even as we idolize the object of our affections, do we idolize ourselves: if we separate him from his fellow mortals, so do we separate ourselves, and, glorying in belonging to him alone, feel lifted above all other sensations, all other joys and griefs, to one hallowed circle from which all but his idea is banished . . . (Vol. II, p. 87)

Here Shelley is remarkably lucid and honest about the egoistic nature of love and, in particular, its self-deluding powers; but she did not come to realize this until later.

At a very early stage of their relationship Shelley was desperately eager for the poet's approbation and was often rewarded with praise. PBS wrote:

> I did not – for I could not, express to you my admiration of your letter to Fanny. The simple & impressive language in which you clothed your argument – the full weight you gave to every part, the complete picture you exhibited of what you intended to describe – was more than I expected. How hard & stubborn must be the spirit that does not confess you to be the subtlest & most exquisitely fashioned intelligence: that among women there is no equal mind to yours – and I possess this treasure: how beyond all estimate is my felicity. Yes! I am encouraged. I care not what happens I am most happy.[1]

PBS might be forgiven for congratulating himself on winning Shelley's love, but at the same time it is clear that he viewed her mind and its development as his exclusive project. Her openness to his views characterized their relationship at this time; he did not hesitate to direct her political expression or her general studies. In fact, her first piece of mature work – an exercise in political writing – reflects PBS's overwhelming influence on her at this stage of her intellectual and literary development. Following is a detailed examination of Shelley's first attempt at political writing and a discussion of PBS's role in its production.

The Bodleian Library's Abinger deposit c.477[2] is an extraordinary piece of writing by Shelley that has been neither described nor discussed. The unfinished essay looks like a first draft, written apparently at great speed with few corrections or crossings-out. The essay, divided into three sections, is a colloquial paraphrase, with a running internal commentary, of parts of the Hebrew Testament, taken mostly from Genesis and Exodus. It seems to represent a systematic anti-semitic diatribe in that it goes beyond a mere critique of religion to evoke racial stereotypes current in Shelley's day. Researchers have until now either ignored the essay, sandwiched as it is between the drafts of *Frankenstein*, or found it too crude to examine in detail. The "History of the Jews", as I have called it, is included in its entirety in Appendix A.

Anomalous as the essay appears at first, the "History of the Jews" belongs to a favourite and familiar Jacobin mode. The divine origins of the Hebrew Testament are 'disproved' by the recital of "absurdities", inconsistencies and "falsehoods"; the narrative is redefined in secular terms as the history of a brutal and savagely nationalistic people. Shelley's underlying aim was to strike a blow at Christianity by undermining its older foundations. She rose to PBS's exhortation, "Let the axe/Strike at the root, the poison-tree will fall . . . "[3]

The "History of the Jews" needs to be examined in the context of Shelley's own career, her intellectual circle, the political climate of the time and, most importantly, within the context of PBS's powerful influence. Initially, it shows a young and highly suggestible mind struggling with the radical currency of the day. Though the essay is very rough and apparently never assumed a second draft, it is an example of Shelley's professional approach to all her work – she undertook, and was to undertake, a great variety of literary tasks with (sometimes misplaced) confidence. Perhaps more importantly, the essay represents that period in her intellectual development during which she was most vulnerable to the influences of her circle. The essay seems to have been written under the direct tutelage of PBS and may be her earliest mature project. However, it also suggests a very early date for her unease with the radical ideals of PBS and thus has direct implications for *Frankenstein*.

The quality of the writing and argument suggests that the essay dates from very early youth and from the beginning of the Shelleys' relationship, between the two trips to Europe in 1814 and 1816, probably in 1815. The 1810 watermark (only 13 in 1810, Shelley was undoubtedly using old paper) also points to an early composition. The paper may well have come from her father's home and it is unlikely that she took it with her when she fled Skinner Street in the early hours of July 28, 1814. Her writing during those weeks on the Continent seems to have been confined to the bound joint journal purchased in Paris, though the story that she evidently wrote during the return to London – *Hate* – has been lost. It is also unlikely that she would have taken her father's old paper with her to Europe in May 1816; she left England from her own household at Bishopsgate. Perhaps a more reliable means of dating the piece is to examine Shelley's reading lists and get some idea of the intellectual influences at work upon her.

Most of the books she read at this time were plainly the programme of reading prepared (and to a large extent shared) by PBS. This was the period when his influence with Shelley was at its height and she took his confidence in her capacities as seriously as he did. Her energies at this time were fired by his approval and encouragement. She was also deeply and emotionally attached to the works of her mother and though there is no proof that she would have wholeheartedly supported her politics, she romanticized her lost parent and indeed, found PBS a kindred spirit because of his similar devotion to Wollstonecraft's life and works.

If one understands Shelley's iconoclastic "History of the Jews" as a radical exercise, then it coincides neatly with her intellectual adventures of 1814 and 1815; she was clearly interested in the radical cause and the generation of Jacobins that preceded her. She read several Jacobin histories, essays and novels including her mother's *Posthumous Works* (1798), edited by Godwin, *A View of the French Revolution* (1794), *Mary, A Fiction* (1788) and *Maria, or the Wrongs of Woman* (1798); her father's treatise *Political Justice* and the novel which is its companion piece, *Caleb Williams* (1794). She studied 'Godwinism' carefully and read "Godwin's Miscellanies", (identified by Frederick Jones as *The Enquirer: Reflections on Education, Manners and Literature* (1797)).[4] She records Matthew Lewis's blasphemous and explicit attack on religion and the church in the novel *The Monk* (1796), a tale of corrupt nuns, a lustful priest and the supremacy of the arch-fiend.[5] The list for 1815 includes Sallust, who had inspired the intellectual leaders of the American Revolution. Robert Bage was likewise sympathetic to that cause and she read his radical novels *Man as He Is* (1792) and *Hermsprong: or Man as He is Not* (1796). She also records the novels of Mme. de Staël, Godwin's *St. Leon* (1799) and *Fleetwood* (1805), Thomas Holcroft and Ann Radcliffe.

But of particular relevance to the "History of the Jews" are Southey's *Thalaba the Destroyer* (1801), *Madoc* (1805) and *The Curse of Kehama* (1810), epics which fascinated and provoked PBS; they, more than any other example of Southey's beliefs and political affinities established him as one of PBS's ideological enemies. With that in mind, Shelley read all three epics in 1814, exotic adventure stories which take place in the Middle East, ancient Wales, South America, and finally India. In each case Southey points out the abominations associated with non-Judæo-Christian religions. In *Thalaba* Southey treats the religion of Islam as a kind of honorary Christianity with the virtuous and stalwart Thalaba redeeming his people from the sorceresses of the underworld. However, Southey's tolerance for Islam is sustained only within the context of the story. His voice enters the narrative at Book V to offer his support of forced conversion – "So one day may the Crescent from thy Mosques/Be pluck'd by Wisdom, when the enlighten'd arm/Of Europe conquers to redeem the East!" (83–85).[6]

In the preface to *The Curse of Kehama* Southey makes his intended message clear when he explains that " . . . the religion of the Hindoos . . . (is) of all false religions . . . the most monstrous in its fables . . . ".[7] He is pointing out the evils of polytheism, implicitly by contrast with the social and ethical tenets of monotheism; the gods of the Hindoos, he might have elaborated, behave with even less decorum than the gods of the ancient Greeks.

Southey displays the brutality of the custom of sutee (self-immolation of the widow on the husband's funeral pyre) and at the same time, the absurd cruelty of gods who act on the side of supplicating evil. Kehama's curse is honoured by the gods as it comes in the form of a prayer and the innocent Ladurlad is forced to bear undeserved suffering. Southey shows the individual gods as feeble and weak, unable to repel the ambitions of a mere mortal and we see the ineffectualness, cruelty and absurdity of polytheistic society. Southey's poem was part of a campaign (associated with the Evangelicals under Wilberforce) to send Protestant missionaries to India. It implies that Christianity alone can make Indian society humane and progressive. In direct opposition to this, PBS's essay, "A Refutation of Deism" (1814) seeks to illustrate the cruelty of the God of the Hebrew Testament – " . . . bloodthirsty, grovelling and capricious . . . ".[8] He takes Southey's own argument and subverts it to prove his radical and anti-religious point, that vindictive cruelty is also characteristic of Christianity. Likewise, in his *Essay on Christianity*, probably written sometime between 1812–1815,[9] PBS attempts to extract the original, pristine behaviour and teachings of Jesus from the encrustations of corrupting church dogma.

Of course Southey was a man of the established church. In *Madoc* Christian "Britons" (the Medieval Welsh) emigrate to South America where is practised the bloodthirsty religion of the Aztecas. Madoc conquers the Aztecas, frees their captives and converts them to Christianity. He is hailed as a saviour, Great White Prince, Lord of the Ocean. The vanquished tribe leave their home (as Madoc and his own people did) to reestablish their nation and religion elsewhere. Again Southey's missionary (and imperialistic) zeal is made plain when he adds at the poem's conclusion:

So in the land
Madoc was left sole Lord; and far away
Yuhidthiton led forth the Aztecas,
To spread in other lands Mexitili's name,
And rear a mightier empire, and set up
Again their foul idolatry; till Heaven,
Making blind Zeal and bloody Avarice
Its ministers of vengeance, sent among them
The heroic Spaniard's unrelenting sword.
　　　　　　　　　　　　　(XXVII, 386–95)[10]

As Marilyn Butler has pointed out, it is for this reason – Southey's proselytizing on behalf of monolithic Christianity – that PBS and Peacock would have reacted so strongly to his work. By implication he would have condemned the religion of the ancient Greeks. They themselves employed that paganism, in 1817, with its 'human' gods and enthusiastic celebration of life, in order to expose the alleged "ascetic and life-denying tendencies of Hebraic Christianity",[11] and to point out the evils of monotheism.

We know from Shelley's later work that she willingly participated in her husband's campaign to criticize Christianity by pointing out the merits of Hellenism instead. During the months at Marlowe in 1817 PBS and Peacock developed their "cult of sexuality"[12] and their celebration of the variety of Greek gods in the natural world. This formulation of his position on Hellenism and myth was part of a developing continuum of interest on PBS's part which expressed itself, but not for the last time, in 1820[13] with the Shelley-PBS collaboration on the two mythological dramas *Proserpine* and *Midas* (unpublished until 1922). Shelley, studying Greek at the time, provided the text and PBS the four lyrics; the "Hymn of Apollo", the "Hymn of Pan" and *Arethusa* were all published in the *Posthumous Poems* (1824) but the "Song of Proserpine" did not appear until 1839. The Hellenism of the dramas – celebrating paganism – represent an implicit attack on Christianity, an attempt altogether more subtle and artistically successful on Shelley's part than the "History of the Jews". What she had attempted, nearly five years earlier, but failed in doing, she largely achieved in the collaborative effort. In the same year PBS indulged his pleasure in mythology in *The Witch of Atlas* (1820) as Keats had done in *Endymion* (1818) and Peacock in *Rhododaphne* (1818).

During this same period Shelley wrote two short stories, dated by

Charles Robinson 1819 and the mid-1820s respectively (but never published during her lifetime), with a similar theme. In *Valerius: the Reanimated Roman*, the eponymous hero returns to modern Rome after hundreds of years of suspended animation and finds the city desecrated by Christianity: " . . . Alas! Alas! Such is the image of Rome fallen, torn, degraded by a hateful superstition . . . ".[14] In *The Heir of Mondolpho* Shelley's resourceful heroine finds inspiration and comfort in her flight from unjust captivity when she stumbles into the ruins of the pagan temple of Paestum.

Shelley's own attachment to Greek mythology and classicism was more aesthetic and emotional than ideological. She always loved Rome and considered it her spiritual home. The classical ruins that she and PBS visited with such enthusiasm in their youth remained her favourite places and she accompanied her son there in 1842, her enthusiasm unabated.

Shelley expressed her love of classical mythology in contra-distinction to Christianity once again by responding to a challenge issued by Byron to PBS. Byron had been impressed by Charles Leslie's book *A Short and Easy Method with the Deists* (1820) and wanted PBS to compose an essay of refutation. Emily Sunstein has pointed out that while PBS responded with a serious argument (one that he did not finish),[15] Shelley offered a humorous refuta-tion of what Byron believed to be Leslie's very convincing argu-ments for the veracity of the Scriptures and proof of the revealed nature of Christianity. Shelley proposes an argument based on Paine and Voltaire that the pagan religions must be equally as true as Christianity. Though the essay is light-hearted in its approach and really no more than a rough outline, it is more 'successful' than the "History of the Jews". In it, Sunstein explains, Shelley "argues for the superior virtues and authenticity of the revelations of the Greeks over the Jews, desacralizes Virgil, attacks the proposition that only revealed religion is true, and ends by disproving what even Spinoza believed incontrovertible, that God revealed himself to Moses".[16]

In addition to the radical texts that inspired the early "History of the Jews", Shelley's playful outline, included in its entirety in Appendix B, indicates the expansion of her reading into classical texts. Sunstein points out:

> The draft reveals her knowledge and love of classical literature, which she studied in the original from 1815, when she read Ovid's *Metamorphoses* and Sallust, to the early months of 1822

when she was reading Homer and Tacitus. It also reveals her knowledge of scripture and her Deist concerns, which are evident in her reading through the years and in particular in her course of study between August 1819 and June 1820, when she read systematically through Jewish and Christian scripture.[17]

The outline, rough though it is, also indicates how Shelley's views, or at least her approach to such a project, had matured. This time, after the space of five years, she was altogether more relaxed in her efforts and in greater command of her sources and references.

But the "History of the Jews" has other concerns as well. It is preoccupied with cruelty, and with the cruelty moreover of religious people. That is the legacy of Southey in the essay, and it is the theme that powerfully supports a date close to that of *Queen Mab* (1813).[18] Shelley's brooding on violence, and her ambivalence towards it as expressed in the essay gives us an early origin for one of *Frankenstein*'s major themes. Southey suggests that the brutality of the Spanish Conquistadores is justified because of the religion that they bring. Shelley ironically reverses this notion with the suggestion that in the face of national freedom – not religion – violence may be acceptable:[19]

From time to time there arose to the aid of the people some bold conspirator who delivered his countrymen from their oppressors – murder & the violation of laws otherwise sacred was in old times deemed pardonable in the avenger of his country and as the Jewish laws peculiarly inculcated that hatred and destruction of ones enemies so contrary to the theory yet so consonant to the practice of [?Moderns] – it is not to be supposed therefore that these barbarians spared either bloodshed or treachery in the pursuit of <liberty> freedom . . .   Do not let them be reprobated for this let us sympathize even with these bloodthirsty robbers in an ardent love of liberty Let us admire the daring assassin that entered the labour of the king . . . and let us excuse the ungentle Deborah when she drove the nail into the head of Sisera but while we approve of the murders of a petty arrabian tribe shall we reprobate those acts preformed by civilized beings who horror struck even in the very deed shed the blood of man for the benefit of man – who have commited unhallowed acts for the love of their country & who while their bosoms panted for

Liberty shrunk with human feelings from that deed which was
to ensure its blessings to so many fellow creatures. (p. 13)

Shelley compares the cruel God of the Biblical Jews to the
bloodthirsty Mexitili. She declares the political motivation of the
essay at its conclusion in her description of the "sacrifice" of
Jephthah's daughter following his successful campaign against the
Philistines: [20]

> . . . Could the man love that God at whose alter he shed the
> life blood of his innocent child no – a cold shuddering fear
> must have frozen his feelings the Deity must have appeared a
> cruel & remorseless fiend whom he <dared not disobey> could
> most please by the offer of a human victim & whom he dared
> not disapoint of his promised prey – These are the genuine
> works of Religion. Mexitili – Jehovah – ye have have all of ye
> your worshippers – Religion is the triumphant & bloodstained
> emperor of the world – who with canting hipocrisy casts his
> crimes on superstition – a shadow – a name who acts a part
> in hiding from the wellmeaning & credulous the enormities
> committed by the daemon king. [21]

Though she seems to be saying that political freedom could justify
cruelty if anything could, Shelley's distaste for murder, even in
the case of the "just war" is unmistakable. She is clearly troubled
by the "ungentle Deborah". This rejection of violence is a theme
traceable throughout her fiction. Much later, in *The Last Man*,
Shelley addresses this issue first raised in the "History of the
Jews"; she condemns justifiable war. After vanquishing the Turks
in a latter-day Greek war of independence Lionel Verney, a member
of the successful army muses:

> But now, in the midst of the dying and the dead, how could
> a thought of heaven or a sensation of tranquillity possess one
> of the murderers? During the busy day, my mind had yielded
> itself a willing slave to the state of things presented to it by its
> fellow-beings; historical association, hatred of foe, and military
> enthusiasm had held dominion over me. Now, I looked on the
> evening star, as softly and calmly it hung pendulous in the
> orange hues of sunset. I turned to the corse-strewn earth; and
> felt ashamed of my species. (pp. 130–31) [22]

Jean de Palacio also detects this train of thought in Shelley's work: "La peinture des dèsastres de la guerre est un thème souvent developpé dans son oeuvre litteraire"[23] and points to a letter that Shelley wrote to Maria Gisborne in 1833:

> what is the use of republican principles and liberty, if Peace is not the offspring? (. . .) War is the companion and friend of Monarchy – if it be the same of freedom – the gain is not much to mankind between a Sovereign and a President.[24]

The ambivalence about the use of violence even in the best of causes, which is first hinted at in the "History of the Jews", forms part of the central moral dialectic of *Frankenstein*. If the Monster does represent, as some critics have maintained, the poor and persecuted classes, then his brutality in overthrowing his rich master and family is wholly reactive and defensive; the moral equivalent of the just war. And yet this overtly Jacobin stance is countered, just as it is in the "History of the Jews", by a second theme, that of the growing unease about the violence inherent in radicalism. This engagement with the fundamental moral dilemma which revolutionary violence poses for the radical also characterizes Mary Wollstonecraft's *An Historical and Moral View of the origin and progress of the French Revolution* (1794). It is interesting that even as early as the "History of the Jews" and *Frankenstein*, Shelley's response to the dilemma is already less antinomian and more conservative.

By contrast it is not clear that PBS unconditionally rejected violence – at least not in his earliest youth. *Queen Mab* certainly condemns war-mongering tyrants and imperialists, but it does not deal with the morality of the violence which would necessarily accompany a revolution like that of France. On the contrary, the poet's activities in Ireland in 1812 gave Godwin some cause for concern. Godwin found PBS's *An Address to the Irish People* and his desire to organize associations for political activism deeply immature and a dangerous incitement to mob violence. He wrote to his young protégé in Dublin:

> . . . your pamphlet . . . has no very remote tendency to light again the flames of rebellion and war. It is painful for me to differ so much from your views on the subject, but it is my duty to tell you that such is the case . . . associations, organized societies, I firmly condemn; you may as well tell the adder not to

sting . . . as tell organized societies of men, associated to obtain
their rights and to extinguish opposition, prompted by a deep
aversion to inequality, luxury, enormous taxes and the evils of
war, to be innocent, to employ no violence, and calmly to await
the progress of truth. I never was at a public political dinner,
a scene that I have not now witnessed for many years, that I
did not see how the enthusiasm was lighted up, how the flame
caught from man to man, how fast the dictates of sober reason
were obliterated by the gusts of passion . . . [25]

The young and ardent PBS was not to be dissuaded from his
associations and in his next letter to Godwin, justified his action in
the name of *Political Justice,* but less than sensitively suggested that
Godwin's magnificent treatise had still not precipitated vigorous
activity on the part of reform, twenty years later. Godwin, still more
alarmed, responded again:

. . . I cannot but consider your fearful attempt at creating a chain
of associations as growing, however indirectly and unfairly, out
of my book . . . I shall ever regret this effect of my book; and I
can only seek consolation in the belief that it has done more good
to many other persons, and the hope that it may contribute, with
other mightier and more important causes, to the melioration of
future ages.
  You say, 'What has been done within the last twenty years?'
Oh, that I could place you on the pinnacle of ages, from which
these twenty years would shrink to an invisible point! It is
not after this fashion that moral causes work in the eye of
him who looks profoundly through the vast and, allow me to
add, venerable machine of human society. But so reasoned the
French Revolutionists. Auspicious and admirable materials were
working in the general mind of France; but these men said, as
you say, when we look on the last twenty years, 'we are seized
with a sort of moral scepticism – we must own we are eager that
something should be done.' And see what is the result of their
doings! . . . you are preparing a scene of blood![26]

Shelley herself must have agreed with her father and felt wary
of the poet's affinity with the earlier revolutionaries – she would
have been more aware than PBS of her father's modifying opinions.
The initial revolution to overthrow a repressive regime may be

justifiable, but as the "History of the Jews" suggests, when the process is constantly repeated – revolution, despotism, revolution – radical politics become an evil and impotent force.

The wantonly destructive Monster of *Frankenstein* is a direct result of Victor's single-minded dedication to a project that he believed would revolutionize the world of knowledge, human relationships and human reproduction. (Victor seems to think the gradual obsolescence of sex a gift to humanity.) He is so focused on the end that he fails to appreciate the means. Perhaps even more damning of revolutionary vision, Victor abandons his creation when it disappoints his original conception. He is personally responsible not only for the monster's birth, but for its subsequent and heretofore preventable turn to violence. And we are not certain that the Monster dies with the novel's conclusion. The Monster tells Walton that he will kill himself, but his promised suicide is the one undocumented event of a very carefully documented story. Revolutionary violence is self-perpetuating.

Moreover, revolutionary literature can be dangerous. With his own reading lists, which include *The Ruins*, Plutarch's *Parallel Lives*, Milton's *Paradise Lost*, and Goethe's *The Sorrows of Werther*, Frankenstein's Monster learns about civilization, sentiment, justice and injustice and identifies himself as Volney's first man – "In the origin of things, man, formed equally naked both as to body and mind, found himself thrown by chance upon a land confused and savage. An orphan, deserted by the unknown power that had produced him . . . ".[27] He is reared on radical idealism and sees those ideals shattered about him as he moves through the world. In fact, the rarified air of exclusive radical ideology ill-equips the Monster for life. Though Shelley signals her radical affiliations by citing these books, she is uneasy about their ultimate value. The Monster is humanized and sensitized by his select education but is spectacularly disillusioned when he discovers the true nature of man and his world.

With *The Last Man*, Shelley had given complete shape to this creeping suspicion first broached in *Frankenstein*, and developed in *Valperga* into a coherent theme that would have left her husband confused and unsympathetic had he lived to read her other novels. Looking back to the "History of the Jews", we can see that the repeated fears about instability which occur in her later work are already intimated by the repugnance she shows to Deborah's blow for freedom.

Shelley's desire to reply to recent anti-revolutionary writing does not account for all the themes in the "History of the Jews". Her essay also belongs to a pre-revolutionary, Enlightenment genre, in which she had evidently read widely. Her earliest ventures under PBS's guidance included the religious sceptics or "Philosophes"; Rousseau, Holbach and Voltaire. She was particularly interested in Voltaire and in 1814 read *Zadig* (1747) and *Candide* (1759). In the former tale one sees a near prototype of the "atheistic" discourse found in Volney's *The Ruins, or a Survey of the Revolutions of Empires* (1791) and in PBS's *Queen Mab* which Shelley also records in her lists for 1814. In *Zadig* Voltaire assembles all the religions and nations of the ancient world together at a market. Arguing amongst themselves on the authority of their respective religions, an Egyptian, Indian, Chinese, Greek, Celt and a Chaldean are finally convinced by Zadig that they all in fact worship the same Supreme Being while at the same time the absurdity of religious ritual is pointed out.

In the following year Shelley read Voltaire's *Micromegus* (1752), the tale of an inter-galactic wanderer-philosopher, and *La Bible enfin expliqué* (1776).[28] This translation of and commentary on the Bible anticipated Shelley's exercise and attempted to explicate the Hebrew and (New Testaments) by denying their divine origins and considering them as the myths and fables of a certain eastern people, very similar in fact to the stories of other ancient peoples and religions. Like Volney and Paine, Voltaire also employed ironic humour in his critique, a quality which Shelley also strived for in her essay.[29]

Shelley also read much of Gibbon's *Decline and Fall*, which, though its concerns are largely with the New Testament rather than the Old, discusses the historical Jews in terms echoed in the "History of the Jews". In Volume II for example, which Shelley probably read in January or February 1815 Gibbon writes:

> A single people refused to join in the common intercourse of mankind. The Jews, who, under the Assyrian and Persian monarchies, had languished for many ages as the most despised portion of their slaves, emerged from obscurity under the successors of Alexander: and, as they multiplied to a surprising degree in the East, and afterwards in the West, they soon excited the curiosity and wonder of other nations. The sullen obstinacy with which they maintained their peculiar rites and unsocial manners seemed to mark them out a distinct species of men, who boldly

professed, or who faintly disguised, their implacable hatred to the rest of human kind.[30]

The Rev. Alexander Geddes's two-volume translation of the *Holy Bible* (1792 and 1797) is among the first of the scholarly works in England that reflected the new school of Biblical interpretation which had begun in Germany with Heyne and Eichhorn.[31] Its prefaces examine the Biblical texts as accreted myth and folklore and attempt to find rational explanation for the events of the Pentateuch and New Testament. Geddes' *Bible* and Volney's *Ruins* do not appear in Shelley's reading lists, but the prominence of Volney in *Frankenstein* shows that she must have read it. Equally, Geddes' prefaces appear to be among the models for Shelley's own "History of the Jews" and for the humorous essay on Leslie's *Short and Easy Method*. In fact, Geddes' work was a controversial *cause célèbre*. As Jerome McGann has pointed out, Geddes' "bible was a work of the English Left and was recognized as such at the time".[32] McGann has also demonstrated the significance of Geddes' translation to Blake's "Bible of Hell"; the subversive work *Urizen* is an alternate and Jacobin Genesis. Geddes asserts that the five Books of Moses are not the word of God at all as both Volney and later Thomas Paine in *The Age of Reason* (1794) demonstrated, but a record of the Hebrew mythology and laws, "compiled from ancient documents".[33] Shelley too speculates on Jewish history:

> The origen of the Jews is <uncertain> doubtful. Nations must rise to a certain degree of eminence before their fellow men will <deign to> trouble themselves with enquiries concerning their existence A nation must be possessed of a force capable of acting in a hostile manner <& by their numbers of opposing some boastful & murderous conquer & then> it must have acquired a capacity for mischief and destruction before <historians can flourish> neighbouring states will take an interest in their history . . . It was not till the Romans had taken an interest in their affairs that they immerged from obscurity. It was not till they had become rebels to this power that they excited any curiosity.

The Jacobin interpretation of the Hebrew Testament saw its stories and miracles as pan-symbolic, founded in common observations of the natural world and developed as a means of explaining or justifying the processes of nature and, significantly, man-made laws. Thus Geddes asserts:

> . . . the Hebrew historiographer invented his Hexahemeron, or six days creation, to introduce more strongly the observance of the Sabbath . . . his history of the Fall as an excellent *mythologue*, to account for the origin of human evil, and of man's antipathy to the reptile race . . . [34]

Likewise, Volney, whose chapter "Origin and Genealogy of Religious Ideas" develops the origins of such myths in detail, concludes, " . . . the ideas of God and religion sprung, like all others, from physical objects, and were in the understanding of man the produce of his sensations, his wants, the circumstances of his life, and the progressive state of his knowledge".[35] He likewise characterized Christianity as the allegorical worship of the sun. Shelley attempts similar reasoning in explaining the Creation but employs a sarcastic tone instead of examples of the universality of ancient myth:[36]

> Thier notions of the sun and moon were of a greater & a lesser light placed in heaven. the one to rule the day the other the night. God they said had created the world in six days – before this time all was void & his spirit floated on the face of the waters – he had ordered light to be & there was light – he had ordered all animals & all plants to bring forth abundantly after their kind & to increase upon the face of the earth – the sixth day he finished his labour & rested on the seventh –
> He then discovered that the earth still needed a being of superior intelligence who might superintend & adorn it – he created man of the dust of the earth & blew into his nostrils the breath of life – But man was alone and as unfortunately he was of a sociable disposition – <of course> he could not be perfectly happy – But God remedied this evil . . .

Though drawing on work that preceded and inspired her own exercise, Shelley's account undermines her radical argument; her humorous tone reflects, as we shall see, a more disquieting prejudice.[37]

In his second preface (1797) Geddes points out the several irreconcilable paradoxes and inconsistencies included in the body of work meant to be the word of God. Thus he concludes, as does

Paine, that the Bible is no more the result of divine revelation than are the works of any other ancient historians. Shelley follows suit by illustrating what she refers to as the "gross falsehoods and inconceivable absurdities":

> Now the Jewish God we must suppose did not foresee what kind of beings men would turn out to be else of course he would have altered the whole plan of things from the beginning – but when he found that his creation which when he first made he declared to be good disappointed his fond hopes in so cruel a manner it repented him that he had ever made man & he determined to destroy them & all other animals, who perhaps took after their masters in their way of life, from off the face of the earth.

Shelley thus derives her assault on the harshness of the Hebrew Testament narrative *and* the unsoundness of her text from Enlightenment scholarship. But in certain respects her emphasis differs. Perhaps because of her inexperience, eagerness to please and dependence on her sources, she introduces a vein of vulgar prejudice and stereotyping that makes uncomfortable reading. Volney addresses the cruelty[38] in the Hebrew Testament but simultaneously assails the Christian precept of Charity. He points out the systematic brutality of the Church over the years during the Crusades, the Inquisition and in the intolerance of missionary practices. Shelley however pins the origin of such cruelty firmly on the Jews, brutalized, so she believes, by their God:

> Now we may suppose that although Noah was very tolerably virtuous in comparison with his wicked fellow creatures he had not entirely escaped the contagion of their vices. Accordingly we soon find that (perhaps in his rapture at his deliverance) he having planted a vineyard *drank of the wine and was drunken.*[*] Such are the feelings of a Jew & befitting the father of their race but surely the sentiments of Deucalion & Pyrrha were of a much milder and more amiable nature when they wept for the loss of their fellow creatures & companions. Soldiers are a brutal and unatural race of men but hard must be the heart of that man who could look with an unmoistened eye on a field after

---

*Bold italic is used here and throughout this book to denote underlining in the original.

the day of battle who would not <sympathize> conjure in his imagination a thousand ties of of affection snapt a thousand dreams of happiness blasted <in their very beginning> for ever. but ten thousand times harder than a rock of flint must that heart be whom a world destroyed a human race cut off for ever from the face of the earth would not lead to meditation & gentleness.

Though the sufferings of mankind might be supposed identical in both myths, Shelley's sympathy is reserved for the Greek characters analogous to Noah and his wife. (This preference of course anticipates her participation in PBS's scheme to celebrate the pagan over the Judæo-Christian traditions.)

Despite this evidence that primitive myths are universal she singles out the problematic ethics of the early books of the Bible and blames the feature on a notion of the Jewish character derived from both ancient and contemporary stereotyping. She regards the stories as lies, a "record of deeds of the most abominable & sanguinary nature", the "extravagant account(s) . . . of their own cruelties" and confuses the point that both Paine and Volney found central to their arguments regarding the tyrannical nature of priestcraft. They do not disparage the writer of the original texts or their subjects, but condemn the dependent, subsequent religions that used the myths to foment mystery and ignorance and to discourage the questioning of authority; Volney's Apparition warns:

> . . . *sacred imposters* have taken advantage of the credulity of the ignorant. In the secrecy of temples, and behind the veils of altars, they have made the Gods speak and act; have delivered oracles, worked pretended miracles, ordered sacrifices, imposed offerings, prescribed endowments; and, under the name of *theocracy* and *religion*, the state has been tormented by passions of the priests.[39]

Even the conservative Southey could point out the evils of priestcraft in *Madoc*. When Shelley does eventually discuss priestcraft or "superstition" in the essay's concluding pages, as quoted above, its association with contemporary prejudice and her attempts to portray both Biblical and contemporary Jews as contemptible obfuscate her potential argument.

Geddes on the other hand takes seriously the belief in Moses as a divinely inspired lawmaker and admires the body of Jewish law, providing as it does for the security of "property, liberty, and personal safety . . . health, prosperity, and population".[40] He notes that unlike the vast majority of other religions, early Judaism did not emphasize "the least hint of future retribution in another world",[41] a liberal doctrine that even the ruthlessly anti-religious Paine (and PBS) would have applauded in their celebration of existing creation and life on earth as the true work of God.[42]

But it is not only in the "History of the Jews" that the young Shelley can sometimes be disquieting in her contempt for other human beings. She wrote in her journal on August 28, 1814:

> We stopped at Mettingen to dine, and there surveyed at our ease the horrid and slimy faces of our companions in voyage; our only wish was to absolutely annihilate such uncleanly animals, to which we might have addressed the Boatman's speech to Pope – "'Twere easier for God to make entirely new men than attempt to purify such monsters as these." After a voyage in the rain, rendered disagreeable only by the presence of these loathsome "Creepers", we arrive . . . [43]

It is difficult to reconcile such sentiments – here apparently expressed aloud, and even shared by her companions within the circle – with a belief in systematic perfectibility or even equality. And Shelley's reference to the tribes of Israel as "a herd of Arrabian robbers", characterized by their brutality, savagery and meanness, betrays not just racial prejudice but an uncharacteristic lack of elementary scholarship.[44] Geddes on the other hand more liberally notes that, "Of the laws of war . . . I shall only say, that some of them appear too sanguinary: but, most probably, they were not more so than the general usage of those times authorized" [45]

Shelley's attack on the Jewish race, past and present, begins with Moses. In describing him as possessing "tenets . . . in every respect those of the most unenlightened savage", she echoes *Queen Mab*[46] and names Moses a murderer. But the note of bigotry special to Shelley's treatment (and *not* a characteristic of *Queen Mab*) becomes unmistakable when she also heaps a disproportionate amount of humorous sympathy on the "good-natured Egyptians" and Pharaoh, whose wise plan of population control (killing the first born of the Jews) is met with such resistance. Further, when she intimates in her comments on the Jewish Eve that Jewish "ladies" are not known for their resistance to sensual indulgence, she invokes an insidious stereotype. Paine in all his vehemence does not particularize Jews in this way. We find that Shelley disregards the positive wisdom of Volney's Apparition in its condemnation of racial prejudice. Speaking of the ancient kingdom of Ethiopia it points out:

> It was there that a people, since forgotten, discovered the elements of science and art, at a time when all other men were barbarous, and that race, now regarded as the refuse of society, because their hair is woolly, and their skin is dark, explored among the phenomena of nature, those civil and religious systems which have since held mankind in awe.[47]

This strikingly modern sentiment left the young Shelley unmoved. Ironically, she appropriated only those elements of Enlightenment argument which did not conflict with immediate personal prejudice.

Shelley's reading lists contain works, such as her mother's and father's novels and essays, which had profound emotional significance for her and which go beyond the mere supply of ideas or information. Such a work was *Queen Mab*, presented to her by PBS as one of his first tokens of love in the Spring of 1814. Though she was later to offer a rational criticism of it, she always treated it as a poem charged with a special private significance and it provided much of the inspiration for the "History of the Jews". Later, she came to understand *Queen Mab* as the unadulterated essence of her husband's beliefs and ideology even though PBS would come to reject some of the cruder elements of the poem, in particular Holbach, the French philosophes and Necessity.[48] Nonetheless Shelley drew on *Queen Mab*, its sources,[49] and the radical literature which she associated with it. But later, in her novels, she would criticize what she came to see as their fundamental inadequacies. But in the "History of the Jews", PBS's influence remains strong.

Shelley did eventually absorb an important and interesting feature of the Hebrew Testament, adding depth and maturity to her later work. The difficult but active relationship between God and man illustrated therein is echoed in Victor's feelings towards his creation, which are variously rejections and obligations. The patriarchs and prophets of the Bible, like the frustrated Monster, are favoured by God's guidance when he speaks to them directly and thrown into despair when he appears to desert them. *Frankenstein* seems to exploit the imaginative possibilities of those relationships and to reflect Shelley's new appreciation of the artistic potential of the Bible, though she does not record reading it until August 1819.

Shelley's essay seeks to discredit Christianity. In *Queen Mab* the naked Ianthe rises from her bed: she is a new Eve, newly born, unobscured, palpable, free of sin, a challenge hurled in the face of religious tyranny – "Each stain of earthliness/Had passed away, it reassumed/Its native dignity, and stood/Immortal amid ruin" (*QM*, I, 135–38). Responding to the new Eve, Shelley's essay attempts likewise to demystify, strip-away and cleanse. In the context of other such works, we understand that she no doubt intended to extend her condemnation of the Jews to religion in general. As it stands, her argument is clouded because she gives her Biblical Jews contemporary racial stereotypical characteristics and her radicalism is undercut by her failure to establish the despotic tendencies in *any* monotheistic religion. But this failure may anticipate the later Shelley who in complete contrast to her husband found it impossible to condemn Christianity. In fact, she had become a church-goer before PBS's death, and after it took comfort in the promise of life after death as the only means to relieve her suffering. More importantly, even the Shelley of the earliest novels did not believe in the possibility of perfection in universal humanity expressed in *Queen Mab* (Canto 3's vision of the future). Indeed, her later novels posit the active presence of evil in the world and in man, an evil that may be destined to triumph.

Only the first glimmerings of this dissent are evident in the "History of the Jews". And yet, the essay remains an interesting index of Shelley's intellectual state of mind before her other works were written; she was, during those early years, strongly influenced by PBS and others. In fact, PBS's intellectual dominance of Shelley was never more complete. Though she addressed the exercise with some skill and humour, she lacked the maturity, generalizing perspective and probably the commitment of the true radical. It is not surprising that she was interested in experimenting in the radical style but over the following years her interest moved away from ideology. Divorced from her husband's vision, her own could develop its distinctive menace.

3

Frankenstein and the "Good Cause"

The birth of *Frankenstein* and of its Monster are among the most celebrated events in literary and popular history. In fact, the latter event occupies a few understated lines in the novel, but the former took place over the course of a long, wet summer that represented a watershed in Shelley's life. The entry of Lord Byron into their circle introduced a new and exciting intellectual stimulus for Shelley. She was impressed by his poetry, intrigued by his life, pleased that he recognized her mother and father's brilliance and that he expected to find it in her. After initiating the famous ghost-story competition he evidently continued to push her for her contribution after the others had lost interest. She was flattered and gratified but more importantly, Byron's irreverence encouraged her to question the radical ideology. Although *Frankenstein* is undeniably a novel constructed out of the currency of the radical movement, it is also a critique of that system and of the personalities of the men who were its proponents. With *Frankenstein* Shelley began to think independently and with the confidence that characterizes all of her projects. In this way it follows on from the "History of the Jews"; she challenges and debates the moral value of many of the ideas that her father (particularly as a young man) and husband cherished. Though PBS played an important role by encouraging the book and editing it, and Shelley was more deeply in love with him than ever, *Frankenstein* is the seedbed of Shelley's doubt and represents the beginning of her original thought. At the same time that she was intellectually tied to PBS, she was testing her own voice and questioning many of the ideas that she had hitherto taken for granted.

As the reading lists have shown, Shelley was well-versed in Godwinism even at the age of sixteen. She absorbed the concepts of rationalism and of perfectibility but whether she was instructed by PBS or by her father she was ultimately to reject those precepts despite both their enthusiasm for them. In most of the criticism that deals with Shelley's novels as a whole, there is general agreement that following her "radical" writings, *Frankenstein, Valperga* and *The Last Man*, Shelley became abruptly conservative and conformist in both her lifestyle and her art. Mary Poovey, in *The Proper Lady and the Woman Writer* is the most recent advocate of this evaluation. Modern, and even her contemporary critics, (such as Trelawny and Hogg), believed that after the completion of *The Last Man*, she 'turned traitor' to the radicals and that this is nowhere more evident than in her revised version of *Frankenstein*. The third edition of *Frankenstein* (1831) was altered by Shelley to a degree more consistent, so her critics believe, with her status as Victorian matron. She did make several changes that appear to pander to 'respectability'. She removed the dedication to Godwin and the suggestion of incest; Elizabeth is no longer Victor's cousin, but a foundling of no relation. Yet the greatest change is represented by the new and extended introduction which replaced the one that PBS wrote for the original (and which remained in the edition of 1823). The new introduction gives an elaborate explanation for the origin of her story and an account of the ghost story competition (including the figure of Byron was a shrewd marketing move), then finally reveals how the story actually came to her:

> When I placed my head on my pillow, I did not sleep, nor could I be said to think. My imagination, unbidden, possessed and guided me, gifting the successive images that arose in my mind with a vividness far beyond the usual bounds of reverie. I saw – with shut eyes, but acute mental vision, – I saw the pale student of unhallowed arts kneeling beside the thing he had put together. I saw the hideous phantasm of a man stretched out, and then, on the working of some powerful engine, show signs of life, and stir with an uneasy, half-vital motion. (p. 9)

But this visionary smoke-screen actually serves to distance Shelley from the responsibility of consciously creating her story; an old trick, used by Coleridge in his preface to *Kubla Khan*. By 1831, Shelley wished to formally disassociate herself from the blasphemous and the radical; she was signaling the separation of her ideas from her husband's and father's. Yet this retrospective distancing has acted as evidence for those who wish to diminish Shelley's role in the creation of her novel; she obliges by denying her responsibility for its invention. They are free to regard *Frankenstein* as the result of automatic writing, in which the application of art was unnecessary. After admitting that PBS was away for most of the novel's composition, that he flatly denied having had any hand in the original drafting of the novel, and that we find his later editorial corrections only on publisher's proofs and in a few places on the original draft, Christopher Small can still ask, "How far his help went in actual composition we cannot be sure".[1] James Rieger epitomizes the reluctance with which many critics are prepared to concede authorship to Shelley. He asserts that PBS "worked on *Frankenstein* at every stage, from the earliest drafts through the printer's proofs . . . We know that he was more than an editor. Should we grant him the status of collaborator?"[2]

But the 1831 introduction also helps to divide Shelley's career neatly in two: her radical youth and her disappointing middle-aged conservatism, to the complete satisfaction of most critics. The greatest grudge held against the poet's widow is that she somehow betrayed her husband's sacred beliefs and prostituted herself to the demands of conventional society. This is a misconception in two respects; Shelley was never a passionate radical like her husband and her later lifestyle was not abruptly assumed nor was it a betrayal. She was in fact challenging the political and literary influences of her circle even in her first work. *Frankenstein* is in many respects a subtle parody of Godwinian rebellion, rationality and perfectibility.

The book is often described as a gothic novel, even as the epitome of that genre. It is also enthusiastically analyzed as a psychological oddity that flowed directly from the author's subconscious onto the page, and all the more interesting because it was written by a teenager. But *Frankenstein* is also a political novel which responds directly to the radical circle from which it came. Written by a politically aware novelist of ideas, *Frankenstein* can be considered as an analytical lever to prise open a door to the recent past. The Terror, though unmentioned, lours over the novel. It is set in and therefore looks back to the 1780s and 90s, and to the literary generation which preceded it, and which produced the Jacobin novel: Elizabeth Inchbald's *A Simple Story* (1791), Thomas Holcroft's *Anna St. Ives* (1792) and Robert Bage's *Hermsprong* (1796) among others.

But *Frankenstein* was written in the post-Napoleonic war years, the years during which the second generation Romantics both mourned the failure of the Revolution and looked forward to new reforms and revolutions across Europe. *Frankenstein* is a product of that disappointment, but it is not necessarily full of the corresponding hope that impassioned PBS and others. At the same time that she signalled her radical associations with *Frankenstein*, Shelley also cast doubt on and rejected outright many of the ideals dear to her husband and to her father. *Frankenstein* anticipates Shelley's own intellectual career and belies the standard and narrow critical evaluation that would reduce it to yet another mouthpiece for the radical ideas of the Shelley circle. Thus, *Frankenstein* is written in a kind of radical code, but it sustains a critique of that same radicalism throughout.

Frankenstein self-consciously associates itself with the Jacobin tradition, the complex of radical literature – the "war of ideas"[3] – which grew up in England as an enthusiastic response to the French Revolution. On its title page, and in its dedication, it signposts itself, quite extravagantly, as part of the radical canon. However, as we shall see later, Shelley undermines those very radical ideals which she initially highlights. In the original 1818 edition *Frankenstein's* dedication read:

To
WILLIAM GODWIN
Author of Political Justice, Caleb Williams, &c.
THESE VOLUMES
Are respectfully inscribed
BY
THE AUTHOR

Godwin's *Enquiry Concerning Political Justice* (1793) proposed an egalitarian future made possible by man's natural inclination towards reason. Godwin believed that once persuaded, humanity would be motivated exclusively by reason and the desire for truth. All government was necessarily hostile to reason. This premise is obviously founded on the optimistic notion of humanity's potential for good and his work attracted, among other idealistic young men, the nineteen-year-old radical Percy Shelley, recently sent down from Oxford for publishing the pamphlet *The Necessity of Atheism* in 1811.[4] But Godwin and PBS met many years after the tremendous popularity of *Political Justice* and the novel *Caleb Williams* were forgotten. In fact, the young atheist was surprised to learn that his hero was still alive.

Caleb Williams dramatizes the principles set forth in *Political Justice*; Godwin had hoped to popularize his radical arguments and make people understand them, if not embrace them altogether. His political convictions were strong and he barely escaped the prosecution and imprisonment that plagued his friends during Pitt's repressive government, when sympathy with the French revolutionaries represented treason (as well as a sinister collusion with Catholicism and Clericism). Holcroft, Robert Thelwell and Horne Tooke were all arrested in May 1794 with the suspension of Habeus Corpus. It is popularly believed that Godwin avoided arrest because of the elitist nature of his work; even he was aware that it was not only the treatise's high price that made it unlikely that it would be appreciated, much less understood, by more than a well-educated few.

Caleb Williams was a success, but perhaps not for the reasons that Godwin had intended. The psychological study of the pursued and the obsessive pursuer impressed its contemporary critics as it does today. The book may have been written for political ends, but its success lies in its transcendence of its genre on the psychological level. It is in fact one of the few, if not the only quintessentially Jacobin novel, which is still read with any popularity today. Gary Kelly has pointed out that "the novel's chief excellence, then as now, is precisely that balance between psychological interest and English Jacobin social criticism which most English Jacobin novels failed to maintain".[5]

The political implications of *Caleb Williams* find their origins in *Political Justice*, a nearly comprehensive theoretical and practical revolutionary handbook. As David McCracken explains, Godwin:

> found virtually all man's institutions radically corrupt and corrupting – not just the monarchy, aristocracy, legislature, court system, and war, but the entire legal system, blame and punishment, *all* forms of government, customary promises, even disease, all these misshapen growths of history were unnecessarily blocking the way of the Godwinian desiderata, reason and justice.[6]

Caleb Williams addresses almost all of these separate but related issues in a manner that fleshes out the austere reasoning of the treatise, making many of the same political points in a complex and sophisticated allegory.[7] *Political Justice* and *Caleb Williams* combined, represent a powerful statement against conservatism and the eloquence of its greatest proponent at the time, Edmund Burke. Godwin's goal, as he himself wrote, was to simplify "the social system, in the manner which every motive, but those of usurpation and ambition, powerfully recommends; render the plain dictates of justice level to every capacity; remove the necessity of implicit faith . . . ". As a result one could " . . . expect the whole species to become reasonable and virtuous".[8]

Broadly, Godwin directed his attack against what he described as the tyrannical and despotic; the entire illegitimate power of government. Thus Tyrrel, the boorish country squire of *Caleb Williams*, has his own set of self-serving laws which supersede those of the kingdom. The "understood conventions of the country gentleman" (*CW*, p. 68) saw that the tenant "was required by his landlord to vote for the candidate in whose favour he had himself engaged" (*CW*, p. 66). What is more, the hypocrisy of these illegal "laws" is such that Tyrrel is condemned by his fellow gentry when he allows his new tenant Hawkins to maintain his independent political allegiance.

In his attack upon government, Godwin claims that injustice is the guiding force of the system, the subversion of justice is the norm. Tyrrel never expects to be challenged in a court by one poorer than himself, firmly believing that "it would . . . be the disgrace of a civilized country, if a gentleman, when insolently attacked in law by the scum of the earth, could not convert the cause into a question of the longest purse . . . " (*CW*, p. 73). Godwin had explained earlier in *Political Justice* that in "many countries justice is avowedly made a subject of solicitation, and man of the highest rank and the most splendid connections almost infallibly carries his cause . . . the man with the longest purse is proverbially victorious" (*PJ*, Vol. I, p. 18). The first magistrate that the falsely accused Caleb turns to refuses to even hear his case against his master, the wealthy and landed Falkland.

In painting Tyrrel as the proverbial tyrant however, Godwin is also careful to show that he is human – he expresses affection for his niece and ward Emily Melville. Thus, Godwin may support his earlier statement from *Political Justice* that man "is not originally vicious", the necessity for governments to exercise authority "does not appear to arise out of the nature of man, but out of the institutions by which he has been corrupted" (*PJ*, Vol. II, p. 210). Godwin implies therefore that men only become evil by succumbing to the corrupting pressures of government, and similarly are capable of great heroism, as in Caleb's case (at least until the end of the second, published version of the novel's conclusion), by defying the imposed system of law.

Particularly striking in its political implications, as well as its relevance to *Frankenstein*, is Godwin's preoccupation with the pursuit of truth. Caleb's decision to assert his autonomy by thinking for himself descends into a Victor Frankenstein-like gratification when his curiosity, "a principle that carries its pleasures as well as its pains along with it" (*CW*, p.122), causes him to pry into the affairs of his master, thus instigating his own destruction. Yet Godwin maintains that it is only through the pursuit of truth that one may challenge the tyranny of government. He portrays this pursuit as a natural pleasure and maintains that the "acquisition of truth, the perception of the regularity with which proposition flows out of proposition, and one step of science leads to another, has never failed to reward the man who engaged in this species of employment" (*PJ*, Vol. I, p. 308). The gaining of knowledge becomes an almost sensual pleasure.

Shelley was to point out the irony of this. Victor is carried away by the intellectual ecstasy of his pursuit, uncovering the ultimate knowledge of life and death. However, he receives no reward for it or even a moment of gratification. On the contrary, he destroys all those he loves and loses his own life prematurely. Victor embraced the Godwinian idea of the noble pursuit of knowledge too eagerly and too uncritically.

Political Justice, with Godwin's firm belief in the perfectibility of man, is unquestionably optimistic. He maintained that the potential for political and social harmony lies naturally within each individual. The means of stimulating that potential, to achieve the final goal of justice, are education and the subsequent desire for truth. In fact Caleb fails to achieve satisfactory justice in both versions of the conclusion to *Caleb Williams*: in the first unpublished ending he dies in jail; in the printed ending, he bears the guilt of Falkland's death, having succumbed to governmental tyranny by seeking justice in a court of law. But Caleb's failure is entirely due to the fact that neither he nor the society in which he lives have attained that state of philosophical grace in which justice would be automatically available. By denying his hero the fruits of his proposed reforms,

Godwin is not saying that they will not achieve the desired results; on the contrary, he is emphasizing how necessary they are.

However, Shelley did not share her father's optimism nor his faith in the necessarily noble potential of man, an idea that was fundamentally unchanged in the modified editions of *Political Justice.* Despite the criticism which assumes *Frankenstein's* ideology to be purely Godwinian, Shelley did not set out to do exactly what her father had done. *Caleb Williams* is Godwin's attempt to shape a popular novel out of a system of political theories. The novel is also a call-to-arms to a public which its author hoped was eager for reform or even revolution. *Frankenstein* is not polemical. Rather, it is a discourse on the value of revolution and reform, *not* simply a recommendation or incitement. While her father was eager to bring about a radical social change, Shelley was interested in the phenomenon of radical change itself, all its potential benefits and dangers.

Shelley studied the theories and systems that her circle embraced (Locke, Hume, Rousseau and others) and her understanding of Godwinism, as illustrated in *Frankenstein,* represents her most complete acknowledgement of systematic radicalism.[9] Burton Pollin has commented, her "first novel particularly revealed a respectable philosophic intent and an intellectual ingenuity, although it was the work of a girl of nineteen".[10] Making use of Godwinian concepts, Shelley begins to take optimism, idealism and revolution subtly to task in *Frankenstein.* In the novels that followed, her criticisms became bolder and more confident.

Nevertheless, the first reviews of *Frankenstein* placed the novel firmly within the Godwin camp. The *Edinburgh Magazine* began its review:

Here is one of the productions of the modern school in its highest style of caricature and exaggeration. It is formed on the Godwinian manner, and has all the faults, but many likewise of the beauties of that model . . . There was never a wilder story imagined, yet, like most of the fictions of this age, it has an air of reality attached to it, by being connected with the favourite projects and passions of the times.[11]

The review went on to point out the novel's specific Godwinian associations, as well as its general political concerns. Other reviews, especially those of Tory journals like the *Quarterly,* reacted with hostility to *Frankenstein's* obvious Godwinian characteristics, and continued its relentless attack on PBS and all his published associates.

The book was dedicated to Godwin himself and most assumed that it was the work of PBS, his notorious disciple (and, as rumour would have it, the buyer, for one thousand pounds, of his two daughters). In fact, PBS's own anonymous review (1818) points out the intentional echoes of Godwin in the new novel:

> Treat a person ill, and he will become wicked. Requite affection with scorn; – let one being be selected, for whatever cause, as the refuse of his kind – divide him, a social being, from society, and you impose upon him the irresistible obligations – malevolence and selfishness . . . The encounter and argument between *Frankenstein* and the Being on the sea of ice, almost approaches, in effect, to the expostulation of *Caleb Williams* with Falkland. It reminds us, indeed, somewhat of the style and character of that admirable writer, to whom the author has dedicated his work, and whose productions he seems to have studied.[12]

The two novels have many thematic similarities, not to mention those of style, pointed out unflatteringly by Kiely who asserts that Shelley's "prose style is solemn, inflated and imitative, an unhappy combination of Godwin's sentence structure and [PBS's] abstract vocabulary".[13] Some evaluations of Godwin's 'contribution' to *Frankenstein* betray a larger prejudice against Shelley as an independent thinker and writer. In addition to citing the "almost deadpan prose that *Frankenstein* inherited from her father"[14] (a prose which Walter Scott specifically applauded for its straightforwardness and simplicity), Locke seems loathe to give Shelley any credit for her novel at all. He maintains that *Frankenstein* is "the archetypal Godwinian novel, more Godwinian than Godwin's own",[15] its primary focus the story of injustice and the corruption of natural goodness. Locke goes on to quote De Quincey who said, "Most people felt of Mr. Godwin . . . with the same alienation and horror as . . . of the Monster created by Frankenstein".[16]

But both novels have at their centre the story of an obsessive pursuit where the pursued and the pursuer exchange roles and as A. D. Harvey has pointed out, have a crucial symbiotic relationship with each other.[17] Falkland and Victor both function and are acknowledged as "father" to their "sons", but Victor the father is similar to Caleb the son in his obsessive quest for hidden knowledge and in his subsequent victimization. At the same time, Caleb is placed in the paternal role when, after discovering his secret, he gains ascendency over Falkland. In fact, the reader is never able to fix clearly on the relative positions; who is the father and who the son, who the master, who the slave, who the people, who the tyrant (or government) in both novels, though *Frankenstein* is particularly fluid in this respect. Victor and the Monster continuously exchange roles after their meeting on the glacier.

First, the Monster commands Victor to create a female and follows him to the Orkney Islands to see that the job is carried out. He is obeyed until Victor rebels and destroys the work in progress. Victor's sense of horror at his gruesome project is not wholly untouched by a familiar proud defiance:

> I thought with a sensation of madness on my promise of creating another like to him, and trembling with passion, tore to pieces the thing on which I was engaged. The wretch saw me destroy the creature on whose future existence he depended for happiness, and, with a howl of devilish despair and revenge, withdrew . . . 'Begone! I do break my promise; never will I create another like yourself, equal in deformity and wickedness.'[18]

The tables turn again. The Monster reminds him:

> Slave, I before reasoned with you, but you have proved yourself unworthy of my condescension. Remember that I have power; you believe yourself miserable, but I can make you so wretched that the light of day will be hateful to you. You are my creator, but I am your master; – obey! (p. 167)

The chase into the Arctic reverses Victor's dominant position in the first half of the novel. Victor pursues the Monster, swearing to kill it and make the world safe. (Once again the vehemence of Victor's personal ambition and egoism is obscured by protestations of altruistic intent.) The Monster leaves food, warm clothes and clues to his direction along the trail and seems to protect his creator on his quest. The Monster is triumphant and provocative during this episode – a complete contrast to his behaviour at Victor's death. Before Victor's corpse he is completely subdued, he feels no sense of victory:

'That is also my victim!' he exclaimed: 'in his murder my crimes are consummated; the miserable series of my being is wound to its close! Oh, Frankenstein! generous and self-devoted being! what does it avail that I now ask thee to pardon me? I, who irretrievably destroyed thee by destroying all thou lovedst. Alas! he is cold, he cannot answer me'. (p. 219)

The Monster is finally cowed by his creator's death and, as he indicates, seeks himself only to die. Victor's ultimate passivity in death removes any possibility of struggle and confrontation with the Monster.

In life, the Monster and Victor are engaged in an endless struggle for supremacy; the notion of resolve or compromise is impossible. The Monster's symbolic rape of Elizabeth on her wedding night seals Victor's humiliation and subjugation and the Monster's (temporary) ascendency – like the practice of a victorious army's systematic rape of their enemy's women. Analogous to a class struggle between the irrepressible proletariat and the ruling class, as Franco Moretti has suggested,[19] the contest between the Monster and Victor can never be productively resolved. In fact, Shelley did not imagine a satisfactory conclusion to her character's fight or to the larger socio-political struggle. She offered no solution, no conclusion, no proof of the Monster's death, no hint that Victor had somehow learned from his momentous errors.

The similarities between *Caleb Williams* and *Frankenstein* are many, but others have found similarities in *Frankenstein* to Godwin's later novels. In his March 1818 review of *Frankenstein* for *Blackwood's Edinburgh Magazine* Walter Scott refers to St. Leon (1799):

assuming the possibility of the transmutation of metals and of the *elixir vitae*, the author has deduced, in the course of his narrative, the probable consequences of the possession of such secrets upon the fortunes and mind of him who might enjoy them. *Frankenstein* is a novel upon the same plan with St. Leon.

St. Leon also features a protagonist whose Faustian ambition is fulfilled with dire consequences, but unlike *Frankenstein* it relies on the supernatural. By contrast, *Frankenstein* is a naturalistic or explained gothic in the manner of the novels of the American Charles Brockden Brown; *Wieland* (1798), *Edgar Huntley* (1799) and *Ormond* (1799). There are no supernatural agencies.

Pollin stresses the fact that both *St. Leon* and *Frankenstein* are set in Switzerland. However, the Alps, like Radcliffe's Pyrennes, became one of the favourite environments of the Gothic and Romantic novel. They seemed to epitomize the sublime in nature and the genuine danger of travelling through them, as well as their forbidding aspect, ensured that their presence in the novel would contribute to a threatening atmosphere. What is more, Shelley's experience of those mountains had made a deep impression on her (and of course on PBS). They figure largely in her journal of the time and in her first published journalistic piece, *History of a Six Weeks' Tour* (1817),[20] following the adventures of her elopement with PBS and Clare Clairmont. Certainly, by the turn of the eighteenth century, the landscape of Switzerland and the Alps was a stock Romantic feature and fascination with the sublime in nature, as epitomized by huge, snow-clad mountains, predates Godwin. Nevertheless, *St. Leon* gives us a magic elixir, Pollin points out, that has the power both to create life and to restore it. What is more, he maintains that like Godwin's *Fleetwood* (1805), *Frankenstein*'s moral is the importance of love and companionship.

In fact, there are a number of literary allusions and sources that may have contributed to the story of *Frankenstein*, though too often comprehensive listings of such sources are offered in place of critical analysis and further contribute to the trivializing of Shelley's authorship. Nonetheless, a sampling of Shelley's wide reading is interesting.

Shelley read Ovid's *Metamorphoses* in Latin in 1815 and in the following year Mme. de Genlis' "Nouvelles Nouvelles" with its story of Pygmalion and Galatea. Marlowe's *Dr. Faustus* was no doubt known to her but it is not included in the lists. *The Rime of the Ancient Mariner*, which Shelley read in 1814 and again in 1821, deeply impressed her. Its implications for *Frankenstein*, not least of all its Arctic scenes, are important, most significantly in the novel's pervasive atmosphere of isolation and alienation. Shelley certainly had it in mind when writing, and drew her readers' attention to the poem in Letter Two and Chapter Five. Also at this time the Royal Navy's search for a North West passage included the unlikely quest for the "Open Polar Sea". It was imagined to be a "temperate ocean, free of ice, surrounding the Pole and walled off from the rest of the world by a frozen barrier".[21] This is the object of Walton's pursuit.

Shelley would have known Artegall's iron-man in *The Faerie Queen* and of automatons, mechanical clockwork dolls, sometimes life-size, which were popular parlour curiosities. What is more, Albertus Magnus (1193 or 1206–1280), one of the "lords" of Victor's imagination, was said to have created a mechanical man. Shelley may also have heard of the legend of the Golem (perhaps from M. G. Lewis), a man of clay animated by the invocation of the secret name of God by a rabbi of sixteenth-century Prague.

Shelley's reading of *The Tempest* in 1818 (and again in 1820), that play which so inspired PBS, may have suggested some aspects of both Victor and the Monster in Ariel and Caliban. Christopher Small has devoted his book to the Ariel-PBS-Caliban relationship which he believes Shelley exploited in *Frankenstein*.[22]

Ketterer also suggests that Shelley was familiar with the sixteenth-century play *The Honorable Historie of Frier Bacon and Frier Bungay* in which the two philosophers create a brass head which they animate with the help of the devil. Shelley did apparently know that Thomas Bungay (or Friar Bungay (fl.1290)) was a Franciscan who lectured on divinity at Oxford and Cambridge, the former the place of Victor and Clerval's visit.[23] PBS's margin notes on the manuscript of *Frankenstein* indicate the story of Bungay and his reputed discovery of gunpowder.

Shelley, like PBS and Byron, was interested in the scientific research of her day. She read Humphrey Davy's *Elements of Chemical Philosophy* (1812) in 1816 and though it does not appear in the reading lists, she was probably familiar with Erasmus Darwin's epic botanical love poem, *The Botanic Garden* (1791) and his prose work *Zoonomia* (1794–96), on the evolutionary principle in plant and animal life.[24]

But *Frankenstein* had other obvious radical associations. By drawing the reader's attention to Godwin, Shelley was also indirectly alluding to her mother, Mary Wollstonecraft, whose memoirs, written by Godwin, had caused a scandal when they were published in 1798. Contemporary readers would have associated *Frankenstein* with *Mary, A Fiction* (1788), Wollstonecraft's novel about the enslavement of marriage and the oppression of women. They would also have been reminded of Wollstonecraft's participation in the "war of ideas" and her pamphlets *A Vindication of the Rights of Man* (1790) followed by *A Vindication of the Rights of Woman* (1792), which entered into the heated debate sparked off by Thomas Paine's *Rights of Man* and Edmund Burke's *Reflections on the Revolution in France*. She was deeply involved with the politics and experience of the French Revolution as her *An Historical and*

Moral View of the Origin and Progress of the French Revolution (1794) shows.

The tell-tale information on the title pages continues with the novel's epigraph and subtitle. In one of its most consistent themes, *Frankenstein* adopts a familiar Romantic preoccupation, that with Milton's *Paradise Lost*, from which the epigraph is taken:

> Did I request thee, Maker, from my clay
> To mould me man? Did I solicit thee
> From darkness to promote me? –
>
> (*PL*, X, 743–45)

The second generation Romantics regarded Milton's interpretation of Genesis as a latent celebration of the defiance of authority and generally shared Blake's view that "Milton was of the Devil's party".[25] Lucifer's defiant act was heroic; challenging oppression and sacrificing personal happiness – a place in heaven – to lead the cause of liberty.[26] Byron was seen as the principle proponent of the "Satanic School" of poetry and Shelley was particularly enthusiastic about his verse dramas. In *Manfred* (1816) the eponymous hero has the powers of a necromancer and summons the spirits of the elements, Arimanes, the Destinies and Nemesis to his castle in the mountains. In *Cain* (1821) Lucifer tempts Abel's murderer with the eternal life forfeited by Adam and Eve and in *The Deformed Transformed* (1822), a humorous verse drama that Shelley fair-copied for Byron, a cripple sells his soul to the devil in exchange for physical perfection. PBS also chose epigraphs from *Paradise Lost* for his pot-boiler *Zastrozzi* (1810) and for Chapter 3 of *St. Irvyne, or, The Rosicrucian* (1810–11).

The character of Victor owes much to Milton's Satan. Victor's vaunting ambition defies God as creator of man. His good intentions become clouded by his own vanity:

> Life and death appeared to me ideal bounds, which I should first break through, and pour a torrent of light into our dark world. A new species would bless me as its creator and source; many happy and excellent natures would owe their being to me. No father could claim the gratitude of his child so completely as I should deserve theirs. (p. 54)

He attempts to usurp the monolithic power of the establishment – God – and assert the supremacy of mortal man. This is Satan's appeal to the radicals. PBS's epigraph selection for *Zastrozzi* expresses the same distaste for a tyrannical God as Shelley in her selection for *Frankenstein*:

> That their God
> May prove their foe, and with repenting hand
> Abolish his own works – This would surpass
> Common revenge.
>
> (*PL*, II, 368–71)[27]

But one is struck by Shelley's choice of quotation – it is not the revolutionary hero Satan but the usually hapless Adam in an uncharacteristic moment of defiance and anger. He is incensed at the cruelty and seemingly arbitrary power of his creator. Milton's God, as represented in this epigraph, is that same cruel manipulator taken to task in Shelley's early manuscript essay; he does not consult his people or consider their desires before imposing his will. It is the same tyrant that PBS's Wandering Jew defies with his rebellious curse and the same reviled in *Queen Mab*. By selecting that passage, epitomizing original defiance against the sting of injustice, Shelley immediately identifies her outward theme and allegiance.

The epigraph is preceded by the novel's subtitle, "the Modern Prometheus", which refers to Victor's role as creator. It also acknowledges Prometheus's dual role, as both creator and defier of the gods, characteristics that he shares with Victor. Victor's misguided ambitions serve to disrupt mankind, whether he is functioning as *Prometheus plasticator* – maker of man, or *Prometheus pyrphoros*, stealer of the gods' fire. Shelley might also have had in mind Ovid and Catullus who implied that Prometheus's work was flawed, as man's nature is base and animal. At least some of Prometheus's efforts *are* undeniably beneficial to man, but always, like Victor, at extreme personal cost.

At the same time that Shelley was working on her novel, Byron wrote "Prometheus" at Diodati, and entrusted her to take the manuscript to John Murray in the autumn. In that poem, Prometheus is a divine hero, but one who inspires common humanity with his own example to defy death:

> Thou art a symbol and a sign
> To Mortals of their fate and force;
> Like thee, Man is in part divine,

A troubled stream from a pure source;
And Man in portions can forsee
His own funereal destiny;
His wretchedness, and his resistance,
And his sad unallied existence:
To which his Spirit may oppose
Itself – and equal to all woes,
And a firm will, and a deep sense,
Which even in torture can descry
Its own concentered recompense,
Triumphant where it dares defy,
And making Death a Victory.

(45–59)[28]

Byron's Prometheus inspires mortal man to defy his narrow measure of existence and Victor *Frankenstein* responds to his call.

As Paul Cantor has pointed out,[29] *Frankenstein* draws upon the two central, western creation myths; the myth of the Greek Titan who moulds mankind, and Milton's account of Christian creation taken from Genesis. Shelley appropriates these two myths to propose a subversive and reflexive version of creation – the role of God is diminished and man celebrated as his own creator. Thus, Prometheus is both divine in his God-like role as creator of man, and the quintessential rebel in his defiance of his own master. Shelley weaves a new Romantic myth from those already established, but she does not accept Prometheus unconditionally as a role model. In *Prometheus Unbound* PBS embraced the Titan as a radical icon, though an imperfect one. Shelley is still more circumspect and weighs the consequences of his action with considerable caution.

Shelley's recreation of Promethean man, celebrated and damned, is not simply a variation of Godwinism or her husband's idealism. Victor's desire to have sole responsibility for his 'son's' creation and his refusal to reproduce in the far simpler and natural way is a desire, Cantor maintains, to see his creation "as solely a projection of himself".[30] He would like to see his entire creative impulse, his very being made flesh, objectified so it may be possessed. However, he is disgusted by the results of the hideous Monster that he had hoped to make beautiful. Cantor reminds us that this gap between inspiration and composition, the idea and the reality, is a recognizable fear in PBS – "Frankenstein beholding his creature is like a Shelleyan poet, disgusted by the fixed form into which his imaginative inspiration has sunk. The corrupting medium of human flesh has distorted *Frankenstein*'s creation into a grotesque mockery of his original vision".[31] In this way, *Frankenstein* is a mockery of PBS's impossible poetical (and political) ideal. And it is also true that Shelley's criticism has a personal element; Mellor identifies Shelley's criticism of the Romantic imagination as the result of her personal dissatisfaction with PBS.

But to return to the features which betrayed *Frankenstein* as a product of radical thought; it departs strikingly from the feminine novel. *Frankenstein* "brought a new sophistication to literary terror, and it did so without a heroine, without even a female victim", points out Ellen Moers.[32] Shelley was not at this period artistically concerned with the social problems of love and marriage, nor did she reaffirm that marriage was the simple solution to all a woman's troubles. Other writers such as Fanny Burney (1752–1840) and Elizabeth Inchbald (1753–1821) had progressive views for women, and they reflected them by allowing their women a wide range of character, education or experience. Nonetheless, they focussed in the main on the heroine and a love story. Even Mary Hays's daring and unconventional eponymous heroine of *The Memoirs of Emma Courtney* (1796) who demands to be as well educated as a man succumbs, at her own admission, to an unrealizable love. In her significant shift of focus away from this convention Shelley was less feminine or ladylike than any of the prominent and radical women writers of her time.

Beneath the obvious radical labels and invocation of radical arguments, *Frankenstein* reveals some scepticism about Godwin's and PBS's beliefs. It certainly speaks to the reader in the parlance of radical circles, yet *Frankenstein* contains a dialectic on radicalism and revolution in general. More narrowly *Frankenstein* is at once a satire and a criticism of the consequences of Godwinism. It is the beginning of Shelley's move away from idealized political theories, or at the very least, her expression of disappointment in those who initially led and then abandoned the Revolution. Though the indications of Shelley's growing independence in *Frankenstein* are subtle, once highlighted they undermine the Godwinian elements in the novel.[33]

David Ketterer and Iain Crawford[34] have suggested that Victor and Henry Clerval's visit to the tomb of John Hampden (1594–1643), a civil war hero, reflects Shelley's disappointment with the revolutionary cause. Victor goes to the tomb in Oxford, keen to be inspired by the spirit of liberty and justice that the figure represented to the radicals and liberals during the period in which the novel is set. The exercise is a failure – "For an instant I dared to shake off my chains, and look around me with a free and lofty spirit; but the iron had eaten into my flesh, and I sank again, trembling and hopeless, into my miserable self" (p. 160). Victor does not find the solace in righteous justice that he had hoped and at the same time, he feels sympathy with the overthrown Charles I, the *opponent*, at Hampden's time, of liberty: "The memory of that unfortunate king, and his companions . . . gave a peculiar interest to every part of the city, which they might be supposed to have inhabited" (p. 159).[35]

Victor *Frankenstein* shares the rebellious characteristics of Satan and Prometheus, two figures of *positive* action to the second generation Romantic psyche. Though Victor and his family appear to be uninterested in religion throughout the novel, like Charles Brockden Brown's Constantia[36] of *Ormond* (1799) – "Religion was regarded by her, not with disbelief, but with absolute indifference"[37] – Victor nonetheless defies the creator in his own attempt and eventual success at giving life.[38] His rebellious instincts are good in Godwinian terms; he celebrates man creating his own life, choosing his own destiny and shaping the world through science (a tool for autonomy) to suit his needs. However, his relentless ambition is a self-delusion, clothed as a quest for truth. He appears to be the dedicated promoter of the Godwinian ideal that would witness the manifestation of political justice. He pursues the "truth" as hotly and as passionately as Caleb Williams, but Victor's intellectual curiosity seeks to satisfy his own vanity. His ambition blots out his entire family, first symbolically than literally – his pursuit of the truth is grotesque in Shelley's novel.

Therefore, Victor's anarchic challenge and the revolution in knowledge that he hoped to bring about – "I will pioneer a new way, explore unknown powers, and unfold to the world the deepest mysteries of creation" (p. 48) – is a failure, not because his endeavour resulted in an unsatisfactory outcome, but because it was ill-conceived. Instead of Victor's scientific advancement contributing to human knowledge and the broadening of man's experience, it leads to capitulation and limitation.[39] Through Victor's example Walton is at first inspired to proceed against the wishes of his crew but finally agrees to return home and forget his intellectual fantasy of a new horizon. He abandons his search for the calm, iceless sea surrounding the Pole (an obvious chimera) and returns to the familiar safety, and claustrophobia, of his sister's parlour. One imagines his return to a sterile, static and predictable world, so unlike the vistas of shifting, floating ice and sea that surround his imaginative quest.

Victor's grandiose challenge, which like the angel Lucifer once sparkled with radiance, has been censured and abandoned. His revolution perpetrates not just a return to the status quo, but the continued descent into an archaic womb of ignorance. If *Political Justice* represents Godwin's vision of potential reality, and *Caleb Williams*, with its depressing warning, is Godwin's spurring-on of the masses, then his belief in a revolution in political and social spheres (even physical, he believed that the entire nature of human disease would change) was fantastically optimistic. Shelley presents this revolutionary optimism in *Frankenstein* but draws her own doomed conclusion for the rebellious spirit.

In fact Shelley's mordant parody of perfectibility looks like her most deliberate blow. Perfectibility was an ideal of PBS's which Shelley always associated with Godwin and it was still dear to her husband's heart while she was composing *Frankenstein*. St. Clair has emphasized PBS's attachment to the concept and to his early 'worship' of Godwin: "The word perfectibility was seldom far from his lips. He longed for the day, he told his friends, when Man would live in accordance with Nature and with Reason and in consequence with Virtue."[40] Shelley explains PBS's notion of perfectibility, as she understood it, in her editorial notes to *Prometheus Unbound*:

> The prominent feature of Shelley's theory of the destiny of the human species was, that evil is not inherent in the system of the creation, but an accident that might be expelled . . . Shelley believed that mankind had only to will that there should be no evil, and there would be none . . . That man could be so perfectionized as to be able to expel evil from his own nature, and from the greater part of the creation, was the cardinal point of his system.[41]

Victor plans for his creation to be physically ideal and gathers the necessary parts from other bodies accordingly. As he explains: "His limbs were in proportion, and I had selected his features as beautiful" (p. 57). The images of the half-crazed scientist (Victor describes a near delirious state) sorting through the dismembered corpses of charnel houses and tombs to select ideal features from dead faces and limbs represent in effect a grotesque satire of perfectibility. It also reminds the reader of the gruesome political cartoons produced in England during the French Revolution depicting, among other atrocities, families of sans culottes feasting on the limbs and entrails of the recently executed aristocracy. Victor uses dead bodies; the very materials for building a new and better humanity, which for both (the early) Godwin and PBS would have meant Reason and Truth, are already filthy and corrupted.[42] The idea that man can take a fundamental and commanding role in the improvement of man is undermined by the doomed and sordid nature of Victor's undertaking. There is no way of starting afresh. All flesh, all spirit, is tainted.

It is ironic too that Victor fails completely to see the merits of his creation, that the Monster is intelligent, eager to learn and affectionate. He is abandoned and let loose, untrained, upon the world. Like the intellectual architects of the Revolution, Rousseau for example, Victor forsakes his project. Shelley was angry not just with the ideals of her immediate family, but, like Byron, as expressed in Canto III of *Childe Harold's Pilgrimage*, with the irresponsible proponents and motivators of the Revolution. Shelley was particularly moved by Byron's (Harold's) ambiguous and complicated reflections on Waterloo and Napoleon's fatal flaw of vanity and over-reaching ambition:

XXXVI

There sunk the greatest, nor the worst of men,
Whose spirit, antithetically mixt
One moment of the mightiest, and again
On little objects with like firmness fixt,
Extreme in all things! hadst thou been betwixt,
Thy throne had still been thine, or never been;
For daring made thy rise as fall: thou seek'st
Even now to re-assume the imperial mien,
And shake again the world, the Thunderer of the scene!

XXXVII

Conqueror and captive of the earth art thou!
She trembles at thee still, and thy wild name
Was ne'er more bruited in men's minds than now
That thou art nothing, save the jest of Fame,

Who wooed thee once, thy vassal, and became
The flatterer of thy fierceness, till thou wert
A god unto thyself; nor less the same
To the astounded kingdoms all inert,
Who deem'd thee for a time whate'er thou didst assert.

XXXVIII

Oh, more or less than man – in high or low,
Battling nations, flying from the field;
Now making monarchs' necks thy footstool, now
More than thy meanest soldier taught to yield;
An empire thou couldst crush, command, rebuild,
But govern not thy pettiest passion, nor,
However deeply in men's spirits skill'd,
Look through thine own, nor curb the lust of war,
Nor learn that tempted Fate will leave the loftiest star.

Byron also expresses his disappointment with Rousseau, whose memory is evoked by Harold's view of Lake Leman:

LXXVII

Here the self-torturing sophist, wild Rousseau,
The apostle of affliction, he who threw
Enchantment over passion, and from woe
Wrung overwhelming eloquence, first drew
The breath which made him wretched; yet he knew
How to make madness beautiful, and cast
O'er erring deeds and thoughts, a heavenly hue
Of words, like sunbeams, dazzling as they past
The eyes, which o'er them shed tears feelingly and fast.

LXXXI

For then he was inspired, and from him came,
As from the Pythian's mystic cave of yore,
Those oracles which set the world in flame,
Nor ceased to burn till kingdoms were no more:
Did he not this for France? which lay before
Bowed to the inborn tyranny of years?
Broken and trembling, to the yoke she bore,

Till by the voice of him and his compeers,
Roused up to too much wrath, which follows o'ergrown
    fears?

LXXXII

They made themselves a fearful monument!
The wreck of old opinions – things which grew
Breathed from the birth of time: the veil they rent,
And what behind it lay, all earth shall view.
But good with ill they also overthrew,
Leaving but ruins, wherewith to rebuild
Upon the same foundation, and renew
Dungeons and thrones, which the same hour re-fill'd
As heretofore, because ambition was self-will'd.

Shelley shared Byron's doubts without being supported by her husband. In fact, in PBS's poem *Julian and Maddalo* (composed in 1818–19, first published in 1824), the PBS character, Julian, though chastened and educated by his experience, finds the Byron character insufficiently radical.

To Shelley, the Monster is the dark, destructive and unrestrained manifestation of the Revolution ("more or less than man"), which, had it not been abandoned by educators and guides, might have been the saviour of mankind. But Victor refuses to educate his offspring, just as his own father neglected to guide him. In this way, Shelley takes Rousseau to task; the Monster is also an attack on the idea of the noble savage. He is given all the politically and aesthetically correct books to read: *The Ruins of Empire* and Plutarch's *Parallel Lives* open his eyes and sensitize him to history and to injustice. Goethe's *Sorrows of Werther* even prepares him for an appreciation and understanding of sensibility and passion. But the Monster still runs amok. In fact, the Monster's 'accidental' education is woefully inadequate and his exclusive dependence on radical texts so ill-equips him for the world that he can only react in the most primitive way. Victor has the same kind of limitations in his own education. His information is too narrow, and the gathering of it unguided. He is left to his own devices and he too wreaks havoc.

Mellor suggests that the date of the Monster's birth and the events of the novel correspond to the key events of the French Revolution and points out that Ingolstadt, the Monster's birthplace, was the home of the revolutionary Illuminati and much Jacobin ferment, underscoring Shelley's deliberate association of the Monster with the bloody progress of the Revolution.[43] She gives another example of this association on Shelley's part. In her memoirs of Godwin, Shelley discussed his early radical politics. As Mellor quotes:

> The giant now awoke. The mind, never torpid, but never rouzed to its full energies, received the spark which lit it into an unextinguishable flame. Who can now tell the feelings of liberal men on the first outbreak of the French Revolution. In but too short a time afterwards it became tarnished by the vices of Orleans – dimmed by the want of talent of the Girondists – deformed & blood-stained by the Jacobins. But in 1789 & 1790 it was impossible for any but a courtier not to be warmed by the glowing influence.[44]

Though Mellor takes no account of Shelley's temporal, emotional and ideological distance, writing in 1836 of *her father's* experience of the Revolution, it is clear that Shelley came to reject revolutionary ideals completely. Instead of bringing humanity into a new age, Victor, like the disappointing Napoleon, plunges it back into darkness.[45]

Shelley's critique of revolution continues. Victor's lack of irony persists beyond his suffering. He warns the ambitious Walton against proceeding with his quest, but at the same time urges on his men. With one voice he appears to accept the supremacy of the quest for truth (as described in *Political Justice*) but tempers it with a caution:

> A human being in perfection ought always to preserve a calm and peaceful mind, and never to allow passion or a transitory desire to disturb his tranquillity. I do not think that the pursuit of knowledge is an exception to this rule. (pp. 55–56)[46]

Victor could be speaking to Caleb, as well as to himself.

Yet Victor's action, as usual, overcomes and obliterates his good intentions. The voice of reason that sees the possibility of emotional and intellectual tranquillity continues to press the worn-out crew to glory; " . . . Are you then so easily turned from your design? Did you not call this a glorious expedition? And wherefore was it glorious? . . . because danger and death surrounded it, and these you were to brave and overcome" (p. 214).

Victor's desire to protect an unfortunately kindred spirit from his own misery is overruled by his passion for defiance and his uncontrollable desire to strike out against conformity – he is enraged by consensus and the will of the many who decide to abandon the dangerous voyage. His imagination, despite full knowledge of its consequences, and an understanding of the benefits of its control, is irrepressible. In all the hundreds of pages of *Political Justice* and in the optimistic belief in man's potential shared by Godwin and PBS, Shelley could not find any treatment of the problem of egoism, personal ambition and the desire *not* to conform or to realize expectations. What proof have they of man's natural inclination towards Reason? *Frankenstein* shows the consequences of this central lacuna at the heart of Godwin's argument. Walton's victorious failure, his decision to abandon the voyage, is a greater achievement in human terms than Victor's 'successful' experiments. However, his victory is won at the cost of the complete suppression of his imaginative impulses. Shelley seems to be saying that no system, least of all her father's, can accommodate the reality of the imagination; one is either its slave or its crushing tyrant.

Finally, we see in Victor's ultimate misery the end result of the persistent quest for truth. As a very young man he selected a goal which he pursued relentlessly. He acquired knowledge systematically and, we are meant to believe, scientifically, until he unlocked the secret of life, the symbol, certainly to the medieval philosopher-alchemist, of all the knowledge of the universe. The eponymous hero of *St. Leon* receives the philosopher's stone and the elixir vitae, which causes his eternal suffering.[47] Victor and St. Leon are doubtless related in this respect but it is the naturalism of *Frankenstein*, its attempt, in what is perhaps a parody of Godwin's emphatic trust in rationality, to rationally explain Victor's work without the supernatural support of Godwin's mythical story which sets it apart. Godwin's view of over-reaching ambition finds expression in classic gothic style. By contrast, Shelley's 'reality' has a purpose. Indeed, when he begins his investigations Victor is at first attracted to such myths and determines to discover the philosopher's stone, only rejecting this course when he turns to science. This also represents, in some sense, Shelley's rejection of her father's fantasy. Shelley presents us with a human being who is destroyed by is own impulses towards knowledge and truth.

Political Justice does not see how the free pursuit of knowledge, truth and perfection can be anything but good. Shelley shows us the dangers of the anarchic personal quest that seems to her to inform *Political Justice*.

Though always considered a radical at this stage in her career, Shelley was already committed to the idea of domestic responsibility and one's accountability to others. The thoughtless rejection of family in the pursuit and perpetration of universal perfectibility deeply disturbed her and it is clear that she often resented PBS, as we shall see later, for his frequent refusal to be intellectually, artistically or spiritually compromised by a family's needs. Her insight into what she may have seen as the insidious implications of *Political Justice* is theoretically grounded, but it is also based on personal experience and emotion. Kiely is correct when he remarks, "Neither her father's trust in system nor her husband's unworldliness seemed satisfactory to her. On the contrary, judging from the events of her novel, both alternatives were too likely to lead to that single-mindedness which, when carried to the extreme, was a kind of insanity".[48]

In *Frankenstein* Shelley initiated a fundamental criticism, not only of her husband, which was emotionally painful, but of Romanticism as she understood it. She saw into and attempted to expose what Cantor calls the Romantic myth. An element of her creative nightmare is the "nightmare of Romantic idealism, revealing the dark underside to all the visionary dreams of remaking man that fired the imagination of Romantic myth-makers".[49] Shelley was not an idealist, her real vision of human potential is dark and pessimistic. An emotional outburst in her journal from October 21, 1838 has often misled prejudiced critics:

> I have been so abused by pretended friends for my lukewarmness in the "Good Cause", that though I disdain to answer them, I shall put down here a few thoughts on this subject . . . In the first place with regard to the "good Cause" – the cause of the advancement of freedom & knowledge – of the Rights of Women &c – I am not a person of Opinions. I have said elsewhere that human beings differ greatly in this – some have a passion for reforming the world: others do not cling to particular opinions. That my Parents & Shelley were of the former class, makes me respect it – I respect such when joined to real disinterestedness (toleration) & a clear understanding; – My accusers – after such

as these – appear to me mere drivellers. For myself, I earnestly
desire the good & enlightenment of my fellow creatures . . . but
I am not for violent extremes . . . I have never written a word
in disfavour of liberalism . . . . I have no wish to ally myself to
the Radicals – they are full of repulsion to me. Violent without
any sense of justice – selfish in the extreme – talking without
knowledge – rude, envious & insolent – I wish to have nothing
to do with them.

Shelley's thoughts on radicalism at this late date are no doubt influenced by the political climate of parliamentary reform of the late
1830s, as well as by her personal desire to disappear quietly from
the limelight of notoriety. But she did not suddenly and inexplicably
embrace conservatism nor did she betray her husband; her life was a
struggle between her unqualified love for him and for the expression
of her intellectual independence. We must take her journal at its
word in this instance, and understand her very early criticism of a
group of values and individuals that she eventually came to reject
completely. Her liberalism could not condone violence – the terror
that the Monster unleashes, despite our feelings of sympathy for him
and our understanding of his frustration, is represented by Shelley
as emotive, arbitrary cruelty. PBS condemned the imperialist's
war but may well have accepted that blood must be shed in the
overthrow of oppression, at least until 1817. Indeed, in his *Essay on
Christianity* he betrays sympathy for Caesar's assassins:

> It was in affection, in inextinguishable love for all that is ven-
> erable and dear to the human heart, in the names of country,
> liberty, and virtue; it was in serious and solemn and reluctant
> mood that these holy patriots murdered their father and their
> friend. They would have spared his violent death if he could have
> deposited the rights which he had assumed. His own selfish and
> narrow nature necessitated the sacrifice they made.[50]

Though PBS changed his mind about acceptable bloodshed,
eventually finding it ultimately unproductive, Shelley always
had profound doubts about this kind of justifiable violence, and
about the inflexibility of radical ideals, and *Frankenstein* remains her
earliest personal debate on the success and morality of radicalism;
in public that is. We have seen that her uneasiness regarding bloody
revolution was manifested very early in the "History of the Jews".

In *Frankenstein* Shelley denies the possibility of man's self-creation, of the success and glory to be found in the remaking of the world and the defiance of God – the essentials of a radical ideal. But at the same time she does not promise fulfilment or happiness in the acceptance of established religion and the worship of God. On the contrary, she refuses to envision fulfillment or happiness at all, most of all in the idealistic theories and fantasies favoured by her circle. We will discover how, in the novels that followed *Frankenstein*, her counter-revolutionary pessimism, as well as her equally firm doubts about the efficacy of establishment ideals, leads her to further studies of decay and dissolution. We will see how her work finally escalates into total global annihilation, the final and natural process of the "workshop of filthy creation" (p. 55) that is her artistic world.

4

"Connected in a Thousand Ways": Mary Shelley and Lord Byron

1816 was obviously an important year for Shelley and her own achievement in the completion of *Frankenstein* in the following year left her with very happy memories of Geneva. Indeed her journal records that time as the happiest of her unhappy life and she looked back to it with retrospective glory well into middle age. Ernest Lovell has suggested that her happiness was largely due to Byron's intervention in the complicated "love triangle" of the Shelley household shaped by Claire Clairmont and that Shelley felt a settling of romantic matters when in proximity to their famous and fascinating new friend.

However, judging from a journal entry of the following spring which looks back to that summer, it is possible to view Shelley's pleasure in a different light. On May 28, 1817, nearly a year after the 'summer of *Frankenstein*' and her first reading of the Canto in manuscript (Claire had made a copy), she records rereading Canto III of *Childe Harold's Pilgrimage*, the epic that had made Byron, quite literally, famous overnight with the publication of its first two cantos in 1812. Shelley was deeply affected with a sense of melancholy and memories of Byron and Geneva:

Dear Lake! I shall ever love thee. How a powerful mind can sanctify past scenes and recollections – His is a powerful mind. one that fills me with melancholy yet mixed with pleasure as is always the case when intellectual energy is displayed. I think of our excursions on the lake. how we saw him when he came down to us or welcomed our arrival with a goodhumoured smile – How very vividly does each verse of his poem recall some scene of this

57

kind to my memory – This time will soon also be a recollection – We may see him again & again – enjoy his society but the time will also arrive when that which is now an anticipation will be only in the memory – death will at length come and in the last moment all will be a dream.

The following day she wrote to PBS:

It made me dreadfully melancholy – The lake – the mountains and the faces associated with these scenes passed before me – Why is not life a continued moment where hours and days are not counted – but as it is a succession of events happen – the moment of enjoyment lives only in memory and when we die where are we?[1]

The profound sense of desolation and isolation in Byron's poem is shared by *Frankenstein*, and must also have helped to shape the dark vision that characterizes Shelley's two subsequent novels. It is not difficult to interpret Shelley's melancholia as an expression of love and longing, but her admiration and emotions are fixed on quite a different aspect of human relationship. "Intellectual energy" was a quality of utmost importance for Shelley. She knew that her mother had possessed it in abundance and it informed much of her relationship with PBS; though critics often discuss their episodes of mutual dissatisfaction, the Shelleys remained intellectually vital to one another. Though her love for PBS almost certainly revolved around the memory of the attachment of her early youth, Shelley's admiration for Byron seems founded on many of the same qualities that first attracted the young lovers to one another – intellectual affinity, great creative power and boundless intellectual curiosity. In fact, as her own political and spiritual instincts developed, she discovered intellectual agreement more often in the works of Byron than in her husband's.

Shelley was in London preparing *Frankenstein* for the press, and the task kept in mind the previous summer, Byron, and the attitudes they shared. Though she was not to see him again until the following year, she remained deeply interested in him, particularly as his daughter by Claire, Alba, (or Allegra as she was also known) formed a much-loved part of her household. Critics have speculated on the nature of Shelley's relationship with Byron, at best considering it simple physical attraction on her part and at worst, evidence of her fascination with the aristocracy. Though it did not fully bloom until the months following PBS's death, it has a richness and seriousness that represent an interesting area of investigation, to further illuminate the circle and Shelley's work.

Students of Romanticism have become familiar with the "Shelley Circle" as a catch-all term for the individual satellites that revolved around a major poet's sun. Built into this term is the method which investigates or attempts to understand those myriad artists and personalities only in relation to the poet. Though the twentieth century has focused on Percy Shelley as the galvanizing force which brought together Byron, Leigh Hunt, Mary Shelley, Matthew Lewis and others, his high literary reputation is a relatively recent phenomenon and owes much to his wife's exhaustive posthumous editions of his poems and prose. Shelley herself achieved far greater popularity than Percy ever did in his own lifetime, Byron of course still more. It also seems clear that Byron's orbital pull was at least as strong as the other poet's and that his draw upon Mary Shelley contributed to her developing intellectual independence and the questioning of her husband's ideals. In some sense, Byron contributed to Shelley's conflicted quest for autonomy.

Shelley found herself a literary star on her return to England from Italy in 1823. She arrived to discover a pirated version of *Frankenstein* a brilliant success as a stage play. As Cameron has pointed out:

> 'The Author of *Frankenstein*' existed in her own right. She was not unsuspected to be Mrs. Shelley; yet the fiction-reading public, then as now, took note of novels and was largely unaware of contemporary poets who had not made the grade of popularity. *Frankenstein, or The Modern Prometheus*, reprinted, translated, dramatized, and screened, has become a by-word with thousands who could never name its author, whereas *Prometheus Unbound* remains, on a general viewing, unread . . . [2]

The early nineteenth-century readership had an immense appetite for biography, and an even greater taste for scandal, preferably from the pens of those who had been on intimate terms with the subject. The public was eager to read of Shelley's glamorous and notorious friends and her subsequent novels were often read by those more interested in her life and the lives of those that surrounded her, than in their literary efforts.

In fact, Shelley became a touchstone not just for the posthumous reputation of her husband, but for Byron's as well. After the poet himself, she did more than many others to feed an eager public with information about their diabolical hero. *Valperga* (1823), *The Last Man* (1826), (actually described as a *roman* à clef), *Lodore* (1835), and *Falkner* (1837) take the Byronic hero as their central characters. Yet Shelley did not simply pander to sensationalism; her understanding of the poet was profound. She knew his work intimately and during what appears to be a short but intense period, formed a professional, intellectual and emotional relationship that shaped the direction of both of their respective work.

Central to the traditional understanding of the dynamics of the Shelley Circle is the summer of 1816. PBS and Mary Godwin had intended to go to Italy but at the encouragement of Claire Clairmont found themselves at Lake Geneva, neighbours of the famous Lord Byron. Claire had introduced herself to Byron by a series of letters and successfully seduced him. As he later wrote to Douglas Kinnaird: "I never loved nor pretended to love her – but a man is a man – & if a girl of eighteen comes prancing to you at all hours – there is but one way . . . ".[3] Claire was eager to continue the liaison, but did not yet realize that she was pregnant with Byron's child. During this summer, save for a few weeks in Venice in the autumn of 1818 represented in PBS's *Julian and Maddalo*, PBS and Byron enjoyed the highpoint of their friendship. It was shortly to sour after Byron's irresponsible and tyrannical treatment of Claire and their daughter Allegra, who eventually died of typhus in April 1822, in the isolated convent where Byron had placed her.

The conventional wisdom of Shelley Circle studies is to assume that PBS and Byron's conversations (joined briefly by Matthew "Monk" Lewis) on galvanism, electricity, ghosts and the new science, were the amorphous materials that came together as the inspiration for Shelley's *Frankenstein*. Shelley's own retrospective comments on that variety of inspiration in the introduction to the revised 1831 edition of *Frankenstein* also advance that misconception:

> Many and long were the conversations between Lord Byron and Shelley, to which I was a devout but nearly silent listener. During one of these, various philosophical doctrines were discussed, and among others the nature of the principle of life, and whether there was any probability of its ever being discovered and communicated. They talked of the experiments of Dr. Darwin . . . who

preserved a piece of vermicelli in a glass case, till by some extraordinary means it began to move with voluntary motion. Not thus, after all, would life be given. Perhaps a corpse would be re-animated; galvanism had given token of such things: perhaps the component parts of a creature might be manufactured, brought together, and endued with vital warmth . . . (pp. 8–9)

Critic after critic, commenting on the novel, reinforces this picture of a silent and passive Shelley soaking up the knowledge, talent and ideas of the great men. "Quite suddenly", Cameron maintains, "Mary's mind seems to have expanded".[4] She is represented as so impassive that one is forced to picture a kind of oracle, moved by a disembodied inspiration to record a history over which she had no control. Her relationship to the two men, Byron in particular, is portrayed as one of emulation and idealization. Critics like Cameron have even claimed that Shelley was a shameless admirer of the aristocracy and was "dazzled" by Byron's title.[5] Lovell has suggested that she was in love with him and remained fascinated by his character throughout her life. He even sees the Byronic figures in her novels (underestimating the significance of the adventurer Edward Trelawny who as a model "out-Byroned" Byron),[6] as evidence of her psychological obsession with the poet and her true preference for him, both sexually and emotionally, over her husband.[7]

There is substance in some of these claims. Byron's own ghost story, that of the vampire, remained unfinished, but that creature had already appeared in the Sultan's curse upon the eponymous hero of *The Giaour* (1813):

> . . . on earth as Vampire sent,
> Thy corse shall from its tomb be rent;
> Then ghostly haunt thy native place,
> And suck the blood of all thy race,
> There from thy daughter, sister, wife,
> At midnight drain the stream of life;
> Yet loathe the banquet which perforce
> Must feed thy livid living corse:
> Thy victims ere they yet expire
> Shall know the daemon for their sire,
> As cursing thee, thou cursing them,
> Thy flowers are wither'd on the stem.

(755–66)

The spirit of that early Byronic vampire persists in *Frankenstein*. Victor comments, "I considered the being . . . nearly in the light of my own vampire, my own spirit let loose from the grave, and forced to destroy all that was dear to me" (p. 77). Like the Giaour condemned in the curse to slaughter his loved ones, Victor must stand passively by as the Monster kills first William, Justine, Clerval and then Elizabeth.

On the other hand, the aristocratic vampire of Byron's fragment[8] (as recorded, elaborated on, and concluded by John Polidori and published by him as *The Vampyre*) bears little resemblance to Victor *Frankenstein*. His preoccupation is largely sexual. In Polidori's adaptation of the story, he devotes his evil efforts to dishonouring and ruining promising young heiresses. He is also a supernatural creature, his corpse disappears unaccountably, reappearing in England to claim the innocent sister of the doomed hero. Victor's sexuality, if at all present, is suppressed to say the least and his relationship with Elizabeth remains passionless and sterile.

If there is a literary link between the two writers here, it operates at a deeper level than that of the sourcing of a simple plot. The concept of incest, which informs the criminal vampire who feeds on his own family, is associated with Byron himself. Shelley might have been aware of the rumours that drove Byron from England in 1816; in addition to cruelty to his wife, it was whispered that he had engaged in a sexual relationship with his half-sister Augusta Leigh. His devotion to her was certainly well known. The subject of incest surfaces in more then one of Shelley's novels and short stories and once again suggests a complex relationship between Shelley and her own father. It is only with the 1831 edition of *Frankenstein* that Elizabeth assumes the safe distance of a foundling where no impropriety could be attached to her marriage to Victor.

Incest held a certain fascination for the Shelleys. It figures repeatedly in PBS's poetry, in *Laon and Cythna* and in *The Cenci* for example. Shelley's own novella *Mathilda* (unpublished until 1959) features a father's obsessive love for his daughter and what is more, her willingness to reciprocate that love. In her "History of the Jews" Shelley even playfully suggests that incest is somehow justified by the Bible; Adam and Eve's children must have "married". Her short story *The Mourner*, published in *The Keepsake* in 1830, features an extraordinarily close father-daughter relationship where she explains, "the love of a daughter is one of the deepest and strongest, as it is the purest passion of which our natures are capable . . . ".[9] Shelley and PBS were also well aware of the rumours which circulated about their own ménage à trois, though strictly speaking they could not be accused of real incest. During the Geneva summer, Byron was at work upon his verse drama *Manfred*, inspired by the spectacular Alpine scenery, but even more so by his relationship with Augusta; Manfred himself is tortured by the memory of his criminal relations with his own sister who had since died. The artistic possibilities of incest were evidently enthusiastically shared by the group, an enthusiasm heightened further by the presence of a genuine Manfred.

There is considerable evidence of friendship between Byron and Shelley based on mutual admiration and respect which, instead of portraying Shelley as the peripheral, blind admirer of a famous poet, shows a serious-minded intellectual who was rather at the centre of her milieu. Shelley's impact on her circle was not just of a practical or domestic nature, though she constantly came to the aid of friends with money, advice, housekeeping, child-minding and nursing. Her role, particularly in regard to Byron, is wider and more profound.

The relationship between Shelley and Byron developed over the years 1816 to 1823 and Byron's departure for Greece. It coincided with Shelley's growing doubts about her husband's brand of political radicalism and idealism. In purely political terms, Byron represented an alternative approach to the question of reform, one that was no less thrilling or attractive than PBS's, but which, beneath its iconoclasm, was somewhat more tolerant of conventional social and political structures – and thus more likely to be truly acceptable to Shelley. But the relationship was deeper in artistic terms than it was in political ones: nor did the influence flow entirely one way. Byron's dramas continued to appear long after the completion of *Frankenstein* and it is possible to trace some characteristics of Victor in the later Byronic heros of *Cain, Sardanapalus* (1821), *Heaven and Earth* and the unfinished *The Deformed Transformed*. Of equal interest is the relationship between some of the dramas which Shelley was fair-copying during or immediately following completion of her own copying-out of *Valperga* in 1821, and the characters of Evadne in *The Last Man* (which Shelley began work on in 1824) and Euthanasia, the noble, nationalistic Countess of *Valperga*. The former is a Greek noblewoman and patriot who dies on the battlefield, dressed as a warrior, fighting for her country. Her passion for liberty and action in arms is reminiscent of Byron's Greek Myrrha (predating *The Last*

Man) who stands with sword in hand, urging on the defenders of Assyria and Sardanapalus the king. Yet Myrrha, in turn, is predated by Shelley's feudal countess,[10] symbol of liberty, who fights to the destruction of her castle and status rather than submit to the imperialistic tyrant Castruccio.

By the summer of 1823 Shelley often found Byron mean, petty and cruel, but as she herself admitted almost regretfully to another member of the circle, Jane Williams, she still had to admire his work. As executor of PBS's estate, Byron was to some extent responsible for Shelley's finances and legal rights, a job that he applied himself to with varying degrees of commitment. He acted forcefully for Shelley when she was confronted by Sir Timothy's determination to support his grandson only if she would surrender him to a foster home of his choosing. Byron argued successfully for some support without that sacrifice – Shelley would under no circumstances give up her only child.

Writing to Jane Williams, Shelley offered some rather tart opinions about the poet's handling of other aspects of her affairs, but also expressed a complex sense of gratitude and admiration for him. She also reveals the workings of her unique talent for pleasing him. On April 10, 1823 she wrote to her friend in England:

> LB. strongly advises my return [to England] . . . he is still very kind to me & makes offers of a *generous* nature. He will profit by the *will* & therefore every motive will induce him to keep his word. But he piques himself on giving good advice & I must follow it, or lose my credit with him – which stands greatly I believe on my known admiration of his writings and my docility in attending to him . . . but I am grateful to him for his kindness to me and if he continues as he promises my gratitude will prevent my being angry with him. I shall see when I depart if his actions are on parr with his professions, & if they are why, my dear Jane, I shall be very glad – truly obliged – not a little surprised & not less *reconnaissante*.

But the friendship of Shelley and Byron deteriorated just before his departure for Greece and her own for England in July 1823. Predictably, it was due to the problems inherent in a friendship complicated by business and financial considerations. Byron reneged on his promise of funds for her return trip to London. It is this misfortune, rather than jealousy or the feelings of a rejected lover

(Shelley's regard for the poet approaches the fraught but fundamentally close relationship of family) which sheds light on their strange behaviour. But the story is even more complex. Just days before his departure, angry letters passed between Hunt, Shelley and the poet. In a fit of generosity Byron had promised to sponsor a journal that Hunt was to publish, thereby providing the much encumbered man – six children and a sickly wife – with a dignified income. The project that might have flourished under PBS's patronage collapsed with the last of Byron's patience. Hunt never forgave Byron for his financial withdrawal, as well as his public claim that *The Liberal's* real function was as a charity, and he revenged himself in print in *Conversations with Lord Byron and Some of his Contemporaries* (1828). Byron's execution of the will further complicated matters. His attempts to clarify the will only increased its ambiguities, and anger, particularly Hunt's, inevitably erupted over the allocation of certain bequests. Shelley was also disappointed by Byron's lapse of integrity but Byron's mistress Teresa Guiccioli did her best, in a series of conciliatory letters, to smooth over the antagonism between the two.

Nonetheless, before this rupture in their friendship Shelley figured prominently in Byron's life following the death of PBS. Bennett has located twenty letters from Shelley to Byron over the period from 1817 to 1823 (one of these is a postscript to PBS's letter to the poet from Marlow in 1817). Ten of these letters were written in the late winter and early spring of 1823, the most intense period of their relationship, when they moved to Albaro, a suburb of Genoa. Byron shared the Casa Saluzzi with the Countess Guiccioli, her father and brother and Shelley the Casa Negroto with the Hunts and their many children. Though we have only five letters from Byron to Shelley during that time and Shelley's journal records no meetings with Byron (in fact, the journal entries for the year 1823 total only seven in number), it is clear from her letters to the Casa Saluzzi that they met regularly by the springtime. She wrote on March 5, 1823:

> I have received a letter from my father today, & should be glad to see your Lordship, if possible before the Post goes out to England. If it be not inconvenient to you would you come up this evening at your usual hour? or will you mention a convenient time when I can see you at your own house?

Perhaps the most telling details of their relationship are found in the set of letters that Shelley wrote on the subject of Leigh Hunt's journal the *Liberal* and Byron's letter to John Murray ridiculing both the man and his project. Hunt's nephew saw the letter in London and immediately took offence on behalf of his uncle. Needless to say, Hunt was deeply hurt. Shelley explains in her letter to the defiant Byron that he should win back Hunt's regard and renew their valuable friendship. The letter is a masterpiece of diplomacy and understanding of Byron's complex personality:

> I am induced to say a few words to your Lordship on this affair of Hunt's. I wish indeed that I could *say* them, as these things are always better said; but I will not venture on a second intrusion & dare not inflict upon you the pain of paying me a visit. Hunt did not send those letters to his nephew that he sent for you to read, and this delay has made him reflect. Indeed, my dear Lord Byron, he thinks much of this & takes it much to heart. When he reflects that his *bread* depends upon the success of this Journal, & that you depreciate it in those circles where much harm can be done to it; that you depreciate him as a coadjutor, making it . . . appear (pardon the quotation) that his poverty & not your will consents – all this dispirits him greatly. He thinks that an explanation would come ungracefully from him, but that it would come gracefully from you. He is very much vexed that his Nephew noticed these reports, but they are noticed, Murray may publish, or give free circulation to your letter, and that places him in a kind of degrading point of view. For "his sick . . . wife & six children" are alledged – not your friendship for him. He said this evening that he thought of writing to you about this, but I offered to write instead, to spare him a painful task. He does not see my letter.
>
> Consider that however Moore may laugh at Rimini-pimini,[11] that Hunt is a very good man. Shelley was greatly attached to him on account of his integrity, & that really your letter *does* place him in an awkward situation. The Journal is now a work of charity – a kind of subscription for Hunt's family – this must hurt the work. Do not you then think that a few words from you in explanation or excuse such as could appear, are due to your literary companionship with him? It would be a goodnatured thing – & a . . . prudent thing – since you would stop effectually the impertinence of Murray, by shewing him that he has no power to make you quarrel with your friend, & that you do not fear his treason.

It is a painful thing for me to put forward my opinion. I have been so long accustomed to have another act for me; but my years of apprenticeship must begin. If I am awkward at first, forgive me. I would, like a dormouse, roll myself in cotton at the bottom of my cage, & never peep out. But I see Hunt annoyed in every way. Let us pass over his vanity. What if that has been pampered – little else about him has – & qualms have visited him even upon that tender point. But here even the independence of his character is in some measure staked – Besides the success of his Journal – & consequently his very existence. So I would fain do a little to make him easy again. You asked me the other evening, why I had not sent you a note about it; I do so now. So do not think me impertinent; if you do not know that I am timid, yet I am so; – it is a great effort to me to intrude with my writing upon you. But if I can make Hunt have less painful feelings by inducing you to soften the effect that your letter must have had in London, why for that I will even risk being impertinent . . . Again I beg your Lordship to excuse my annoying you . . . (November 16, 1822)

Byron responded by outlining his pompous distinction between true friendship and "men-of-the-world-friendships"[12] and by defending his behaviour. Shelley answered on the same day with another self-effacing, gently coaxing letter. It is clear that Shelley understood Byron's character and the best way of influencing him; she guessed that her decidedly 'anti-Blue' demeanour (Byron detested the "Blues", or supposedly aggressive literary ladies) secured her in his affections. Yet very few of Byron's friends would have felt free to correct him on his dishonourable behaviour. Shelley also knew how to stimulate Byron's whims; he usually felt gratified when he could, with his money or influence, do favours for his friends and she attempted to direct his benevolence (or vanity) towards Hunt.[13] Her inside jokes also help to disarm the seriousness of the letter; they had all laughed at Hunt's poem *Rimini* and its dedication to Byron, and the "dormouse" was an early nickname for Shelley that Byron must have been familiar with. Thomas Medwin evidently thought that Shelley could be of some use in his proposed (money-grubbing) biography of the poet immediately after his death. Perhaps wishing to flatter her into assisting him he wrote to her in October 1824 that she knew the poet "perhaps better than any person living".[14]

By the end of November Shelley was no longer as angry with

Byron. He had been acting on her behalf by dealing with Sir Timothy's lawyers in an attempt to secure her an annuity against her
son's eventual inheritance (an inheritance that came far later than
any expected, Sir Timothy living inconveniently into his nineties).
Her letters and journal at this time show an easy familiarity which
must have been reciprocated. She wrote to him:

> . . . it is always a pleasant thing to receive kindnesses; and I need
> not say how truly I thank you for those that you have shewn me. I
> am quite of the *old school* with regard to gratitude & I feel it very
> deeply whenever my friends are good enough to shew affection
> for me and I am not afraid of being misinterpreted when I express
> it . . . " (November 27, 1822)

During the previous months, still much affected by PBS's recent
death, Shelley sheds an interesting light on her feelings for Byron.
As she states in the letter above, she was not afraid that her affection
would be misunderstood, presumably as romantic love. In a journal
entry for October 19, 1822 she reflects on her affection for Albe, for
so she and PBS had called Byron:

> I do not think that any person's voice has the same power of
> awakening melancholy in me as Albe's – I have been accustomed
> when hearing it to listen & to speak little; – another voice, not
> mine, ever replied . . . when Albe ceases to speak I expect to hear
> *that other* voice, & when I hear another instead, it jars strangely
> with every association . . . when Albè speaks & Shelley does not
> answer, it is as thunder without rain . . .   The above explains that
> which would otherwise be an enigma, why Albe has the power
> by his mere presence & voice of exciting such deep & shifting
> emotions within me . . . when in company with Albe, I can never
> cease for a second to have him (Shelley) in my heart & brain with
> a clearness that mocks reality . . .

She repeats the same sentiment in a letter to Maria Gisborne on
November 22, 1822: "Lord Byron reminds me most of [Percy] in a
certain way, for I always saw them together, & when LB. speaks I
wait for [Percy's] voice in answer as the natural result . . . ".

Byron and Mary Shelley were "connected . . . in a thousand
ways".[15] They were close enough for Shelley to give her unsolicited
advice and at the same time be content to allow Byron to handle

her affairs. Byron had also given her his diaries to read – those later burned by Moore and Hobhouse at John Murray's. She claimed in a letter to Trelawny (July 28, 1824), that there "was not much in them I know, for I read them some years ago in Venice". Byron and Shelley were also close enough to squabble, for both to be hurt, and for Shelley to maintain her respect and affection for Byron in the midst of her exasperation.

However, there is further evidence which points to a more positive contribution to the Circle on Shelley's part, and that is in the form of her friendship with the Greek "Prince" and patriot Alexander Mavrocordato (1791–1865).[16] Independently of PBS, Shelley was introduced to the Greek on December 2, 1820. She had begun Greek exercises in July of the same year and read Greek nearly every day. By the time that Mavrocordato arrived she must have been nearly proficient. From that time she studied every day and saw the Prince almost twice a day (except during a short absence), until he left for Greece on June 26, 1821. Mavrocordato gave Shelley Greek lessons in exchange for English and the two became close friends. Yet judging from journal entries and letters, PBS did not see as much of the Prince. Iris Origo suggests that he even disliked him, and by many accounts, the Prince's English needed little attention.[17] Mavrocordato called on Shelley and she on him without any indication of PBS's company. Some critics have taken this as evidence of Shelley's attempt to get back at her husband for his preoccupation with the beautiful and seemingly tragic Emilia Viviani.

There is no doubt that the Prince had great affection for Shelley. He wrote on April 3, 1821:

> Très chère et genereuse Amie! . . . vous ne devez pas doubter que les seuls moments qui me paraitront encore supportables pendant mon court séjour en cette ville, seront toujours ceux que je passerai avec vous.[18]

However, in much the same way that her relationship with Byron is trivialized, critics have failed to see the importance of her near exclusive association with Mavrocordato and its subsequent impact on the circle.

The Prince was a well educated and urbane man, the model of the romantic Greek patriot that Byron himself must have emulated (though he was too European and apparently too reasonable for

Trelawny – he didn't wear "Greek" costume, he was too cautious, nor did he trust the colourful warrior-chiefs that Trelawny so admired). PBS dedicated Hellas to him, found him intelligent, dignified and no doubt an inspiration for the circle's enthusiasm for Greek freedom. Byron had been stirred by Greek patriotism earlier, probably from his first trip to the Levant. He wrote to Trelawny June 15, 1823 of Greece, "it is the only place I was ever contented in".[19] But he did not decide to support the Greek cause with his money and his person until Edward Blaquiere of the London Greek Committee came to see him in Genoa in 1823.

Shelley's interest in Greece may date from the Shelleys' "Greek revival" at Marlow of 1817:

> It is plain that the group [including Hunt and Peacock] always interpreted their shared taste for what they thought was characteristically Greek – comic, elegant and harmonious – as a deliberate rejection of the taste for the German which Coleridge was advocating in 1817 in *Biographia Literaria*,[20]

and which Mme. de Staël delineated in *De l'Allemagne* (1810, translated into English 1813). They formed a "cult of laughter"[21] which Shelley reawakened, practically, in 1821. Mavrocordato fed her enthusiasm and they passed many evenings discussing Greek politics. On March 14, 1821 she recorded, "Prince Maurocordato in the evening – I have an interesting conversation with him concerning Greece . . . " and the following month, "[Mavrocordato] calls with news about Greece – he is as gay as a caged eagle just free . . . " (April 1, 1821).

Though Byron did not arrive in Genoa until after Mavrocordato's departure, he joined him at Missolonghi in January 1824. Byron had given £4,000 to the Greek government to launch a fleet, this bequest ensuring the elevation of the prince to Commander-in-Chief and governor of Western Greece. Marchand has pointed out that except for Mavrocordato, Byron mistrusted the Greeks and would only respect and rely on the Prince's tested honour and honesty.

Shelley's friendship continued by post after Mavrocordato's departure. There are eight letters from the Prince to Shelley recorded in *Shelley and Mary*, and one from Shelley on February 22, 1825, written with affection and continued interest in Greece – "To tell you with what interest I am occupied with the affairs of Greece. – How I rejoice with each victory your country wins, and with each honor that comes to you – will be to tell you a very long and very old story – as long as the list of your renowned feats, as old as our friendship".

Shelley had continued her Greek lessons after a temporary hiatus while she copied *Valperga*. On November 29, 1821, she recorded in her journal, "I mark this day because I begin my Greek again – and that is a study which ever delights me – I do not feel the bore of it as in learning another language, although it be so difficult – it so richly repays one . . . ".[22]

Mavrocordato, introduced into and maintained in the circle by Shelley, was a galvanizing force in Byron's subsequent actions. Casting about for something to do, Byron, inspired by Mavrocordato's many gifts (as well as by Trelawny's promise to accompany him), fixed on Greece as the focus of his energies. However, the gross mishandling of the war on the part of the revolutionary Greek government and the London Greek Committee's deception both contributed to the fiasco that Byron's expedition became. St. Clair has pointed out that:

> the essentially genocidal nature of the war was suppressed, and the assumption that the Greeks were a united people struggling to assert their right to independence as a nation state was scarcely challenged.[23]

But this same misconceived and misguided expedition rehabilitated Byron's savaged reputation in England and made him a hero and champion of liberty. In England both conservative and liberal shared the romantic enthusiasm for the Greek cause. Shelley's influence on Byron's decision to support the cause of the Greeks helped to wipe away the sins that he had carried with him from England.

Finally, Shelley's relationship with Byron had a specifically professional element. She fair-copied many of his poems – his greatest poems – from his drafts. Her fair-copies, in most cases, would then have been sent back to John Murray in London, with Byron's additional corrections or changes. She began in 1818 with "Ode on Venice" and *Mazeppa*. In a letter to Byron in Venice, on the 3rd or 4th of October (evidence conflicts between the letters and journals), she returned the drafts, (which had been delivered by the poet on 28 September) and the completed copies.[24]

In the letter of 3–4 October Shelley also offered to transcribe the first canto of *Don Juan* which she knew Byron had recently completed. Bennett suggests that Byron may have expressed to her what he wrote to Thomas Moore in September: "the bore of copying it out is intolerable; and if I had an amanuensis he would be of no use, as my writing is so difficult to decipher".[25] Indeed, Shelley apologizes in her letter, "I hope not many errors and those partly from my not being able to decypher your M.S . . . .". Even as late as December 1822, after she had copied six cantos of *Don Juan*, she found Byron's hand occasionally difficult: "Your Lordship's MS. was very difficult to decypher, so pardon blunders & omissions".

Despite her occasional complaints about his handwriting, Byron came to depend on Shelley, particularly in the copying of *Don Juan*.[26] She began working for him with Canto 6 and stayed with it until the last complete canto – (16) – came into her hands only days before his departure for Greece. Yet it is clear that her contribution was not simply mechanical. Jerome McGann has pointed out, in his introduction to Volume Five of *The Complete Works*:

> we know that she often introduced small changes into Byron's text. We also know that Byron expected and even welcomed such minor interventions in his text by friends who supplied him with editorial and copying help . . . The surviving Mary Shelley transcripts of DJ [only 6, 7 and 8 have been located] show that when Byron corrected her copy he would sometimes allow her minor revisions to stand uncorrected . . . ".[27]

Shelley's contributions in fact go even farther than this. In several cases Byron offered his copyist alternative endings to stanzas, in some cases, as many as three. Shelley then chose the stanza which she found most appropriate. The full details of Shelley's editions of Byron's texts – and her support of *Don Juan* when publisher and friends urged him to stop writing – needs greater amplification than there is room for in this chapter; accordingly, they appear in Appendix C.

Shelley evidently enjoyed transcription. She was genuinely enthusiastic about Byron's poetry and solicited as much work from him as she could. She had finished the copying and correction of *Valperga* by the end of November 1821 and in January 1822 she read *Werner* and *Sardanapalus* as if in anticipation of another assignment from the poet. Shelley sent Byron many assurances that she was pleased to do the work that he had come to rely on; " . . . allow me to hope that it will not be long before you employ me on my usual interesting task" (Pisa, April 12, 1822).

On October 30, 1822 she wrote: "You could not have sent me a more agreable task than to copy your drama [*The Deformed Transformed*, published February 20, 1824, one month before *Don Juan* Cantos 15 and 16], but I hope you intend to continue it, it is a great favourite of mine." She was delighted with *The Deformed Transformed*, her first assignment after the long interval that followed *Mazeppa* and "Ode on Venice". Byron sent her the completed first section in a letter on 14 November[28] – "I send you the completion of the *first* part – of the drama – as I think it may be as well to divide it – although *intended* to be *irregular* in all its branches". She wrote back with the completed copy on the 16th of November:

The 'Eternal Scoffer' seems a favourite of yours. The Critics, as they used to make you a Childe Harold, Giaour, & Lara all in one, will make a compound of Satan & Ceasar to form your prototype . . . I delight in your new style much more than in your former *glorious one*, & shall be much pleased when your fertile brain gives my fingers more work.

In January Byron sent a few more scenes of *The Deformed Transformed* to be copied. After completing those sections she returned them to the poet with her praise on February 2, 1823:

The more I read this Poem that I send, the more I admire it. I pray that Your Lordship will finish it. – It must be your own inclination that will govern you in that, but from what you have said, I have some hopes that you will. You never wrote anything more beautiful than one lyric in it – & the whole, I am tempted to say, surpasses "Your former glorious style" – at least it fully equals the very best parts of your best productions.

At a time when Byron's "sublime" and dramatic poetry, *Childe Harold's Pilgrimage* and the Oriental Tales for example, was by far the most popular and critically acclaimed body of his work, Shelley's high estimation of his satirical verse, *over* his previous 'inflated' style, anticipates the criticism of Byron's work today. At present *Don Juan* is considered his masterpiece, almost to the exclusion of those works which made and supported his fame during his lifetime and immediately after his death. Shelley's enthusiasm was tempered by some insightful criticisms of the pieces that she read and was given to copy. Her letters to others on Byron's latest work are often more critical (usually depending on the state of their personal relations) than those that she sent to the poet. They are none the less astute and anticipate her editing of PBS's poems.

In the spring of 1823, Shelley resumed her work on *Don Juan*. She continued enthusiastically on 30 March:

> The 15th Canto was so long coming even after I heard that it was finished, that I began to suspect that you thought that you were annoying me by sending me employment. Be assured however on the contrary, that besides the pleasure it gives me to be in the slightest manner useful to your Lordship, the task itself is a delightful one to me.

As soon as she had completed the 15th, she offered her services for the next canto – "I hear that you have begun Your 16th Canto. I trust that your Lordship will make use of me, in the only way I can be of service to you . . . " (April 2, 1823). The following year, on March 22, 1824, she wrote to Trelawny after these cantos were published:

> Opinions vary very much with regard to these last Cantos of Don Juan; they are usually considered as a falling off – & so they are in many respects, they want the deep & passionate feeling of the first – but they are unequalled in their strictures upon *life* & flashes of wit.

Shelley was impressed by the gusto of *Don Juan* and Byron must have been gratified. She was one of his few friends to encourage the poem's satirical passages when most had urged him to suppress or give up the work altogether. Even his faithful publisher John Murray had washed his hands of the controversial, not to say inflammatory poem, when Byron refused to compromise. Shelley, who has been deemed something of a prude by history, supported him throughout. She wrote to Jane Williams on October 15, 1822, " . . . I have copied for him the 10th Canto of Don Juan. It is not in his *fine* style, but there are some beautiful & many witty things in it . . . the most severe satire I ever read . . . ". Later that month, working on Canto 11 she wrote to Byron, " . . . I have nearly finished your *savage* Canto – You will cause Milman to

hang himself . . . I was much pleased with your notice of Keats
– Your fashionable world is delightful . . . " (October 21, 1822). By
October 24 Shelley had copied Canto 11. Between the 7th and 14th
of December she copied Canto 12 and commented:

> I like your Canto extremely; it has only touches of your *highest*
> style of poetry, but it is very amusing & delightful. It is a comfort
> to get anything to gild the dark clouds now my sun is set –
> Sometimes when very melancholy I repeat your lyric in "The
> Deformed", & that for a while enlivens me . . . (? December 14,
> 1822).

By May 21, 1823, Shelley had copied Cantos 13–16 (and more
scenes from *The Deformed Transformed*) and thus ended her on-going
assignment. Upon his departure for Greece in July Byron instructed
his new publisher John Hunt (Leigh's brother), to use the fair copy
of Canto 16 as printer's copy, as there was no time to send and
correct proofs. Byron trusted Shelley's copies – and the corrections
and slight alterations that she consistently made. His respect for her
intelligence and skill was complete. He used no other amanuensis'
services as consistently or with as much confidence. For her part,
Byron's strong influence, particularly during the months of her
deepest grief, supported her emotionally and encouraged her intellectually. She found that a new intellectual affinity was possible.

5

"That Masterpiece of His Malice": *Valperga*

Shelley's adored son William died at the beginning of her composition of *Valperga* and PBS was drowned in July 1822 just after its conclusion. It is perhaps a reflection of the devastation that she felt at her losses that *Valperga* remains the darkest and most profoundly pessimistic novel that she ever wrote. That very pessimism contradicts what she learned from PBS; even given the gradual modification of PBS's early unqualified optimism in regard to perfectibility by the adoption of a measure of scepticism, he would never have embraced the bitter realism of *Valperga*. There is no hint in the world of *Valperga* that humanity has the potential to improve itself or to significantly better its lot. Shelley's excruciating grief – her journal shows just how extreme and persistent it was – did not retard the development of her intellectual independence. Nor did any guilt that she must surely have felt at her bid for independence and intellectual purpose.

On the contrary. The Monster who disappears into the arctic wastes at *Frankenstein*'s conclusion, but *not necessarily to die*, reappears in *Valperga* and even in *The Last Man*. And so, in the former, does a developed and modified Victor Frankenstein, but a Frankenstein whose creativity is no longer morally ambiguous. The character of Castruccio in *Valperga* is unequivocally destructive, he does not even dream of making a contribution to humanity. The Monster and his creator are reborn in the shape of the deceptively beautiful and refined warrior.

It is ironic that Victor had thought, with the Monster's first animation, that his "labours would soon end" (p. 56). It was only the beginning of his suffering and the first articulation of Shelley's own doubts about idealistic and rigid political solutions *and* about

76

her own fears about authorship and romantic creativity. *Valperga* followed *Frankenstein* by five years. In this second self-consciously political novel, her ambiguity towards the idealism of her father and husband and the terrors of the uncontrolled imagination takes shape.

Castruccio, the hero of the historical romance *Valperga*, is, with significant developments, the inheritor of Victor Frankenstein's ambition. It is interesting to consider briefly the history of this new character. In a letter to Maria Gisborne, June 30, 1821, Shelley explains that she first conceived of *Valperga*, or Castruccio as the novel was then to be called, as early as 1817 in Marlow, at about the same time that PBS began his revolutionary epic *Laon and Cythna*. She did not begin the novel until the spring of 1820, just a few months before PBS wrote *The Witch of Atlas* (in August 1820), with her journal recording "write" on April 7. Between 1817 and the beginning of the novel's composition in 1820, Shelley and PBS had moved to Italy in self-imposed exile and became preoccupied with local and national political concerns.

The Shelleys' removal to Italy placed them at the epicentre of a new pan-European revolution in ferment. They had left England in disgust at the rigidity of the Castlereagh government. Despite the repression of the Metternich regime and of the Papal States, the Italian people had already tasted the comparative progressiveness of the Napoleonic regimes that had preceded it. As K. N. Cameron has pointed out, the seeds of the movement that resulted in the unification of Italy under Garibaldi and Mazzini over 40 years later were already planted in the Shelleys' time.

The Shelleys went to Tuscany because of its relative liberalism, a legacy of the Napoleonic reforms which also attracted many exiles from other Italian states. PBS was immediately occupied in literary attacks on the reactionary governments of Austria and Britain. Shelley also shared his disgust. She wrote to Maria Gisborne from Florence on January 12, 1820:

> Are you yet reconciled to the idea that England is become a despotism? The freedom with which the newspapers talk of our most detestable governors is as mocking death on a death bed. The work of dissolution goes on, not a whit slower – And cannot England be saved? I do hope it will . . . The rich alone support the government – The poor, and middling classes are, I believe, to a man, against them – But we have fallen, I fear, on

evil days. There are great spirits in England. So there were in
the time of Cesar and Rome. Athens flourished but just before
the despotism of Alexander – Will not England fall? I am full of
these thoughts . . .

In a letter to Marianne Hunt of 24 March, her diatribe grows more
heated:

Not that I much wish to be in England . . . I am too much
depressed by its enslaved state, my inutility; the little chance
there is for freedom; & the great chance there is for tyranny
to wish to be witness of its degredation step by step, & to
feel all the sensations of indignation & horror which I know
I sh^d experience were I to hear daily the talk of the subjects
or rather the slaves of King Cant whose dominion I fear is of
wider extent in England than any where else . . . No – since
I have seen Rome, that City is my Country, & I do not wish
to own any other untill England is *free* & *true* that is untill
the throne *Cant* the God or if you will the abominable idol
before whom at present the english are offering up a sacrifice
of blood & liberty, be overthrown. Cant has more power in
parliament, & over the Kingdom than fear or any other motive
– a man now in England w^d as soon think of refusing a duel
as of not listening to & talking the language of *Cant* & from
the same motive – he w^d be afraid of being turned out of
society . . . But do not think that I am unenglishifying myself
– but that nook of ci devant free land, so sweetly surrounded by
the sea is no longer England but Castlereagh land or New Land
Castlereagh, – heaven defend me from being a Castlereaghish
woman . . .

Local events fired the Shelleys' enthusiasm. Byron had become
personally involved with the shadowy Carbonari,[1] a secret society of revolutionary-minded aristocrats which sought to liberalize
the Church States and oust the Austrians. Living in Ravenna, he
joined the Gambas, father and brother of Teresa Guiccioli, in an
effort to establish contact with the Neapolitan revolutionaries far
to the south. The Neapolitan uprising drew the Austrian army
south through Ravenna and the Papal states in February 1821.
The Carbonari tried, unsuccessfully, to cut off the Austrian artillery
and when the Gambas were discovered and forced into exile at

Florence, Byron joined them. PBS's "Ode to Naples" celebrated the uprising of 1820 in that city and its spiritual if not practical success.

In March 1820 PBS heard of the January revolution in Spain which had bloodlessly removed the despotic Ferdinand and formally ended the Inquisition. He celebrated the news in the "Ode to Liberty". He likewise expressed his support for the Greek war of independence in *Hellas* and predicted the downfall of the Austrians in "Lines Written Among the Euganean Hills".

PBS and Byron conceived the journal *The Liberal* in response to the Tory *Quarterly* and to reflect the new currents of liberalism and reform that they believed were prevalent in Italy. PBS believed that English panic in the face of the Napoleonic Wars and its consequent persecution of the Whigs and Liberals was over. He thought that reform was possible across Europe, as well as in England, and offered his optimistic views in "A Philosophical View of Reform" (composed 1820, unpublished until 1920). It is clear from the essay's 'practical' outlining of political liberty that PBS, if not Shelley herself, was convinced that the very same potential for productive revolution existed in Italy in the same way that it had in pre-revolutionary America and France. Cameron points out that, "Paine, Godwin and the others [Condorcet, Volney, Wollstonecraft] were read by [PBS] not as intellectual exercises but as political guidebooks, for the issues of the age of the American and French revolutions continued into his own century: war, revolution, dictatorship, colonialism, and parliamentary reform".[2] Nonetheless *A Philosophical View of Reform* is rather conservative for PBS. Its goals are reform rather than violent revolution. In it he addressed a liberal rather than a radical audience and thereby hoped to avoid alienating too many potential readers.

Thus, the atmosphere surrounding the composition of *Valperga* was highly charged politically, specifically with reference to contemporary Italy. Shelley places her story in the Italy of the late Medieval city states; this period in Italian history had political parallels with Shelley's present. During both periods the country seemed to be straddling a fence between the victory of nationalism and liberty (and also in Shelley's day liberalism) and the continued domination of an opportunistic, despotic power. Castruccio, the villain of *Valperga*, offers his strength to the invading German emperor. The Shelleys, as well as participating in the margins of the struggle, witnessed the revolutionary activity that sought to oust the control of another alien dictator in the form of Metternich.

Shelley's novel is also in some sense prophetic. Though it does not present the victory of liberty – quite the contrary in fact – the plot depends on the possibility of such an achievement. Though a Ghibelline and supporter of the German Emperor, Castruccio is nonetheless in love with and betrothed to Euthanasia,[3] a Guelph allied to the Papal throne and representative of the city of liberty and Italian nationalism – Florence. She is the patron of that city and her loyalty to it exceeds her love for Castruccio. To the radicals and liberals of Shelley's day, profoundly influenced by Sismondi's *L'Histoire des républiques italiennes du moyen âge* (1809–18), Florence, centre of the relatively liberal Tuscany, represented a modern incarnation of the glory of ancient Athens, itself a beacon of liberty and the civic ideal. Indeed, Sismondi celebrated the figure of Dante as the Medieval incarnation of the ideal Attic citizen: artist, individualist and patriot. As Marilyn Butler has pointed out:

> What Athens had represented at the very close of the eighteenth century, fourteenth-century republican Florence also represented from about 1805. The two city-states and their cultures were seen as markedly similar . . . the rise of the Italian republics was felt to signalise the break-up of the hegemony of feudal monarchs and an obscurantist church, the long post-classical Dark Ages . . . The true achievement of Venice and especially Florence was liberty; the great art which they produced was the natural expression of a new and nearly ideal social organisation, the small republic of free citizens.[4]

In the figure of Euthanasia, Countess of Valperga, Shelley presents a parallel to Sismondi's Dante.[5]

But *Valperga* is prophetic in another way. It anticipates and undeniably influences George Eliot's *Romola* (1863), a novel set in the same period as Shelley's and with the same plot dynamic: one ultimately corrupted opportunist and two women of contrasting character and symbolic significance. Romola, spirit of Rome, looks to national unity and beyond to the accomplishment of the Risorgimento which Eliot herself witnessed. Romola's husband Tito, like Castruccio, is completely self-serving and disloyal. Both Euthanasia and Romola are devoted to learning, scholarship and education and to the fulfilment of the legacy of their fathers. Both of the women's lovers become attracted to naive, ignorant and 'primitive' women, the antitheses of themselves.

Over the three and a half years from *Valperga*'s conception to the start of its composition, Shelley had lost three children; a premature infant, the year-old Clara, and, most devastatingly, the three-year-old William. "I never shall recover that blow . . . the thought never leaves me for a single moment – Everything on earth has lost its interest to me", she wrote in her despair to Amelia Curran on June 27, 1819. When she finally regained her interest in life, she attacked the project of Castruccio with vigour, and PBS wrote to Peacock in November of the following year, "Mary is writing a novel, illustrative of the manners of the Middle Ages in Italy, which she has raked out of fifty old books. I promise myself success from it; and certainly, if what is wholly original will succeed, I shall not be disappointed".[6]

Valperga, or the Life and Adventures of Castruccio, Prince of Lucca was completed in the Autumn of 1821 and published in February 1823 by G. and W. B. Whittaker of Ave-Maria-Lane, London. Among the "fifty old books" from which Shelley "raked out" her research are those that appear in her preface: Machiavelli's "romance" of the life of Castruccio and Sismondi's more factual *Histoire des républiques italiennes du moyen âge*, a book which as we have seen, influenced the novel in other ways.

Because Lackington, the publishers of *Frankenstein*, would not agree to her terms, Shelley, through PBS, turned to Ollier who proved too hesitant in making a decision. Shelley finally turned over the manuscript – and all rights – to her father, to edit and to see into publication. It is clear from his letters that he took considerable advantage of his carte blanche. Announcing its publication, Godwin wrote to his daughter in February 1823:

I have taken great liberties with it, & I fear your amour propre will be proportionably shocked . . . The whole of what I have done is nearly confined to the taking away things that must have prevented its success. I scarcely ever saw any thing more unfortunately out of taste, than the long detail of battles & campaigning, after the death of Beatrice, & when the reader is impatient for the conclusion.[7]

Godwin continued:

Frankenstein was a fine thing; it was compressed, muscular and firm; nothing relaxed and weak; no proud flesh. Castruccio is a work of more genius; but it appears, in reading, that the first rule you prescribed yourself was, I will let it be long. It contains the quantity of four volumes of *Waverley*. No hard blow was ever hit by a woolsack.

William Walling has concluded that Godwin's contribution was largely to pare down the manuscript and remove considerable excess. Godwin did let stand one of Shelley's more obvious excesses, a lengthy chapter describing a picturesque festival at the castle of Valperga with tournaments, ballads and *al fresco* dining. The episode has no bearing on plot, character or mood, rather, it seems a catalogue of folk traditions that had enchanted Shelley in her research and that she felt compelled to use.[8] This suggests that Godwin's work on the manuscript was largely beneficial – he probably removed many such unnecessary diversions.

Shelley's zeal, in an attempt perhaps to displace her grief, a grief that none of her friends and family seemed to sympathize with or even respect,[9] also resulted in a new character, one of more dangerous consequences for mankind than Victor. Castruccio, like other ambitious, power-hungry men (Mary had witnessed the devastation of France first-hand in 1814) rationally chooses the selfish and evil path; his passion is not romantically thrust upon him by fate. His decision, as an intelligent and brave man, to waste and destroy human love, demonstrates by the end of the novel a new and profoundly dark view of man, one that makes for a parody of perfectibility as Shelley herself understood it and of a generally optimistic belief in man's moral potential.

Valperga is very different from *Frankenstein* in narrative shape and style. It was originally intended to centre around Castruccio himself, but as Bonnie Neumann has suggested, its focus shifted during composition towards the two central female characters; the razing of the castle of *Valperga* became the climax of the novel.[10] This change of focus is significant. Shelley decided, despite the novel's sub-title, to move away from the absolute primacy of the predestined male hero (the essential feature of *Frankenstein* that made it uncategorizable as a "women's" novel) to a complex structure in which the two women play more important roles than Castruccio, and become the vehicles for subtle political allegories.

Valperga is best summarized by PBS in his letter to the publisher Ollier whom he hoped would take on the novel. On September 25, 1821 he wrote:

The romance is called "Castruccio, Prince of Lucca" and is founded (not upon the novel of Macciavelli under that name, which substitutes a childish fiction for the more romantic truth of history, but) upon the actual story of his life. He was a person, who from exile and an adventurer, after having served in the wars of England and Flanders in the reign of our Edward the Second, returned to his native city, and, liberating it from its tyrants, became himself its tyrant, and died in full splendour of his dominion, which he had extended over the half of Tuscany. He was a little Napoleon, and, with a dukedom instead of an empire for his theatre, brought upon the same all the passions and errors of his antitype. The chief interest of his romance rests upon Euthanasia, his betrothed bride, whose love for him is only equalled by her enthusiasm for the liberty of the republic of Florence which is in some sort her country, and for that of Italy, to which Castruccio is a devoted enemy, being an ally of the party of the Emperor. Euthanasia, the last survivor of a noble house, is a feudal countess, and her castle is the scene of knightly manners of the time. The character of Beatrice, the prophetess, can only be done justice to in the very language of the author. I know nothing in Walter Scott's novels which at all approaches to the beauty and sublimity of this – creation I may almost say, for it is perfectly original; and, though founded upon the ideas and manners of the age which is represented, is wholly without a similitude in any fiction I ever read. Beatrice is in love with Castruccio and dies; for the romance although interspersed with much lighter matter, is deeply tragic, and the shades darken and gather as the catastrophe approaches. All the manners, customs, opinions, of the age are introduced; the superstitions, the heresies, and the religious persecution are displayed; the minutest circumstances of Italian manners in that age is not omitted; and the whole seems to me to constitute a living and moving picture of an age almost forgotten. The author visited the scenery which she describes in person; and one or two of the inferior characters are drawn from her own observation of the Italians, for the national character shows itself still in certain instances under the same forms as it wore in the time of Dante. The novel consists, as I told you before, of three volumes, each at least equal to one of the "Tales of my Landlord", and they will be very soon ready to be sent.[11]

After he and his family are exiled from Lucca by the Guelphs, the young Castruccio Antelminelli consecrates his life to the attainment of power and above all, to vengeance, which he later claims, "is among those few goods in life, which compensate for its many evils" (Vol. III, p. 233). From an early age Castruccio had a "goal for which he panted" (Vol. I, p. 131), ambition "was the ruling feeling of his soul" (Vol. I, p. 161). Also, like Victor, he is notionally attracted by the prospects of domestic happiness and love and becomes betrothed to his childhood friend, Euthanasia. It is only at his return to *Valperga* to claim his betrothed that Castruccio no longer suppresses the destructive nature of his ambition and the would-be hero consciously becomes a villain. He rejects love for the sake of his campaign. He is corrupted by his own relentless will into a grotesque tyrant. Machiavelli's Prince is made flesh and the consequences of his actions laid bare.

Some critics have claimed that Shelley used the characters of her husband and close friends as models for the central figures of the novel as a means of courting commercial success; they go on to offer this as proof of her limitations as an artist. Elizabeth Nitchie maintains that the character of Castruccio is based almost entirely on Byron:

> In appearance he is the typical hero, beautiful as a god, with soft yet bright eyes. He is marked by Byronic pride and arrogance, bold in action, careless of danger, ambitious of glory. Yet he is too fond of pleasure, too unstable to be a wise ruler. He is not as admirable as the later Raymond and Lodore. Although he is softened and romanticized from the tyrant of history, in him can be recognized, as the story develops, the Byron who disappointed and alienated Shelley (Euthanasia), and coldly rejected the claims of Claire (Beatrice).[12]

Aside from ignoring the lineaments of Edward Trelawny (who joined the Shelley circle in 1822), which certainly contributed their own share to the character of Castruccio, Nitchie's rather simplistic approach trivializes and underestimates Shelley's skills as a writer of fiction. Though it is true that Shelley's characters are often composites of herself, PBS, Claire and Byron, they shift and change throughout the story, much as Victor and the monster's roles are constantly exchanged. The real human beings inspire the fictional characters; they are not simple models. The character of Castruccio and the 'real' Byron are particularly interesting in this respect. Shelley saw in both the poet and in the historical Castruccio a complex nature of great magnanimity, style and intelligence merged with a pettiness, vanity and cruelty difficult to reconcile in one person. With her new narrative style she weaves the thread of Castruccio's biography in and around the lives of the two women. Each is brought forward in prominence as the other recedes and Shelley presents her characters as both human and symbolic. Castruccio's consciousness in particular is carefully examined. His education and the fostering of his early plans for revenge shape his overall motivation throughout the novel. However, in *Valperga* Shelley unmistakably arrives at a subtle condemnation of certain aspects of PBS's and Godwin's political philosophy and behaviour and in delivering her disapproval, she declares her opposition.

With Castruccio's careful and considered choice to reject his beloved Euthanasia in order to pursue his bloody ambitions comes a change in Shelley's voice to one darker and more pessimistic than ever before. Frankenstein was a victim of destiny, we are repeatedly told, and his imagination obliterated those instincts that would have ensured his domestic and emotional, if not intellectual desires. Castruccio's corruption is not left to fate. He decides, with complete self-possession, to give up his love. When he returns from a long campaign and from his liaison with the beautiful prophetess Beatrice, Euthanasia desires to know if the rumours of his ambition to conquer her native city Florence, and ultimately Italy, are true. She herself has sworn an oath, she "made a deep and tremendous vow, never to ally herself to the enemy of Florence . . . she waited for the return of Castruccio to Lucca, so to learn if he could clear himself, or if indeed he were that enemy to Florence against whom her vow was made" (Vol. I, p. 213). Confrontation is anticipated and prepared for on both sides.

Shelley draws and highlights the reunion scene carefully, playing it out beneath a magnificent thunderstorm, an element of the sublime that she often employed to underscore crisis, moments of discovery – the oak shattered by lightning that so inspires Victor – and moments of intense emotion. Byron too favoured the dramatic splendour of lightning and expressed its imaginative hold over him in Canto Three of *Childe Harold's Pilgrimage*:

XCVI

Could I embody and unbosom now
That which is most within me, – could I wreak
My thoughts upon expression, and thus throw
Soul, heart, mind, passions, feelings, strong or weak,
All that I would have sought, and all I seek,
Bear, know, feel, and yet breathe – into one word,
And that one word were Lightning, I would speak;
But as it is, I live and die unheard,
With a most voiceless thought, sheathing it as a sword.

Likewise the party at Geneva in 1816 admired the persistent electrical storms over the lake with great enthusiasm. Critics have made much of the storms that illuminated the summer of *Frankenstein*'s birth, so much so that it is popularly – and erroneously – assumed that a storm accompanies the actual moment of the Monster's animation in the novel. Shelley identifies the scene of Castruccio's and Euthanasia's mutual rejection with the rage of nature and nature's sublime disapproval of the consequences of that rejection. At the same time she suggests an irreligious (or pan-religious) reaction from nature herself by drawing on both the pagan and Judaeo-Christian associations of thunder and lightning. Thus we are alerted to the significance of the couple's decision: a crime against nature *and* the spiritual life:

The white lightning sped in forked chains around the sky, and without pause or interval, deluged the midnight heaven with light, which shewed to her, as she stood at the window of her apartment, the colours of the trees, and even of the few flowers which had survived to witness the advent of the storm. The thunder broke in tremendous and continued peals, and the rain awoke in a moment the dried up sources of the mountain torrents; yet their liquid career was not heard amidst the tumult: for, if the thunder paused, the echoes prolonged the sound, and all nature seemed labouring with the commotion . . . the first sound alien to the storm that visited her sense, was her own name pronounced in a well known and soft voice . . . (Vol. II, pp. 139–40)

"Are you mine", Castruccio asks Euthanasia. "If you are your own", she replies, with an extraordinary firmness of purpose (Vol. II,

p. 141). Unlike the hapless Victor, Castruccio, sadly, is "his own" for "ambition, and the fixed desire to rule, smothered in his mind the voice of better reason" (Vol. II, p. 146). The dissolution of their betrothal marks a profound change in Castruccio's character and the point at which he parts from Victor's path. It also opens out the political allegory and marks the joining of the fate of the two women. The author's ambiguity towards her first protagonist – Shelley never completely resolves her attitude towards Victor's persistent bad judgement – is finally clarified. Castruccio willfully chooses the path of destruction. His devotion is solely directed towards self-advancement and the consolidation of power. He cannot even express the bitter remorse that haunts Victor Frankenstein as he sees his family systematically cut down. Castruccio's decision to choose the path to supposed glory over that of love demonstrates that he can control his own fate; there is no question of predestination in *Valperga*. "Ambition had become the ruling passion of his soul, and all bent beneath its sway, as a field of reeds before the wind" (Vol. II, p. 173).

Victor is undeniably egocentric and isolationist, most notably in his prolonged absence from his home. He professes great love for his family, but abandons his loved ones for several years, neglecting even to write. But his egocentricity is in fact quietism; his decision to separate himself from others is completely passive. By contrast, Castruccio confronts the temptation of domestic happiness and rejects it; "love was with him, ever after, the second feeling in his heart, the servant and thrall of his ambition" (Vol. II, p. 174).[13] At the same time he rejects Euthanasia's patriotism and the republican system that she proposes, practiced, in actual fact, as a kind of utopian monarchy:

> Euthanasia had many occupations, and among them the glorious and delightful one of rendering her numerous dependents happy. The cottages and villages over which she presided, were filled by a contented peasantry, who adored their countess, and knew her power only by the benefits she conferred on them. (Vol. I, p. 245)

The excuse she offers to Castruccio for not relinquishing control of her peasantry to form their own independent state reflects her ironic patriarchal role. Encouraging their independence by abdicating her authority she believes, would leave them vulnerable to domination by a perhaps cruel power. They are safer and happier she believes, under her protection.

But the ties that bind the lovers from youth are severed. Castruccio goes on his way a cruel tyrant, and Euthanasia is confirmed in her role as his moral opposite, an indomitable spirit of liberty, nationalism and whiggish paternalism.

Castruccio's infidelity is an imaginative parallel of PBS's actual behaviour and Shelley's subsequent resentment. Shelley eventually became impatient with PBS's thoughtless infatuation with other women. She grew to resent the beautiful but ultimately frivolous Italian Emilia Viviani and even Claire may be recognized in the prophetess Beatrice's profusion of black hair and raving fantasies. Shelley's condemnation of Castruccio's sexual infidelity may also express resentment of PBS's very early encouragement of a love affair between Shelley and his friend T. J. Hogg. This early test of PBS's commitment to his advocacy of free love probably never came to fruition; Shelley's letters to the eager Hogg in 1815 during her first pregnancy seem to have put off the consummation of their affair indefinitely. The scheme was never mentioned again but it is not inconceivable that Shelley may have grown increasingly indignant about PBS's manipulation of her naïveté and emotional dependence on him to test and further his political ideals.

Castruccio's betrayal of Euthanasia is compounded. He enters the impregnable fortress of *Valperga* with his army through the hidden postern gate that had formerly allowed him access to his lover; " . . . discovered by his love, now used to injure and subdue her whom he had loved . . . " (Vol. II, p. 230). His metaphorical and actual violation of their love leads ultimately to the destruction of the castle and of Euthanasia's sovereignty. The ruins of her ancestral home and the corpses of her loyal peasants greet the eyes of the conquered Countess. She is completely stripped of her power, station and self-will. Her privileged position as a matrilineal chieftain is nullified. Her unique status, as a woman more powerful and respected than most of the men surrounding her, is dissolved by martial force as a result of base opportunism rather than freely surrendered in a marriage of equals that she would have embraced. In Shelley's fictions (particularly true of her late sentimental novels) men control and subdue women. Shelley is cynical about the ideal of an equal marriage. In fact, her pessimism in this respect would have shocked her parents. As proposed by both Wollstonecraft and Godwin, intelligent men and women could live together in an ideal relationship based on intellectual equality and mutual respect; Shelley mocks such utopianism with the blasting of her fictional relationships. Even her own relationship, undeniably based on sound Wollstonecraftian principles, did not live up to the original ideal of its model.

Shelley repeats this pattern of betrayal, both sexual and political in her next novel. Lord Raymond of *The Last Man* destroys his wife by first returning to the corrupting political world that he had abandoned and, later, by an adulterous affair. At his death she commits suicide, the existence of her small daughter not reason enough to live without the all-powerful husband that gave her life its meaning. But *Valperga* gives us powerful and striking female characters, and even something of the ideal in Euthanasia.

EUTHANASIA

The dynamic between Castruccio, Euthanasia and Beatrice highlights what the women represent politically. The naive and uneducated Beatrice is hopelessly confined by the chains of ignorance and superstition. Her appeal to Castruccio is physical and primitive and, unlike the Countess, she is obviously vulnerable. She has no will of her own, nor the means to control her over-indulged imagination. Euthanasia is her antithesis. She is strikingly modern. She is powerful, both materially and psychologically, confident and highly intelligent, in fact, Shelley's most intelligent and well-educated character. She is devoted to learning and to a form of liberal government exemplified by her own local rule. She has ideals for a free and independent Italy, unoppressed by outside powers. But she has often struck readers as merely an idealized portrait of PBS. Critics cite the superficial affinity of the Countess's stated philosophy with that of the poet in descriptions of her sensibility: "she felt as if she were a part of the great whole; she felt bound in amity to all" (Vol. II, p. 165). Later, in *The Last Man*, the intellectual Adrian will be described in similar terms: " . . . he felt that he made a part of a great whole. He owned affinity not only with mankind, but all nature was akin to him" (*TLM*, p. 31). But these passages are also reminiscent of the descriptions of nature in *Childe Harold's Pilgrimage*, a poem that Shelley found deeply compelling. In Canto III, which Shelley first read in 1816, Harold travels through the Alps to Lake Leman. This identification with nature is of course pure Wordsworth:[14]

LXXII

I live not in myself, but I become
Portion of that around me; and to me,
High mountains are a feeling, but the hum
Of human cities torture: I can see
Nothing to loathe in nature, save to be
A link reluctant in a fleshly chain,
Class'd among creatures, when the soul can flee,
And with the sky, the peak, the heaving plain
Of ocean, or the stars, mingle, and not in vain.

LXXV

Are not the mountains, waves, and skies, a part
Of me and of my soul, as I of them? . . .

Many also point to Euthanasia's unrealistic goodness as a further attempt on Shelley's part to deify her husband. Neumann goes so far as to say that she is the first Shelley character to be pure victim, bearing no responsibility for her suffering [15] and viewed uncritically, it is easy then to draw a simple parallel between the fictional character and PBS in Shelley's mind. If this simple parallel does exist, and Shelley is giving us a portrait of her husband, then critics have overlooked an essential and very telling flaw in Euthanasia's character which in turn reflects a subtle criticism of PBS. Unwavering principle and idealism governs all of Euthanasia's decisions and actions. They are the source and power of her nationalism and like PBS she is obsessed with the exaltation of the ideal over the necessary disappointment of reality. She explains to Castruccio:

> I have lived a solitary hermitess, and have become an enthusiast for all beauty. Being alone, I have not feared to give the reins to my feelings; I have lived happily within the universe of my own mind, and have often given reality to that which others call a dream. I have had few hopes, and few fears; but every passing sentiment has been an event; and I have marked the birth of a new idea with the joy that others derive from what they call change and fortune. (Vol. I, pp. 192–93)

Euthanasia's philosophy is an unmistakable echo of that of Julian's in PBS's poem *Julian and Maddalo* (composed 1818–19, first published 1824). In that poem PBS partially drew on his relationship with Byron (Maddalo), highlighting some of the two poets' conflicting philosophies. Julian asks "Where is the love, beauty and truth we seek/But in our mind?" (174–75); his character is associated with that of Euthanasia's.[16]

Euthanasia's defiance of Castruccio's demand that she surrender her castle and domain – "he is resolved to spare no exertion, and to be stopped by no obstacle, until he has reduced into his own hands *Valperga* and all its dependencies" (Vol. II, pp. 221–22) – epitomizes her inflexible idealism. She responds to the formal declaration of war, and Castruccio's offer of compensation and protection with a statement which reflects both her character and her significance as a political symbol:

> I will never willingly surrender my power into his hands: I hold it for the good of my people, who are happy under my government, and towards whom I shall ever perform my duty. I look upon him as a lawless tyrant, whom every one ought to resist to the utmost of their power; nor will I through cowardice give way to injustice. I may be exasperated beyond prudence; but right is on my side: I have preserved the articles of my alliance with him, and I will hold them still; but, if he attacks me, I shall defend myself, and shall hold myself justified in accepting the assistance of my friends. If I have not that right, if indeed I had pledged myself to submit whenever he should call upon me to resign my birthright, what an absurd mockery is it to talk of his moderation towards me! . . . Valperga stands on a barren rock, and the few villages that own its law are poor and unprotected; but this castle is as dear to me as all his dominion is to him; I inherited it from my ancestors; and if I wished to despoil myself of power, it would be to make my people free, and not to force them to enter the muster-roll of a usurper and a tyrant. (Vol. II, pp. 222–24)

Euthanasia's 'masculine' integrity is commendable, but she has, unlike any of the men of power, an inflexible idealism and nationalistic pride as powerful as the relentless ambition that overshadows Castruccio's passion for her. Just as Victor is so self-absorbed that he interprets the Monster's warning, "I shall be with you on your wedding-night" (p. 168), as a threat to himself alone, the lovers of *Valperga* fail to see that they are sacrificing other people to an idealism not wholly divorced from egoism. Their respective obsessions with principle and with glory are equally damaging.

When she momentarily considers capitulating to love, Euthanasia's "accustomed feelings returned to press her into the narrow circle, whence for her all peace was excluded" (Vol. II, p. 170). At the very moment that she makes her self-destructive decision, Castruccio's fate is sealed and he becomes all in all to himself. In a subversion of the climactic act of love, beneath the thunder and lightning, they each embrace, not the other, but their own isolation from each other, to continue in a life of self-will, bounded by their own thoughts – a wholly egotistical existence. They are alike in their denial of that which they force themselves to consider as a baser need – domestic love.

Euthanasia is completely self-contained and intellectually self-sufficient. She even shares one of Castruccio's most damning characteristics; she is all in all to herself. She too is single-minded and denies her need for domestic love. She is equally responsible for breaking off her betrothal. As a patriot of Florence and Italy, "the high independence and graceful pride of her nature would never permit her, to stoop beneath the mark she had assigned as the object of her emulation" (Vol. II, p. 164). Having 'created' or imagined for her exclusive reality the Castruccio that she is prepared to love and respect, she refuses to accommodate his deviation from that ideal. She is as rigid in her determination to live up to her own self-image as is Castruccio. As he has sworn vengeance for his family, she has sworn to maintain her father's lofty principles, to their mutual detriment (it is impossible to avoid a comparison here with Shelley and her own beloved but difficult father): "I love you; – but I have other duties besides those which I owe to you, and those shall be fulfilled. My father's lessons must not be forgotten . . . I am a Florentine; Florence is my native country; nor will I be a traitor to it" (Vol. II, pp. 142–43).

Castruccio is dedicated to the pursuit of power, and Euthanasia to the fulfillment of her unrealistic life-plan, both to the exclusion of any realistic happiness. She is unable to compromise her principles or envision a solution to the moral dilemma that her marriage would create. In the same way that PBS may be criticized for familial negligence while tirelessly working for others – it is probable that Shelley blamed her husband for the death of their daughter Clara because his attentions were focused on Claire – Euthanasia betrays herself and her lover through an egocentric devotion to her own ideal. But she also epitomizes Shelley's paradoxical feelings for her beloved husband. On the one hand Shelley worshipped

PBS for his integrity and sense of purpose, and on the other she resented its correspondent, ironic rigidity. His idealism ruled out any domestic tranquillity and its passion seemed to engulf her own intellectual programme. Euthanasia is certainly Shelley's most positive character, but she is not without her significant flaws and special meaning for her creator.

But Castruccio's relationship to Euthanasia is still more complex. His schizophrenic attitude to his own conscience underscores the unnatural, divided nature of both characters. Even though he has alienated Euthanasia and lost her respect, he depends on her to retain his spiritual goodness; he knows that she cherishes her vision of him in his pre-corrupted state. He establishes her, saviour-like, as the keeper of his soul. She becomes the talisman that can prevent his complete corruption. Misunderstanding her role in a plot to usurp him, Castruccio is deeply distressed:

> She knew, she must have known, that in spite of absence and repulse, she was the saint of my life; and that this one human weakness, or human virtue, remained to me, when power and a strong will had in other respects metamorphosed me . . . I believed, that, if she died, like Dante's Beatrice, she would plead for me before the throne of the Eternal, and that I should be saved through her. (Vol. III, pp. 234–35)

He had always felt free to continue his evil activities believing that his essential being would be safe.

This idea of transposed spiritual protection finds its corollary in "The Veiled Prophet of Khorassan", the first story in Moore's four-part verse allegory of superstition, priestcraft and religion, *Lalla Rookh* (1817). Zelica, an impressionable and ignorant beauty becomes the physical and psychological slave of an evil and false prophet. Her vow of emotional and sexual loyalty is extorted by the prophet's strange magnetism but her self-delusion is finally revealed and, like Beatrice, she finds herself degraded and corrupted:

> Are all my dreams, my hopes of heavenly bliss,
> My purity, my pride, then come to this? –
> To live, the wanton of a fiend! to be
> The pander of his guilt – O infamy!
> And sunk, myself, as low as hell can steep

In its hot flood, drag others down as deep!

(pp. 26–27)[17]

Just as Castruccio wants Euthanasia to bear his uncorrupted soul, Zelica is concerned for the moral soul of her original lover. She feels that he has been damaged through her own supposed corruption, and must flee him (an idea, in relation to the crime of Beatrice Cenci, that PBS vigorously refutes in his preface to *The Cenci*). Part of her lover Azim's pleasure in Zelica was to see himself in her eyes: "He would have seen himself, too happy boy,/Reflected in a thousand lights of joy".[18] His self-love, it would appear, like Castruccio's, is at the root of his love for another. Yet Castruccio is blind to his own corruption, confident to continue his evil ways with the knowledge of Euthanasia's supposed protection of his pre-lapsarian state. He successfully deludes himself that she is his spiritual salvation.

In a wider context, Euthanasia represents the motherland conquered and devastated by an invading force. Euthanasia in her power was a protector of the poor and universal provider to the dependents of her domain, as well as a nurse and counsellor to her friends. Her grief at losing her castle is surpassed only by that for the death of her loyal people in its defence. Shelley had witnessed the devastation of Europe in 1814 and the appalling poverty and degradation of French peasantry was fixed in her mind. She recollected that journey through France in her travelogue, *History of a Six Weeks' Tour* (1817):

> Nothing could be more entire than the ruin which these barbarians had spread as they advanced; perhaps they remembered Moscow and the destruction of the Russian villages; but we were now in France, and the distress of the inhabitants, whose houses had been burned; their cattle killed, and all their wealth destroyed, has given a sting to my detestation of war, which none can feel who have not travelled through a country pillaged and wasted by this plague, which, in his pride, man inflicts upon his fellow.[19]

Famine deliberately induced as a military tactic is a repellant example of nature victimized by man. Shelley's condemnation of war, a recurrent theme, is also echoed by Byron's moral disgust at the field of Waterloo in *Childe Harold's Pilgrimage* Canto III and in the Siege of Ismail in *Don Juan* Cantos VII and VIII. It is also vividly described in PBS's *A Philosophical View of Reform*:

> Visit in imagination the scene of a field of battle or a city taken by assault, collect into one group the groans and the distortions of the innumerable dying, the inconsolable grief and horror of their surviving friends, the hellish exultation and unnatural drunkenness of destruction of the conquerors, the burning of the harvests and the obliteration of the traces of cultivation . . . [20]

Shelley's own horror of war reaches its climax in *The Last Man*. Adrian Windsor, who resembles PBS in many respects, illustrates the reality of war in the face of his friends' discussion of the Greek War of Independence and in so doing, echoes Shelley's earliest reservations about justifiable war in the "History of the Jews":

> I shall not be suspected of being averse to the Greek cause; I know and feel its necessity; it is beyond every other a good cause. I have defended it with my sword, and was willing that my spirit should be breathed out in its defence . . . But let us not deceive ourselves. The Turks are men; each fibre, each limb is as feeling as our own, and every spasm, be it mental or bodily, is as truly felt in a Turk's heart or brain, as in a Greek's . . . Think you, amidst the shrieks of violated innocence and helpless infancy, I did not feel in every nerve the cry of a fellow being? They were men and women, the sufferers, before they were Mahometans, and when they rise turbanless from the grave, in what except their good or evil actions will they be the better or worse then we?[21]

Castruccio's conquering ambition lays to waste not just his intimates, but entire populations that live off the contested land. Castruccio's abused women represent the country, or the very earth that he has profaned by his insatiable thirst for vengeance and his hunger for power. His ambition knows no bounds, least of all a sense of national responsibility; he allies himself to any outside power that may assist his own local ambitions.

If Euthanasia's inflexibility and implicit egocentricity suggest a criticism of the PBS/Godwin radical prescription,[22] her love of knowledge marks her out equally as an exemplar of what Shelley thought was the best of her father and husband's ideology. Like

Adrian in *The Last Man*, Euthanasia assumes her strength and power through her commitment to learning, the central focus of her existence. In Shelley's fictions, as well as in her life, reading and the gaining of knowledge is the means of achieving modern enlightenment. This is Wollstonecraft's most profound legacy to her daughter.

A little learning can be a dangerous thing, however; and Shelley certainly believed that an education undertaken with insufficient guidance, or with a narrow and unrepresentative reading list could prove worse than useless. Thus Victor is doomed by his early, unguided selection of Paracelsus, Cornelius Agrippa and Albertus Magnus as his sole source of information about the world and his father is equally at fault for not guiding him properly in his reading. Shelley also suggests that there is an innate virtue in a devotion to knowledge which renders a character morally good. For women in particular, it may be the only means of achieving security and even power above and beyond marriage. And equality in marriage, along the lines of Mary Wollstonecraft's *Vindication*, might also be achieved in the same way. Eliot's Romola is morally superior to her husband and to others because of her devotion to both the wishes of her father and to the library – the knowledge – that she has been entrusted with. It is no mistake that Castruccio's knowledge comes exclusively from the men, both virtuous and wicked, who became, haphazardly, mentors, guardians or friends during his youth and early manhood. He is shaped by personal influence and principle and never learns, through the independent study of history and literature, to shape his own morality. He is fed the same kind of information that Machiavelli offers the would-be prince and tyrant. He adopts the morals of others as convenient to his schemes of domination. Thus, Castruccio

> hardly believed the simple sincerity of Euthanasia; he understood well and judged with sagacity the balancing objections in a question of interest; but the principle of decision was always with him, that which would most conduce to the fulfilment of his projects, seldom that of the good or evil which affected others. (Vol. I, p. 247)

But in some sense, Euthanasia's sincerity *is* simple and it is marked with the unrealistic idealism of PBS. Shelley seems to be saying that to trust in love and family and one's own intellect implicitly is as unlikely a scheme for happiness as Castruccio's relentless quest for power.

Nevertheless, Euthanasia's devotion to study is a clear indication on Shelley's part that she is to be taken as an essentially good character, though, because she is a woman intellectual, one doomed to have no role. Shelley's own relationship with PBS seems to have been grounded in their mutual pleasure in and dedication to study. The journal records not just the extensive reading lists that they shared, but that she maintained intellectual pursuits throughout her life, even after PBS's death. Despite the problems they may have encountered in their physical and emotional relationship prior to his death, an area of much controversy among scholars,[23] the couple seems to have remained intellectually engaged. Indeed, after his death, Shelley mourned not only the loss of a husband, but that of a teacher, critic and intellectual equal. In a journal entry of January 1824, after four months in England, she is starved of discourse and imaginative expression:

> My imagination is dead – my genius lost – my energies sleep . . . seeing Coleridge last night reminded me forcibly of past times – his beautiful descriptions, metaphysical talk & subtle distinctions reminded me of Shelley's conversations – such was the intercourse I once dayly enjoyed – added to supreme & active goodness – sympathy of affection, and a wild picturesque mode of living that suited my active spirit & satisfied its craving for novelty of impression.

Shelley always remained committed to learning, the legacy of her mother and father. Some critics point to the Monster's 'education' as evidence of the influence of Rousseau in *Frankenstein*. But Shelley entirely rejected the idea of the noble savage, that nurture and culture were unnecessary. As Elizabeth Nitchie has pointed out, she firmly believed in a proper education (preached but not always practiced by her father), with careful, personal guidance through wide and eclectic reading. Euthanasia is the Monster's (and Victor's) educational opposite; she has had the benefit of wide reading and excellent guidance. The Monster's accidental education in the De Lacey's woodshed is woefully inadequate and its exclusive dependence on radical texts so ill-equips him for the world that he can only react in the most primitive way – by lashing out against that which he cannot understand.

Like Edward Waverley of Walter Scott's novel (1814), which Shelley read in 1815, Victor is led astray by the literature that fancy alone has selected, but the consequences of his misguidance are far darker than those adventurous dangers that Waverley encounters. Indeed, Catherine Morland of *Northanger Abbey* is a parody of those heroines whose steady diet of romantic novels have justified the self-indulgence of their imaginations. But the horrors that she only dreams of are realized by Shelley's characters. The outright rejection of love may be on par with, and also more realistic than, the mysterious disposal of an unwanted wife. The theme of ill-directed and mismanaged education was popular in the fiction of Shelley's period. Only Shelley was prepared to follow it to its darkest conclusions.

Shelley also presents us with the vigorously educated individual who is untrammelled by emotion. Undoubtedly a partial self-portrait, in that it reflects a facet of Shelley's character of which she was all too aware, Miss Jervis, the governess in *Falkner* (1837), is the perfect teacher and disciplinarian. Her blend of dispassionate but kind insistence on scholarship, comprehensive study and feminine graces represent an ideal that has been taken to an extreme. She is unmarried, childless, and somewhat cold. Later, the heroine outgrows her teacher. In *Lodore,* Shelley gives the reader another exemplar of the educational ideal with the character of Fanny Derham, independent and well-educated. Mellor has pointed out, "Fanny Derham embodies a female potentiality that Mary Wollstonecraft had described, and her presence in the novel is Mary Shelley's homage to her mother's radical feminist convictions".[24] But Mellor's evaluation is incomplete. Fanny is also an expression of Shelley's profound frustration with her own position. Fanny's education has been the ideal, as represented by both Wollstonecraft and Godwin. Yet, like the ill-educated Monster, she is doomed to have no place in the world. She is emotionally and intellectually strong, independent and good, but she is also awkward and isolated. She will never marry and her life must be reconciled to unhappiness.

Though she represents a facet of the Shelleys' relationship and, in many respects, both halves of the couple, Euthanasia is not an impossibly idealized figure. On the contrary, Shelley's attitude to her is ambivalent. Her steel-like integrity is an embryonic manifestation of the monster of inflexibility that is the Duchess of Windsor in *The Last Man* and the cameo self-portrait of Miss Jervis. The Duchess, like Sir Timothy Shelley with his lifelong hatred of his son's wife, is deeply offended when her only daughter marries Lionel Verney. She cannot countenance Idris's disobedience and her association with a commoner, nor the thwarting of her own political ambitions. She is so rigid in her rejection of her daughter and son-in-law, that forgiveness comes too late. Like Euthanasia she denies herself happiness by refusing love and reconciliation. The Duchess is such an extreme example of the submission of imagination and desire to fixed self-image, duty and pride, that as a character she verges on the grotesque. She is variously described as possessing a body "like a machine" to do her will, and "seemed not to belong to flesh and blood" (*TLM*, p. 52). The two-dimensional character of the Duchess is shaped out of one facet of Euthanasia's more complex personality. Nevertheless, she highlights a very real characteristic that Shelley found both outwardly dangerous *and* self-destructive. She may even be expressing fears and guilt about her own coldness, a characteristic which friends and even PBS complained about in her personality. But this same inflexibility in Euthanasia's character also reflects a disturbing aspect of PBS's idealism. He may have modified his radical views as he grew older and replaced Godwinian influences with others (Platonism for example), but to Shelley's eyes PBS remained committed body and soul to a cause that often petrified, as in Euthanasia's case, that flexibility that a lover, husband, father and intellectual partner should have.

BEATRICE

Though Shelley's criticism of Euthanasia, Castruccio and Victor is founded, in part, in their self-isolation and rejection of love, she does not accept the introduction of passionate love as a panacea, (nor, perhaps, would she have accepted the idea of love that PBS came to embrace as a kind of substitute for his earlier confidence in reason). In fact, in the case of Beatrice the Prophetess, passionate love, both for religion and for Castruccio, becomes a crippling obsession, based as it is on a fundamental immaturity. As both a character and as a symbol Beatrice is Euthanasia's opposite. She is impulsive, sensual to the near exclusion of her intellect, and ill-educated. She is without objectivity or principle. She represents the undeveloped and primitive state of humanity *and* womankind which Euthanasia has manifestly rejected.[25] But despite her inutility, Beatrice is a powerful and frightening symbol. She is passion and creativity gone mad, the potential end result of the unrestrained and impractical Romantic imagination. And such an imagination, whether recognized in herself as an artist, or in her husband's apparently difficult poetry and behaviour, disturbed Shelley and inspired the dark fates of her characters.

Beatrice is a fascinating character, certainly Shelley's most sensational, and she gained the reviewers' attention over the other characters in the novel. Reviews of *Valperga* were generally favourable though the Shelleys were expecting a greater uproar over the unshrinking blasphemy of Beatrice's insane ravings. It was given serious consideration in *The Examiner*, *The Literary Chronicle*, and *The Literary Gazette*, though *Blackwood's*, in whose pages Walter Scott had so admired *Frankenstein*, was more qualified in its praise of the second novel. However, in March 1823 *Blackwood's* quietly expressed the generally held view that, "It is impossible to read it [Beatrice's speech expressing her heretical, Paterin beliefs and how she came by them] without admiration of the eloquence with which it is written, or without sorrow that any English lady should be capable of clothing such thoughts in such words".[26] The reviewer's controlled outrage is very similar to that expressed over *Frankenstein* when it was discovered that its author was a young woman. The surprise seems located in the sex of the author, rather than in the horrifying hereticism or broad hints at sadism presented in Beatrice's narrative.

It is possible to identify Shelley's own fears about the power of the imagination to overcome the individual in the character of Beatrice. Where Euthanasia offered Shelley's public views about the possibilities of political and social progress for women as well as men, Beatrice offers an insight into the personal implications of authorship and the artistic imagination. She is the focal point of Shelley's anxiety about her identity as an artist, author and female intellectual. She is Shelley's own awareness of herself as an evil prophet, who represents the evil potential of the imagination. Indeed, Beatrice's suffering is deemed the result of " . . . her imagination, that evil pilot for her . . . " (Vol. III, p. 135). Beatrice speaks for Shelley when she elaborates on God's cruel tricks in her speech to Euthanasia: "He, the damned and triumphant one, sat meditating many thousand years for the conclusion, the consummation, the final crown, the seal of all misery, which he might set on man's brain and heart to doom him to endless torment; and he created the Imagination" (Vol. III, p. 47). And indeed, as if to illustrate

Beatrice's "creed", the message of *Valperga* and of *The Last Man*, the novel that immediately followed, is one of annihilation.

But Shelley's fears were not purely reflexive. She could see that those around her, PBS in particular, could be victims of their own imaginations, ignoring the practicalities of a domestic life with a responsibility to others. Indeed, PBS could imagine himself into a complete terror, as when he fled from the room during a recitation of *Christabel*, convinced that a pair of eyes stared at him from Mary's breasts. His other "visions", such as the hideous creature that he believed had come to kill him at Tremadoc in Wales, are equally famous. His relationship with Claire, resented by Shelley, was characterized by their mutual pleasure in creating, through pure fancy, atmospheres of horror. Claire even took advantage of her terror, and its associated hallucinations, to invade the Shelleys' bedroom. Later, Shelley was to describe her anxiety about PBS's extravagant imaginative tendencies in her notes to her editions of his poems; her chief complaint against *The Witch of Atlas* was its over-fanciful imagery. Beatrice stands as an early manifestation of the destructive nature of the unchecked imagination, the force which motivated PBS in his greatest works and at the same time compelled him to behave destructively. Beatrice is irresponsible *and* mad, she both embodies and articulates her author's fears.

Beatrice is described variously as looking like a "painted . . . Virgin", "an Ariadne" and as the "unfortunate Beatrice Cenci" (Vol. II, pp. 17–18), (the heroine of PBS's historical tragedy and his most successful work). Thus, at the same time she is divine, pagan and hopelessly human and tragic. She is the embodiment of the extremes of imagined women – goddess/saint, lover and victim. Indeed the encapsulated description is prophetic. During her short life Beatrice becomes all three women. It is significant that this description is our first view of Beatrice, seen through the eyes of the fascinated Castruccio. Before her fall, he is struck by her great beauty and charisma. She believes herself to be "the *Ancilla Dei*, the chosen vessel into which God has poured a portion of his spirit . . . a Donna Estatica . . . an inspired woman" (Vol. II, p. 43). Daughter of the executed heretic, Wilhelmina of Bohemia, "the Holy Ghost incarnate upon earth for the salvation of the female sex" (Vol. II, p. 26), the orphaned child is brought up by a devout and affectionate bishop who desperately tries to disabuse the girl of her supposed prophetic powers, and the legacy of her blasphemous mother.

The convergence of Christianity and paganism in Beatrice's life informs the character with tension. The bishop's education is as useless and even damaging as the heretical legacy of her mother. In *The Cenci* PBS's doomed Beatrice can find no consolation in the prospect of paradise after death. She replies to Lucretia's "Trust in God's sweet love,/The tender promises of Christ . . . " (Act V, iv, 75–76) with:

> . . . I know not why, your words strike chill:
> How tedious, false and cold seem all things. I
> Have met with much injustice in this world;
> No difference has been made by God or man,
> Or any power moulding my wretched lot,
> 'Twixt good or evil, as regarded me.
> I am cut off from the only world I know,
> From light, and life, and love, in youth's sweet prime.
> You do well telling me to trust in God,
> I hope I do trust in him. In whom else
> Can any trust? And yet my heart is cold.
>
> (V, iv, 79–89)

Before her own death, Shelley's Beatrice is likewise unconsoled, trusting in nothing but the supremacy of evil.

In fact, Beatrice's religiosity is confused from the beginning. She is pious and a Christian but in the margins where established religion becomes cult worship; in the manner of pagan devotions (the earliest Christian gnostic practices for example), Beatrice is the focus of a fervent following, fascinated by her beauty as well as by her divine eloquence. Her followers are superstitious and ignorant and Beatrice herself becomes duped by her own "powers". Through the influence of her guardian, the auto-da-fé, devised by the Inquisition for her public exposure and punishment, is rigged to prevent her injury. Walking across the burning coals without effect, Beatrice becomes convinced of her own exalted status:

> the air resounded with the triumphant *Te Deum* of the monks, and the people pressed around, awed, but joyful. They endeavoured to touch the garment of the newly declared saint; mothers brought her their sick children; the unhappy intreated her for prayers . . . the nobles pressed round the prophetess, kissing her hand, and the hem of her garment; while she, modest,

half abashed, yet believing in her right to the reverence of her friends, smiled upon all. (Vol. II, pp. 62 and 64)

Castruccio, worshipping her beauty rather than her supposed powers, takes full advantage of her self-delusion. He is not malicious, but selfish, never considering the consequences of his seduction before her ruin. Beatrice believes, with the same unruly imagination that convinced her of her visionary powers, that their mutual desires are sanctified by God. "I loved him", she later explains to Euthanasia, "beyond human love, for I thought heaven itself had interfered to unite us" (Vol. III, p. 69). In *The Last Man*, Perdita makes a similar error in her love for Raymond – she "erected a temple for him in the depth of her being, and each faculty was a priestess vowed to his service" (p. 65). Beatrice's Christianity becomes hopelessly confused with the religion of her own device. In fact, her only mode of understanding is a mystical one. She is mired in superstition and ignorance, exacerbated by her own fantasies. The fact that she turns from a fervent devotion to God's goodness to a confident but equally 'religious' conviction of His evil suggests her total dependence on the world of superstition. One form of religious devotion is easily replaced by another.

With Victor and Castruccio Shelley represented masculine ambition and self-isolation as destructive and dangerous. With Beatrice as a model, Shelley begins to explore the character of her own imagination. From the "flower of paradise" (Vol. II, p. 35), Beatrice becomes "the eloquent prophetess of Evil" (Vol. III, p. 51) when, after her fall, she preaches her new "religion" to the horrified Euthanasia. When Euthanasia responds to her friend's distress, trying to calm her and convince her of God's beneficence to his "children", as Lucretia to Beatrice Cenci, the girl cries: "His children? his eternal enemies! Look I am one! He created the seeds of disease . . . he created man – that most wretched of slaves; oh! Know you not what a wretch man is? and what a storehouse of infinite pain is his much-vaunted human soul?" (Vol. III, pp. 45–46).

Her enthusiasm for voicing good, after physical and emotional violation, is replaced by enthusiasm for God as an evil creator – we hear the echo of the embittered Monster rejected by his own maker. We hear too the echo of the entranced poet in Coleridge's *Kubla Khan* who "on honey-dew hath fed" when Beatrice speaks of God – "that power who sits on high, and scatters evil like dew upon the earth, a killing, blighting honey dew" (Vol. III, p. 43). The deranged Beatrice is not unlike Coleridge's poet, "His flashing eyes, his floating hair!" – " . . . her eyes were not the same . . . they now, like the sun from behind a thunder cloud, glared fiercely from under her dark and scattered hair . . . " (Vol. III, p. 43). Shelley associates the mad woman with the romantic ideal of the inspired poet, satirizing and rejecting at the same time the masculine creative ideal it implies.

Beatrice's conviction that the imagination is exclusively malevolent is particularly striking in its vehement repudiation of the familiar romantic imagination. In her frenzied speech to Euthanasia she explains of God:

> the imagination, that masterpiece of his malice; that spreads honey on the cup that you may drink poison; that strews roses over thorns, thorns sharp and big as spears; that semblance of beauty which beckons you to the desart; that apple of gold with the heart of ashes; that foul image, with the veil of excellence; that mist of the maremma, glowing with roseate hues beneath the sun, that creates it, and beautifies it, to destroy you; that diadem of nettles; that spear, broken in the heart! He, the damned and triumphant one, sat meditating many thousand years for the conclusion, the consummation, the final crown, the seal of all misery, which he might set on man's brain and heart to doom him to endless torment; and he created the Imagination. (Vol. III, pp. 46–47)

Shelley's blasphemy is extreme. The recitation of Beatrice's creed is coloured by key words of the Last Supper and the Passion; "cup", "thorns", "spears", "desart", "the veil", "diadem of nettles", "spear broken in the heart", "the final crown". To Beatrice the Imagination is God's spiteful gift of his son, the male Messiah, "that masterpiece of his malice."

In a similar parody, Shelley gently satirizes PBS's idea of the beauty of the imagination as expressed in *The Witch of Atlas*, a poem that she did not like. The Witch, dark-haired and beautiful like Beatrice first draws the animals to her cave: "The magic circle of her voice and eyes/ All savage natures did imparadise" (103–104). Shelley's Beatrice likewise attracts dumb animals – the down-trodden ignorants, fascinated by her physical beauty, who are her first followers. She then spreads her seductive net over the nobility. However, the Witch offers a panacea to the world that would simultaneously ease life and strip away the hypocrisy of priestcraft and religious ignorance. Beatrice, on the contrary, offers a message of evil.

But Beatrice's suffering, if she is to be believed, is not just the result of her own confused imagination. In her wild ravings to Euthanasia, she speaks from actual experience. She becomes, like Childe Harold, "guilty of the knowledge of crime, which it would seem that fiends alone could contrive" (Vol. III, p. 85). Also like Harold's own suggestion of an ambiguous crime, but perhaps even more daringly, Beatrice hints at sexual depravity. In an episode which echoes the experiences of De Sade's Justine in the prison-monastery of Sante-Marie-des-Bois, Beatrice is imprisoned by a debauched and sadistic tyrant who keeps her and other young girls for nightly orgies. (Shelley may well have heard of de Sade's novel from Lewis and Byron, and PBS apparently read *Mémoires pour la vie de F. Petrarque*). Beatrice's captor is an evil figure:

> he bore a human name; they say that his lineage was human; yet could he be a man? During the day he was absent; at night he returned, and his roofs rung with the sounds of festivity, mingled with shrieks and imprecations. It was the carnival of devils, when we miserable victims were dragged out to – . . .
> (Vol. III, pp. 85–86)

Like the vampire, Beatrice's nemesis appears only at night and she, like the cursed Giaour, is condemned to witness all. Shelley was not adverse to treating her readers to a completely gothic interlude in her altogether serious work. Her nameless master and the dark castle that he inhabits are reminiscent of those that imprison Ann Radcliffe's heroines and wordlessly threaten some unnameable sexual misdeed. Shelley remains just short of specific detail, approaching "Monk" Lewis in her suggestion of violation and sexual slavery in Beatrice's dark words to Euthanasia, "what I saw, and what I endured, is a tale for the unhallowed ears of infidels, or for those who have lost humanity in the sight of blood . . . It has changed me, much changed me, to have been witness of these scenes; I entered young, I came out grey, old and withered . . . " (Vol. III, p. 85).

But like Zelica's irresistible attraction to the evil Veiled Prophet, Beatrice finds herself mesmerized by her captor whose eyes "had a kind of fascination in them" (Vol. III, p. 84). Shelley underscores the sexual frisson when Beatrice continues her description: "There was something about him that might be called beautiful; but it was the beauty of the tiger, of lightning, of the cataract that destroys" (Vol. III, pp. 86–87). In a similar episode, the beautiful and aristocratic Juliet is mesmerized by the promises of salvation from the plague as well as by the dark magnetism of a self-proclaimed holy man in *The Last Man*. Like Zelica she becomes his slave, his victim and she is "left in the fangs of this man of crime, a prisoner, still to inhale the pestilential atmosphere which adhered to his demoniac nature" (*TLM*, p. 286). Shelley, the professional writer, is certainly offering her readers a near-illicit Gothic thrill, but the (former) above description, employing later eighteenth-century images of the sublime, also owes something to *Childe Harold's Pilgrimage* and the early Oriental tales. She exploits not only Byron's own 'commercial' self-image, but her public's knowledge of her own relationship with Byron.

The unrelenting blackness of Beatrice's fate is a clear challenge to PBS and the uncompromised Godwin that he had imbibed so early. How might a world where such depraved behaviour (albeit, behaviour familiar in terms of a highly sensationalized variety of fiction) exists also support the potential for universal human improvement? Though PBS grew more sceptical about perfectibility from 1818 or 1819, and would probably no longer have supported his description as an unqualified atheist, he nonetheless always rejected the idea of sin (and the church and church dogma). His optimism for humanity was not significantly checked; as Desmond King-Hele has pointed out, PBS celebrates the idea of an earthly heaven in *Prometheus Unbound*. The eminently reasonable Euthanasia cannot support such optimism for humanity, even in the face of Beatrice's demanding questions and even with her superior education, she cannot offer a satisfactory answer. After presenting her evidence for the irrefutably evil inclination of humanity, Beatrice raises the spectre of something like sin by asking rhetorically, "what was the influence that hung alone over the mind of man, rendering it cruel, hard and fiendlike?" (Vol. III, p. 86).

Yet Beatrice's destruction is largely self-inflicted. In much the same way, the Greek noblewoman Evadne of *The Last Man* is inflamed by the 'disease' of romantic revolutionary fervour as a result of her unrequited love for Lord Raymond. She is destroyed by her dream. When she is discovered disguised as a soldier, dying on the field of battle, one is reminded of Byron's Myrrha,

of *Sardanapalus* (1821), and her ardently held ideal of Greek freedom. Evadne's love for the ambitious Raymond, moreover, like
her patriotism, is obsessive; "Overpowered by her new sensations,
she did not pause to examine them, or to regulate her conduct by
any sentiments except the tyrannical one which suddenly usurped
the empire of her heart. She yielded to its influence" (*TLM*, p. 31).

But Beatrice is aware of her transformation from innocence to
corruption as a result of her own uncontrolled imagination. In
this passage, with Beatrice at her most ill and most inspired, we
again see Beatrice Cenci, but a Beatrice Cenci who has not been
able to overcome her corruption. PBS's stated belief in his preface
to the play, that "no person can be truly dishonoured by the act
of another",[27] is vehemently rejected by Shelley's Beatrice whose
dishonour is so complete that she is transformed in a few years
from a beautiful young woman to one withered and white-haired
– the fate of Moore's Zelica. What she took for divine passion was
basely human. Describing her recurring vision of evil, a ruined
tower surrounded by water in a dark plain, finally realized by
the castle of her tormentor and captor, the prophetess calls it "my
genius, my daemon" (Vol. III, p. 82).

The prophetess feels profound relief after her outbursts; the horror
of her imagination, its urgency and forcefulness, is appeased in the
telling. Beatrice is oppressed by what she knows and, like the
Ancient Mariner, is forced to relate her tale of suffering forever.
To Euthanasia Beatrice insists, "you must know all . . . why do
you balk me? indeed I do best when I follow my own smallest
inclinations; for when I try to combat them, I am again ill, as I was
this morning" (Vol. III, pp. 68–69). She is powerless against the
force of her own imagination and, like the sinful Mariner, compelled
to testify.

The concept of the all-consuming force of the imagination has
implications for Shelley's own thoughts of herself as an artist. In
one of the few extended journal entries which precedes PBS's death,
Shelley describes a visionary mood in her journal, on February 7–8,
1822, just a few months after the copying and correcting of *Valperga*
was complete:

> During a long – long evening in mixed society, dancing & music –
> how often do ones sensations change – and swift as the west wind
> drives the shadows of clouds across the sunny hill or the waving
> corn – so swift do sentiments pass . . .   It is there that life seems

to weigh itself – and hosts of memories & imaginations thrust into one scale makes the other kick the beam. You remember what you have felt – what you have dreamt – yet you dwell on the shadowy side and lost hopes, and death such as you have seen it seems to cover all things with a funeral pall. The Time that was, is, & will be presses upon you & standing in the centre of a moving circle you ' – slide giddily as the world reels' . . . The Enthusiast suppresses her tears – crushes her opening thoughts and –

But all is changed . . . Sometimes I awaken from my ordinary monotony & my thoughts flow, until as it is exquisite pain to stop the flowing of the blood, so is it painful to check expression & make the overflowing mind return to its usual channel . . .

Shelley's imagery, though it clearly lacks the violence of Beatrice's prophecy of evil, is nevertheless acutely aware of the destructive potential of the imagination, which must be constantly restrained and "return(ed) to its usual channels". It must be controlled and directed to banish the ever-impending threat of a universal funereal darkness.

Shelley develops and articulates her early unshaped fears in Beatrice's central speech on the ascendancy of evil. Beatrice tells the horrified Countess that she shares the Paterin beliefs, an heretical religion based on the principle that God purposely designed evil. She adopts the faith after being rescued in her wanderings by a hermit Paterin following her escape from bondage. His tutelage and gentleness, which ironically parallel her education by the pious bishop, guide her in the direction of blasphemy. She is as easily swayed by a new mentor, from good to evil, as was the young Castruccio. She joins the Paterin faith; "I learned that creed which you hold in detestation, but which, believe me, has much to be said in its behalf" (Vol. III, p. 95). Though her thinking verges on the irrational, the reader can sympathize with the fundamental logic of the suffering girl's conversion. Her choice of this warped belief, and rejection of her original piety, is a response to a series of traumas, caused by the combination of an excessive imagination and physical and mental abuse. However, it is Beatrice's characteristic response. She does not enquire deeply, but simply seeks protection within the framework of another, apparently interchangeable, faith. For her, God is malicious, a grotesque version of the God of the Hebrew Testament,[28] and therefore not unrelated to Shelley's earlier exploration of that Jacobin concept. Beatrice's new creed provides not just a radical argument, but an explanation for her own suffering, a concept all too familiar to Shelley herself. If Shelley could see the seeds of wanton and self-perpetuating evil already sown in the world, an idea dating back to the "History of the Jews", Beatrice sees its complete and utter ascendency. She goes much further than Beatrice Cenci in definitively damning the creation.

However, Beatrice's corrupted voice is not simply that of a lunatic. She explains to Euthanasia, who tries to console her with thoughts of childhood, that through her experiences she has undergone a kind of subverted rite of passage. She deplores the evil of her self-deluded youth: "My childhood! . . . what to become again a dupe, a maniac? to fall again, as I have fallen? . . . days of error, vanity and paradise! My lessons must all be new; all retold in words signifying other ideas than what they signified during my mad, brief dream of youth" (Vol. III, p. 53). In this remarkable speech (and one cannot escape speculation on Shelley's retrospective thinking about her own youth) she expresses a semiotic confusion. The damage done by her imagination and to her psyche has been so great that she must assume a new language in order to function in a world of new realities. The world of her own creation has been shattered. In this she again echoes PBS's Beatrice who, after the outrage of rape by her father exclaims: "Am I not innocent? . . .   Oh, what am I?/ What name, what place, what memory shall be mine?/ What retrospects, outliving even despair? " (III, i, 70, 74–76).

Euthanasia's reply to the prophetess makes it clear that she has endured a similar change, as a result of her own self-imposed principles, "I have passed the fearful change from dream to reality" (Vol. III, p. 56). Likewise, Perdita of *The Last Man* must be 'reeducated' after her husband Raymond's betrayal. After his departure she is "still questioning herself and her author, moulding every idea in a thousand ways, ardently desirous for the discovery of truth in every sentence" (*TLM* Vol. I, p. 114).

Coming of age, in the sense of a Bildungsroman, is in Shelley's world a necessarily destructive process. The two women find no reward in maturity despite the efforts of their respective educators. Indeed, experience has been the agent of their ruin. The reality of the world that they must take a place in, dominated by men who dismantle and crush their power, cannot be accommodated in the dreams that they have created for themselves. Though he was not always directly involved in the education of his daughter, Godwin's highminded educational practices, as spelled out in *Political Justice*, equipped Shelley, like Euthanasia and Beatrice, with tremendous expectations about her place in the world, what was expected of her, and what she assumed was her due.

Both Beatrice and Euthanasia seem to exemplify Shelley's great disappointment. In his introduction to the 1965 edition of *The Last Man*, Luke suggests that Shelley's view of the way that human life progresses was exactly opposed to that of Wordsworth. The poet saw a maturation from infant unity with nature, to adolescent alienation, to unity again as an adult (not dissimilar to PBS's images of complete self-dissolution into nature). Shelley's scheme moves from infant alienation to unity with another, and concludes with adult alienation.

But Euthanasia understands the dynamic of the imagination and her elaborate allegory of the cave of the mind illustrates just how precarious is the imaginative individual's hold on reality. She describes a cavern, with the personified figures of Consciousness, Joy and Sorrow at the entrance, and further back but

> still illumined by the light of day sit Memory . . . grave Judgement . . . and Reason. Hope and Fear dwell there, hand in hand . . . But beyond all this there is an inner cave, difficult of access, rude, strange, and dangerous. Few visit this, and it is often barren and empty; but sometimes . . . this last recess is decorated with the strongest and most wondrous devices . . . But here also find abode owls, and bats, and vipers, and scorpions, and other deadly reptiles. This recess receives no light . . . nor has Conscience any authority here . . . This is the habitation of the madman . . . But it is here also that Poetry and Imagination live; it is here that Heroism, and Self-sacrifice, and the highest virtues dwell . . . and here dwells the sweet reward for our toil, Content of Mind, who . . . rules, instead of Conscience, those admitted to her happy dominion. (Vol. III, pp. 99–102)

The proximity of imagination and poetry to madness, within the cavern, becomes Shelley's paradigm for the process of her own imagination, so that when she came to write *The Last Man*, she prefaced the story with the cave of the Cumean Sibyl. As the introduction to the novel relates, she penetrated the secret chambers of the cave with her companion and came upon the sibyl's

scattered leaves which, translated and ordered by her, became the
novel which follows; "Scattered and unconnected as they were,
I have been obliged to add links, and model the work into a
consistent form. But the main substance rests on the truths contained in these poetic rhapsodies, and the divine intuition which
the Cumaean damsel obtained from heaven" (*TLM*, pp. 3–4). The
sibyl, an echo of the mad prophetess of *Valperga*, as well as a
remnant of the Shelleys' earlier celebration of pagan culture and
Hellenism, produces the creative raw material for the story. The
pagan sibyl precedes Christianity, but she is an element of the
universal myths and legends of the ancient world that Geddes,
Paine and others saw as the basis of many of the Old Testament's
stories. In the same way that the pagan is separated from established
Judaeo-Christianity, Shelley carefully divides her imagination; the
isolated, secret and perhaps insane sibyl is a distinct creative entity
who is not the writer, the professional and conscientious recorder
of events. The anonymous novel, *The Last Man, or Omegarus and
Syderia, a Romance in Futurity* (1806),[29] often cited as a source for
Shelley's novel, also begins with the ostensible author visiting a
mysterious cave and receiving his orders to record a certain history
– that of certain individuals at the end of the world.[30] In Shelley's
world and in Euthanasia's allegory the writer or the subject may
try to keep her distance but nonetheless teeters on the brink of
insanity.[31]

In *Valperga* Beatrice finally dies in a state of madness. She suffers
a relapse into violent self-delusion, believing that she can recapture
the heart of Castruccio through the machinations of a purely malicious witch. Mandragola, as a kind of parody of the beneficent Witch
of Atlas, hopes to perpetrate as much evil as possible before her
death and to bring down the supremely powerful Castruccio. The
witch is a kind of grotesque counterpart to Castruccio's ambition
(and to PBS's witch); she desires power for its own sake and despises
the world. She seeks vengeance for all and for nothing. Yet it is the
young woman, "she, once the loveliest, now the most lost, the most
utterly undone of women" (Vol. III, p. 154), who suffers the fate
that Shelley so feared. Near death Beatrice cries, "Save me! . . . save
me from madness, which, as a fiend, pursues and haunts me . . . "
(Vol. III, p. 144). She dies without regaining lucidity and the last
rites are administered "mercifully" without her knowledge. She
dies therefore an unrepentant heretic, closely followed by the death
at sea of the likewise unabsolved Countess. Both women, formerly

powerful and beloved, die without leaving any accomplishment. At Euthanasia's death, "Earth felt no change . . . and men forgot her" (Vol. III, p. 262). They leave nothing behind to mark their passage on earth – even the seat of the Countesses of *Valperga* which had stood as monument to the family for generations is "scathed ruins" (Vol. II, p. 285). Beatrice is given a lurid, magnificent funeral by the guilty Castruccio. Both women, childless, die excluded from salvation; even their final spiritual states are left blank. They are completely annihilated, the failure of their lives extending into eternity.

By the novel's conclusion we see that the course that Castruccio has appeared to steer between the two women has been no course at all. Though set up in the novel as polar opposites to one another neither woman has been able to influence Castruccio. His struggle between ambition and love is even less convincing than Victor Frankenstein's. But Castruccio is also meant to undergo a struggle for his moral soul and in this respect the women come to symbolize his potential political conduct. Were his love for Euthanasia to overcome his conquering ambition, he would look to the governance of his own home and rule over it with the style of benevolent monarchy that Euthanasia advocates for her own domain of *Valperga*. And more importantly, he would adopt her nationalistic idealism; he would not opportunistically embrace an outside power – the German emperor – for personal gain. He would see the possibilities of a united country and, symbolically, look to the future Italy from where Shelley writes.

Yet, to choose to remain with Beatrice would not simply be to betray Euthanasia, but to accept the world that the prophetess represents: the Dark Ages, the quagmire of superstition and ignorant adoration. Beatrice's power is in her iconic beauty, a beauty that seduces and blinds her followers to her true vulnerability and spiritual emptiness. Her fall, a result of her own impulsiveness and base *humanity*, underscores the reality of misguided religion. Held up as a living saint, she is in reality the incarnation of human frailty. And Castruccio is equally unwilling to participate in the precarious power that she symbolizes, just as he is unwilling to participate in the altruistic, self-sacrificing world of Euthanasia.

Thus, the struggle for Castruccio's soul is full of potential significance, but finally amounts to nothing. He is aware of the choices that he makes but they do not torment him; unlike Victor, he remains serene. He is unaware of mistakes on his part. His soul is merely worn away. Castruccio is the soldier, a "little Napoleon", as PBS characterized him, and his dedication, like that of the famous general and of Victor Frankenstein, is solely to his own aggrandizement. Unlike Victor, who deludes himself into thinking that he pursues his ambition for the benefit of mankind, Castruccio retains no delusions. His education, by warriors, princes and politicians fits him for a single purpose, equally alien to a democratic ideal of government and to a world view shaped by religion, false or otherwise.

Ultimately then, the women and their respective domains have no effect on Castruccio, and even less effect on the world of the novel. The symbol of Euthanasia's power, the castle of Valperga, is completely annihilated and the symbol of Beatrice's power, her apparently transcendent beauty, is blighted and disfigured. Both women die symbolically before their actual physical deaths. Though Castruccio believes that Euthanasia remains the protectress of his mortal soul, it is precisely because her true power has no power to change him. His soul is safe with her because she can do nothing to it and because, as the reader is aware, Castruccio relinquished it with little regret. If Castruccio represents power for power's sake, the spirit of the tyrant, than Shelley seems to be saying that no concerns of humanity may halt or influence his progress; his tyrannical force is precisely that which her husband and father consistently spoke out against and believed could be abolished. She takes up the theme of relentless malevolence – even more removed from human control – in *The Last Man*, where she brings it to its logical conclusion.

6

"The earth is not,
nor ever can be heaven":
The Last Man

With the news of Byron's death at Missolonghi Shelley was finally able to begin writing the novel that she had planned months before. She now felt completely alone and believed (unrealistically, given her wide circle of friends), that she would never engage in exhilarating conversation again, or rather listen to it. Byron's death meant the end of the voice that in her memory always responded to her husband's while she sat in silence. PBS was now finally dead, as was the powerful ghost of his intellectual discourse. Shelley was profoundly sad at Byron's death but with her increased sense of isolation came her first real intellectual breathing space. Her imagination could expand freely and with a new ebullience she could attack a theme grander than any she had attempted before. She was finally independent and no longer needed to define herself in terms of PBS. *The Last Man* is her final (fictional) word on that deeply disturbing intellectual and emotional conflict.

The Last Man is in some sense a tribute to PBS but it is an ironic one, a colossal monument to difficult and frustrating idealism. The fact that *The Last Man* begins with what the poet would have regarded as a politically ideal state, and then that state very quickly breaks down, is an unmistakable swipe at PBS's most cherished ideal. In *The Last Man* England is a republic thrown into disarray, its government rendered impotent in the face of crisis.

Though her expressions of self-pity in both the letters and journal continue unabated, Shelley seems to have plunged into her project with a new enthusiasm. She could perhaps begin to view her widowhood as a kind of freedom and, as head of her own household, she could devote her self to her work. *The Last Man* lays the ghost of PBS and with it, Shelley also subdues her spiritual disquiet. She was exhausted by the novel and never attempted an ambitious theme in fiction again. The struggle with PBS's ideology, it seems, had been the motivating force of her creativity.

Some contemporary critics, among them Mellor, have identified Mary Shelley's primary anxiety as the preservation of the family and intimate love relationships between man and woman against all odds. It is Mellor's thesis in *Mary Shelley: Her Life, Her Fiction, Her Monsters* (1988) that Shelley's creative strivings "to idealize the bourgeois family as the source both of emotional sustenance and of ethical value" are at the foundation of her work.[1] The well-ordered, secure and loving family unit, Mellor maintains, forms the focus of Shelley's fiction, and at the same time is offered as a panacea against all the ills and misfortunes of life. According to Mellor, Shelley believes that within the family's quiet bounds one finds not just security but all the components of a fulfilled life. But this supposition over-simplifies Shelley's anxieties *and* ideals and under-estimates her intellectual ambitions. *Frankenstein* disregards family altogether; and the Frankenstein household remains resolutely at the margins of the story. The deaths in Victor's family, more than anything else, propel the plot, they serve only to motivate him to find and stop the Monster. It is quite clear that, at least initially, the family represents an environment that stifles intellectual growth and curiosity. It is also no simple Gothic device that joins together the hands and the futures of Elizabeth and Victor in the dying grasp of Mrs. Frankenstein. They are betrothed over her death-bed; marriage is in effect sanctified by death. Victor must leave his home in order to pursue his education that, though misguided, was no more so than that passively suggested by his ineffectual father. The explorer Walton, in addition to his intellectual curiosity, appears to pursue his quest in part to escape the closeted and sterile home of his sister.

One cannot help but be reminded of the cramped and tense atmosphere in the Godwin household at Skinner Street and Shelley's gratitude to her lover for rescuing her from its constant frustrations. What is more, Shelley grew to find her position in her new household frustrating in a different way. PBS's connection with Godwin ensured that her father continued to invade her intellectual and emotional life and she must have felt stifled by his 'presence' and perhaps resentful of the relationship that he shared with her husband. What is more, she may have felt an outsider; as a woman she had no real role. Like Euthanasia she was equipped by education and heredity for power and intellectual sway but, because she was a woman, that role was unacceptable. Euthanasia is doomed and destroyed, Fanny Derham is awkward, isolated and, because of her extraordinary independence of thought, will never fit in; she is an outcast like the Monster. Like both these women Shelley would not be fulfilled by a complete home life. On the contrary, life in the home, especially and ironically the home of enlightened intellectuals, was Shelley's intellectual and ideological battleground. She was fundamentally divided in her emotional relationship to PBS; the man who was the focus of her love and admiration was also the ideological figurehead with whom she found it difficult to empathize.

In the two novels that followed *Frankenstein*, the family is glaringly absent. In *Valperga* each of the main protagonists is alone, sole remnant of his or her respective family line. But in *The Last Man* Shelley positively anatomizes the family, mounting both a generalized attack on its near-sacred status, and denying that for the individual it can ever represent fulfillment, especially for an individual of great intelligence. In *The Last Man*, Shelley seems to take delight in setting up a vision of tranquillity and happiness in her first volume, then remorselessly laying it to waste throughout the following two. Ultimately, not only do the families of her protagonists systematically expire, but the entire family of man is wiped from the face of the earth. Lionel Verney, the only survivor of the remorseless plague, finds himself on a deserted globe.

Shelley is *not* simply focused on domesticity. Like Beatrice in *Valperga*, she was searching for some meaning in the apparently blind destruction that she witnessed, in the suffering that characterized her life, and which she subsequently subjected her characters to. As we shall see, the conclusions of Lionel Verney, the Last Man, would have disturbed PBS and Godwin, just as Beatrice so disturbed Euthanasia and the readers of *Valperga*. Shelley offers no panacea, no comfort at all in fact. She explodes the feminine belief in the prevailing strength of love (and indeed, PBS's confidence in the power of love according to his own definition of the word). Her domestic circles are painstakingly established at the beginning of the story; then in a reversal of the normal ordering of the woman's novel, they are systematically blasted apart. As in PBS's "Ozymandias" and in Byron's *Sardanapalus* (1821), with its fall of the Assyrian royal line, former pleasures and glories are unconditionally obliterated, only their grandiose memories remain to mock the present and the future.

The Last Man takes up the curse of *Frankenstein*, as developed and articulated in *Valperga* by Beatrice's ravings and by the desolation of that novel's conclusion, and brings it to its ultimate and logical conclusion – complete annihilation. In fact, Shelley seems to comment on the very irrelevance of words and writing, as Verney determines to record his story, a futile and impotent shout into the earless and eyeless void of the future. Though some critics, particularly her contemporaries, have taken Shelley to task for her unrelenting pessimism, it is clear that her protagonist is searching for reasons for the destruction around him, seeking to understand (but not necessarily to solve) the depressing weaknesses of humanity and its inevitable suffering. His conclusions, as we shall see, represent a kind of proto-existentialism and at the same time depart from the political and philosophical systems that preoccupied Godwin and PBS. *Frankenstein*'s inconclusiveness left Shelley the opportunity to develop her theme, which reaches maturity in *The Last Man*. It is with *The Last Man* that Shelley's vision is finally presented in completion. It is no surprise that the novels that followed are so different from the first three and by comparison, so uninteresting. *Perkin Warbeck, Lodore,* and *Falkner* represent standard genres, the historical and the novel of fashionable life, and suggest that Shelley had perhaps solved some of her earlier philosophical questions and could now write for pleasure and profit.

BACKGROUND TO THE NOVEL

By August 25, 1823, Shelley was back in England, having delayed her departure from Italy for as long as possible. It had become clear that she had to earn a living – Sir Timothy Shelley showed no signs of softening towards his daughter-in-law and grandson. Her copying work for Byron had ended with his departure for Greece and Italy could not provide her with enough work. In October she wrote to Leigh Hunt mentioning plans for another novel. In February she begged Hunt for his promised biography of PBS to be included in the *Posthumous Poems* already at the press. In the same letter she again mentioned a novel, as an antidote this time to her drudgery: "I write bad articles which help to make me miserable – but I am going to plunge into a novel, and hope that

its clear water will wash off the <dirt> mud of the magazines –"
(February 9, 1824). Still composition was delayed. It is evident from
her journals that she was experiencing considerable creative inertia.
A journal entry for May 14 expresses her profound loneliness, her
inability to apply herself to work without PBS's encouragement, and
her homesickness for Italy. She wrote, "The last man! Yes I may well
describe that solitary being's feelings, feeling myself as the last relic
of a beloved race, my companions, extinct before me – ". On the next
day she learned of Byron's death, more than confirming to herself
her desolate condition:

> Byron has become one of the people of the grave – that innumer-
> able conclave to which the beings I best loved belong. I knew
> him in the bright days of youth, when neither care or fear
> had visited me: before death had made me feel my mortality
> and the earth was the scene of my hopes . . .   Can I forget his
> attentions & consolations to me during my deepest misery? –
> Never . . .   What do I do here? Why am I doomed to live on
> seeing all expire before me? God grant I may die young . . . all
> my old friends are gone – I have no wish to form new – I cling to
> the few remaining – but they slide away & my heart fails when
> I think by how few ties I hold to the world . . . (May 15, 1824)

But Shelley evidently took some creative inspiration from her own
immediate situation – news of Byron's death seems to have released
her creative block. She found a publisher in Henry Colburn and,
probably because pirated productions of *Frankenstein* "had prodi-
gious success as . . . drama"[2] and Shelley was herself something of
a literary celebrity – "But lo & behold! I found myself famous!" she
wrote to Hunt on September 9, 1823 – Colburn paid her the large
sum of £300 for the novel. It was published in February 1826 to
largely unenthusiastic reviews, in great contrast to the early triumph
of *Frankenstein*.

It is necessary to summarize briefly *The Last Man*. Lionel Verney's
account begins a few years after the abdication of the King of
England in 2073. Britain has become a republic after the peaceful
deposition of the royal family. Verney himself is an orphaned and
penniless shepherd whose father had been friend and confidant of
the old king. His lonely and brutish life among the Cumbrian hills
is transformed when he meets Adrian Windsor,[3] the quondam heir

to the throne. At the age of sixteen Lionel is elevated to a life of culture, scholarship and intellectual pursuit and losing his rustic savagery, "Poetry and its creations, philosophy and its researches and classifications, alike awoke the sleeping ideas in (his) mind, and gave (him) new ones" (p. 21). He marries Idris, Adrian's sister, against the wishes of their domineering, ambitious and inflexible mother, the Duchess of Windsor. Lionel's own sister Perdita marries the ambitious Lord Raymond. The happy group settles at sylvan Windsor Castle until Raymond is prompted to re-enter political life. In so doing he forms an illicit relationship with the Greek noblewoman and patriot Evadne, former beloved of Adrian, destitute since the death of her father. Rejected by the betrayed Perdita, Raymond escapes his shame by joining the Greeks in their war for independence. But Perdita relents and the first volume ends with Lionel and his sister journeying to Greece to rescue Raymond; lost, believed dead. With the second volume, Raymond leads a successful campaign. He conquers Constantinople where a plague has already devastated the city. Raymond is killed within its walls. His death is followed by that of his wife whose suicide leaves their only daughter, Clara, an orphan. During the ensuing years the plague depopulates the East, Europe and America, and finally reaches Britain. Volume Two ends as Lord Protector Adrian Windsor determines to lead the group of British survivors to the cold climate of the Alps in an attempt to escape the seasonal resurgence of the pestilence. In Volume Three, in Paris, the Lord Protector is challenged by a false prophet, evil leader of a band of desperate survivors, but manages to avoid battle and further depletion of their dwindling numbers. However, the plague returns. By the time that the group reaches Dijon, only eighty remain. Crossing the Alps into Italy, only Adrian, Lionel, his son Evelyn and Clara survive. Evelyn dies of Typhus and then a shipwreck on their voyage to Greece leaves only Lionel Verney to roam the empty world and record his story.

Critics such as Spark, Nitchie and Luke have pointed to some of the "antecedents" to, and specific influences on *The Last Man*. It is clear that the novel owes a debt to many artistic visions of doomsday, not to mention accounts of the plague in novel and historical form that were already popular reading by the time Shelley's novel was published. She almost certainly read Byron's poem "Darkness" (1816) during the Geneva summer, composed while she was at work on *Frankenstein*. It is a bleak and terrifying vision; one that anticipates the tone of the novel and Shelley no doubt recalled its devastated atmosphere when she came to write *The Last Man* eight years later. "Darkness" concludes with a sense of emptiness that suggests the similarly dark theme in Shelley's work:

> . . . The world was void,
> The populous and the powerful – was a lump,
> Seasonless, herbless, treeless, manless, lifeless –
> A lump of death – a chaos of hard clay.
> The rivers, lakes, and ocean all stood still,
> And nothing stirred within their silent depths;
> Ships sailorless lay rotting on the sea,
> And their masts fell down piecemeal; as they dropp'd
> They slept on the abyss without a surge –
> The waves were dead; the tides were in their grave,
> The moon their mistress had expired before;
> The winds were withered in the stagnant air,
> And the clouds perish'd; Darkness had no need
> Of aid from them – She was the universe.
>
> (69–82)

Two striking images from the earlier work are particularly interesting. In Byron's poem the last men on earth comb through the ashes of a ruined church and

> . . . lifted up
> Their eyes as it grew lighter, and beheld
> Each other's aspects – saw, and shriek'd, and died –
> Even of their mutual hideousness they died,
> Unknowing who he was upon whose brow
> Famine had written Fiend . . .
>
> (66–69)

In the novel Verney dreams of the dead Raymond, who, as a phantom, bears upon his "brow the sign of pestilence" (p. 146). Later, roaming the empty world, Lionel wanders into the saloon of a palace. As the sole survivor (and at 36, the same age as Byron in his last year) he sees his reflection in a mirror and is shocked at the image of the "wild-looking, unkempt, half-naked savage"

(p. 331). Though he does not die of fright, nor read death upon his own countenance, the horror evoked when man fails to recognize the face of man – his *own* face – is borrowed from the poem.

In the poem humanity is wiped out and only darkness remains; "She was the Universe". The desolation is complete and without suggestion of salvation, like that of Shelley's emptied world. However, the essential difference lies in Byron's *visionary* apocalypse, as opposed to Shelley's naturalistic and detailed account of the world's scientific or "explained" depopulation. In fact, Shelley subverts Byron's vision when she portrays the world's destruction accompanied by tranquillity and the coming of spring:

> Hear you not the rushing sound of the coming tempest? Do you not behold the clouds open, and destruction lurid and dire pour down on the blasted earth? See you not the thunderbolt fall, and are deafened by the shout of heaven that follows its descent? Feel you not the earth quake and open with agonizing groans, while the air is pregnant with shrieks and wailings, – all announcing the last days of man?
>
> No! none of these things accompanied our fall! The balmy air of spring, breathed from nature's ambrosial home, invested the lovely earth, which wakened as a young mother about to lead forth in pride her beauteous offspring to meet their sire who had been long absent. The buds decked the trees, the flowers adorned the land: the dark branches, swollen with seasonable juices, expanded into leaves, and the variegated foliage of spring, bending and singing in the breeze, rejoiced in the genial warmth of the unclouded empyrean . . . birds awoke in the woods, while abundant food for man and beast sprung up from the dark ground. Where was pain and evil? Not in the calm air or weltering ocean; not in the woods or fertile fields, nor among the birds that made the woods resonant with song, nor the animals that in the midst of plenty basked in the sunshine. (p. 229)

In Shelley's ironic vision, man's demise has no effect on nature; she retains her implacable beauty. Nature mocks; after all man's vanity, he emphatically does *not* control his world. Nature's beauties of spring are the flowers of the field, as well as the corpses of men. The plague is hers, just as the burgeoning buds of spring are hers. The physical world remains plentiful and healthy, the seasons persist and the spring and summer still bring forth their bounty. Life goes on without its supposed master. Shelley uses this poetic irony with great effect. Though the overall style of the novel is often verbose and plodding, the details of the weather, seasonal change, local episodes, characters and personal tragedies, build up a frightening picture of the relentless power of the plague. Shelley constructs an extraordinarily eerie atmosphere of dread.

There are other contemporary or near-contemporary works which share Shelley's novel's name and basic theme. Thomas Campbell's poem "The Last Man" (1823) is a portrait of a biblical apocalypse, one that, unlike the novel, smacks of religious salvation: "This spirit shall return to Him/Who gave its heavenly spark . . . " (61–62).[4]

Thomas Lovell Beddoes' contribution to the theme was in dramatic and very fragmentary form. The poet had a nearly mystical obsession with death, his many attempts at suicide culminating finally in success. Indeed, as his editor H. W. Donner explains: "Beddoes is above all others the poet of death".[5] In fragment 62 of his "Last Man", the dying Dianeme looks to death as an ultimate fulfillment and homecoming – "I am, I have been, I shall be, O glory!/ An universe, a god, a living Ever" (80–81).[6] This positive (though bizarre) notion of death is once again at odds with the spiritual inconclusiveness faced by Shelley's last man.

Thomas Hood also published a ballad of the same name in *Whims and Oddities* (1826). Appearing in the same year as the novel, Hood's ballad is satirical and contains some of the blackest gallows humour of the period. Some contemporary reviewers claimed that Hood's poem said everything that Shelley's novel did in far pithier terms. It is true that of all the group, Hood's ballad seems the most similar in its perspective to the novel. His last man shares the same sense of loneliness and desolation as Lionel Verney; the experience of global depopulation is told from his point of view. In this respect it is also related to two other important influences on the novel: Defoe's account of 1665, *A Journal of the Plague Year*, and the American novelist, Charles Brockden Brown's *Arthur Mervyn* (1799), also the story of a plague.

Hood's poem also contains images that constantly recur in Shelley's novel; the levelling of society when the poor man may occupy the palace, and, the very essence of depopulation, domestic animals occupying the streets and buildings of once great cities. Shelley wrote:

. . . the animals, in new found liberty, rambled through the gorgeous palaces, and hardly feared our forgotten aspect. The dove-coloured oxen turned their full eyes on us, and paced slowly by; a startling throng of silly sheep, with pattering feet, would start up in some chamber, formerly dedicated to the repose of beauty, and rush, huddling past us, down the marble staircase into the street, and again in at the first open door, taking unrebuked possession of hallowed sanctuary, or kingly council-chamber" (p. 313).

Hood's narrator witnesses the same:

> . . . so we far'd that way to a city great,
> Where the folks had died of the pest –
> It was fine to enter in house and hall
> Wherever it liked me best . . .
> The grandest palaces in the land
> Were as free as workhouse sheds.[7]
>
> (99–102, 107–108)

and continues:

> . . . In vain I watch'd, at the window pane
> For a Christian soul to pass!
> But sheep and kine wander'd up the street,
> And browz'd on the new-come grass. –[8]
>
> (129–32)

In fact, an anonymous novel *The Last Man: or Omegarus and Syderia, a Romance in Futurity* (1806), predates them all. This earlier novel, on the surface, has much in common with Shelley's. *Omegarus and Syderia* also begins in the present, with the narrator entering a mysterious cave, echoed by Shelley's preface and her account of her own investigation of the cave of the Cumean Sibyl. At this point the earlier novel takes a supernatural turn as the cave turns out to be the dwelling of the spirit of Futurity who reveals to the narrator the fate of Omegarus, the last man, and his encounter with the Genius of the Earth, described in very Blakean terms: "his eyes, blacker than ebony, diffused a light and his strong muscles resembled burning rods of iron in the furnace . . . ".[9] The narrator is then commanded by Futurity to "celebrate" the story of the earth's last inhabitants. In a parallel account, though maintaining a naturalistic thread, Shelley determines to piece together the scraps of writing on leaves that she finds in the sibyl's cave.

Incidental similarities continue. As in *The Last Man*, the characters of *Omegarus and Syderia* travel by hot air balloon. The "aeronauts"[10] pass over the ruined empires, nations and countries of the world, much as the Apparition had carried the narrator of Volney's *Ruins*.

Omegarus and Syderia is striking in its prophetic character, an adjective often used to describe some of the innovations of Shelley's novel. In the earlier book the world has steadily depopulated as a result of chronic infertility rather than disease. The corresponding degradation of the earth as the result of man's relentless exploitation, over-cultivation, the cutting-down of primeval forests and other outrages against nature seems curiously contemporary.

Yet the two novels remain fundamentally different. Though leavened with pagan imagery and devices and at times a surreal quality, *Omegarus and Syderia* is the story of a Christian apocalypse and resurrection. It is an essentially Christian moral tale evoking the Day of Judgement and the narrator is charged with telling his own world of the last day and salvation. Indeed, the last day as portrayed in the novel is strikingly similar to Shelley's ironic description of how the world does *not* end in *The Last Man*, as quoted above. As we shall see, Shelley has no such conventional spiritual instruction in mind.

AMBITION

The theme of the disruptive nature of personal ambition dominates the first volume of *The Last Man*. Lord Raymond, who seems to inherit Victor Frankenstein's (and Byron's) desire for action in the public realm – though their means are markedly different – also unleashes a malevolent force upon the world. The motif of the animation of a destructive force which Shelley had first explored in *Frankenstein* is at the heart of *The Last Man*: the plague. Before his last battle Lord Raymond despairs of leaving his mark upon posterity and confesses that the "prayer of (his) youth was to be one among those who render the pages of earth's history splendid; who exalt the race of man, and make this little globe a dwelling of the mighty" (p. 141). But when Raymond razes Constantinople, he discovers that the empty, dead city has already given birth to its own "hideous progeny" – the plague – that within a few years desolates the earth.

Raymond has a foil in the character of the Duchess of Windsor. She is relentlessly ambitious, both for herself and for her children. The bitterness that she feels as a result of her husband's abdication colours all her actions. As I suggested in the last chapter, she is described in terms that highlight her lack of humanity and her unmistakable affinity with *Frankenstein*'s monster: "she slept little, and hardly ate at all; her body was evidently considered by her as a mere machine" (p. 52). She is initially aligned with Raymond; he shares in a plan to marry Idris (before he succumbs to Perdita's love) and establish himself and the former princess as king and Queen of England. The Duchess schemes with her henchmen to drug Idris and carry her to Austria, away from the devoted Lionel. Even following the happy marriage of Idris and Lionel she cannot forgive him the thwarting of her ambitions. She remains embittered against Lionel and her disobedient daughter, denying herself the pleasures of family and friends, and only realizes her terrible mistake with Idris's death.

Alone and at night Lionel places Idris's body in the family vault and sees the "banner of her family hung there, still surmounted by its regal crown". In anticipation of the Duchess's remorse only moments later when she comes unbidden to the Windsor chapel, Lionel muses on the royal banner: "Farewell to the glory and heraldry of England! – I turned from such vanity with a slight feeling of wonder, at how mankind could have ever been interested in such things" (p. 260). The Duchess then sees the corpse of her daughter on her bier and her foolishness is revealed to her:

> the perception of the falsehood, paltryness and futility of her cherished dreams of birth and power; the overpowering knowledge, that love and life were the true emperors of our moral state; all, as a tide, rose, and filled her soul with stormy and bewildering confusion. (p. 262)

Shelley makes her suffer for her crime along with Victor and Raymond; though Lionel does, her daughter can never forgive her.

But Raymond remains the heir of Victor and Castruccio's destructive over-reaching. The direst consequence of his egotistical actions, the release of the contagion, becomes an entity in Lionel's dream, born out of the vision of the overly ambitious and failed Raymond:

> Methought I had been invited to Timon's last feast; I came with keen appetite, the covers were removed, the hot water sent up its unsatisfying steams, while I fled before the anger of the host, who assumed the form of Raymond; while to my diseased fancy, the vessels hurled by him after me, were surcharged with fetid vapour, and my friend's shape, altered by a thousand distortions, expanded into a gigantic phantom, bearing on its brow the sign of pestilence. The growing shadow rose and rose, filling, and then seeming to endeavour to burst beyond, the adamantine vault that bent over, sustaining and enclosing the world. (p. 146)

Shelley's vision of despair goes far beyond the end of *Frankenstein*. Raymond's selfish 'achievement' unleashes a nightmare, like that of Victor's, in the mind of the author, and upon the world. Shelley's own dream vision of the Monster, as outlined in her preface to the 1831 edition of the novel, is again made manifest in Lionel's vision of his phantom of the pestilence. In fact, Lionel's description of his transmogrified friend suggests Victor's monster; huge, distorted and threatening. Shelley associates the two over-reachers in the minds of her readers, as well as in the vision that she holds of her own creativity.

THE DESTRUCTION OF THE FAMILY

Institutions are under siege in *The Last Man*. Shelley whittles away relentlessly at the supposedly firm edifice of the family. She fulfils her characters' dreams of domestic love and tranquillity then systematically destroys them. As characters in their desperation erect one redoubt after another against the onslaughts first of politics and war and ultimately of the plague, Shelley undermines the notion that the family can provide refuge and security against the world. Indeed, within her own family that security was a kind of intellectual control from which she struggled to free herself.

In Volume One of the novel the reader finds the orphaned Verney children – Lionel and Perdita – reaching maturity and through the influence of Adrian Windsor, becoming cultivated, domesticated and in Verney's case, intellectual. Perdita is a particular challenge to the civilizing influence and, in this respect she is like Beatrice:

> Yet though lovely and full of noble feeling, my poor Perdita . . . was not altogether saintly in her disposition. Her manners were cold and repulsive. If she had been nurtured by those who had regarded her with affection, she might have been different; but unloved and neglected, she repaid want of kindness with distrust and silence. She was submissive to those who held authority over her, but a perpetual cloud dwelt on her brow; she looked as if she expected enmity from every one who approached her, and her actions were instigated by the same feeling. All the time she could command she spent in solitude. She would ramble to the most unfrequented places, and scale dangerous heights, that in those unvisited spots she might wrap herself in loneliness. (pp. 9–10)

In fact, Perdita the anti-social wanderer is described as a "visionary"; she is a parody of the Wordsworthian solitary. It is precisely because she is alone that her spirituality is raw and unrefined. Exclusive communion with nature has retarded her and it is the effects of civilization, books, music, conversation and luxurious surroundings which redeem her. Even the cottage that she had inhabited at Windsor before her marriage becomes, after her death, an unmistakable double of Wordsworth's *Ruined Cottage*.[11] Shelley would have been familiar with Wordsworth's "Solitary" and Margaret's pathetic story from reading *The Excursion* in 1814 (the year of its publication). The journal records for 15 September: "Mary reads the Excu[r]sion all day & reads the history of Margaret to PBS". Shelley expressed an energetic dislike of *The Excursion* and other Wordsworthian elements which appear in *The Last Man* are subtly satirized. Martha is a solitary wise-woman, a "rustic archon" (p. 196) that Adrian enlists to help nurse the victims of the plague in the neighbouring villages of Windsor. Once freed from the useless existence of the solitary she is of value to the community.

Lionel's boyhood among the hills – the same Cumbrian hills that nurtured the spirit of the young Wordsworth – is solitary, savage and idle. He poaches for spite rather than necessity and is even arrested. In retrospect he comments, "I cannot say much in praise of such a life; and its pains far exceed its pleasures" (p. 8) and later, "I had lived in what is generally called the world of reality, and it was awakening to a new country to find that there was a deeper meaning in all I saw, besides that which my eyes conveyed to me" (p. 21). As PBS did in *Alastor*, Shelley takes the Romantic notion of the solitary poet, exemplified in Wordsworth's early oeuvre, to task. The conclusion of *The Last Man*, misanthropy taken to its ironic extreme, is Shelley's answer to what she and her husband saw as unproductive and life-denying self-indulgence.

Eventually, after becoming part of Adrian's circle at Windsor and overcoming certain obstacles, the Verneys marry their respective lovers. Before the first volume is concluded, they have achieved an unparalleled domestic fulfilment, encompassing passionate love, children, friendship and intellectual stimulation: "Jealousy and disquiet were unknown among us; nor did a fear or hope of change ever disturb our tranquillity. Others said, We might be happy – we said – We are" (pp. 64–65). However, still within Volume One, Shelley shakes the foundations of her characters' happiness and the wall of domestic tranquillity is breeched, first by Raymond's return to political life, and later, by the collapse of Constantinople and the advent of the plague.

Sole "remnant of a noble but impoverished family" (p. 27), Lord Raymond abandons his plans for reinstating the monarchy with the inhuman Countess of Windsor. On the contrary, he falls in love with Perdita and in a step that Shelley intended should exhibit his true nobleness, he forsakes his ambitious plans and marries her. He takes the decision that Castruccio rejected and eloquently expresses his humanity and integrity. At the same time, though it is perhaps dangerous to interpret the novel as biography, Shelley attempts to redeem the character of her friend Byron who did *not* behave nobly in love, nor often make sacrifices for its sake. Shelley's portrayal of him as heroic augmented the improvement of his reputation in England following his death in Greece. After paying her respects to the poet, lying in state at Sir Edward Knatchbull's home at 20 Great George Street, and watching his funeral procession pass her window on its way up Highgate Hill to the North, she wrote about the experience to many of their mutual friends. She wrote to Prince Mavrocordato on February 22, 1825, the "death caused a very great sensation here, and they pay more enthusiastic respect to his memory and his ashes, than to him when alive." Also, given her real sorrow at his death, and in some sense, its triggering of the inspiration of the novel, Shelley may have wished to redress the statements in her letters and conversations (particularly as recorded by Trelawny) that attacked him.

It is also interesting that through Raymond Shelley imagines the life that Byron might have led immediately following his death, if his activities in Greece had met with more obvious success. Indeed, Raymond is lost, feared dead during an early campaign. He is rescued, 'resurrected' by the softened Perdita's care, and goes on to lead the Greek fighters for independence to victory against the Turks. In this extrapolation of Byron's story, Shelley makes no concession to the futurity of the novel. The Greek revolution of the twenty-first century is identical to that of the early nineteenth century. Though Raymond is not a portrait of Byron in the strictest sense, Shelley was clearly commenting on his character. She describes Raymond in early life:

> His voice, usually gentle, often startled you by a sharp discordant note, which shewed that his usual low tone was rather the work of study than nature. Thus full of contradictions, unbending yet haughty, gentle yet fierce, tender and again neglectful, he by some strange art found easy entrance to the admiration and affection of women; now caressing and now tyrannizing over them according to his mood, but in every change a despot. (p. 33)

Shelley wished her readers to know that her information was based on intimate knowledge. She knew that Byron had wished to return to England as a hero, his sins washed clean. She wished to defend him after his death *and* memorialize and idealize his contribution to liberty. In *Falkner*, similarly, the eponymous Byronic hero partially redresses the wrongs he has committed by risking his life to fight in the Greek War of Independence. It is also clear that Shelley's business acumen told her that a public eager for information about the famous poet would find even a fictional account irresistible.

Nonetheless, Raymond is the first to disrupt the years of happiness at Windsor: "A new Lord Protector of England was to be chosen; and, at Raymond's request, we removed to London" (p. 66). Inevitably, Raymond enters the fray:

> The next step was to induce Raymond to confess his secret wishes for dignity and fame . . .   A few words from us decided him, and hope and joy sparkled in his eyes; the idea of embarking in a career, so congenial to his early habits and cherished wishes, made him as before energetic and bold . . .   Perdita reproached

us bitterly . . . She felt, that, once awakened, Raymond would never return unrepining to Windsor. His habits unhinged; his restless mind roused from its sleep, ambition must now be his companion through life; and if he did not succeed in his present attempt, she foresaw that unhappiness and cureless discontent would follow. (pp. 69–70)

Collectively, the men alone instigate the return to public life and all three come to take part in Raymond's government; this is no mistake. The Duchess of Windsor, the only woman in the novel (excepting the love-struck, martial Evadne) to take action and possess 'man-like' ambition is characterized in explicitly inhuman terms.

Perdita's fears are of course realized. Raymond is elected Lord Protector and she joins him in London. Though Lionel and his family remain at Windsor, their idyll is never restored. Raymond deceives his wife through a secret liaison with Evadne. He resigns the Protectorship and departs for Greece to escape Perdita's anger and inflexibility and his own diminished sense of self.

If the initial disruption of the domestic ideal is the result of personal ambition, it would be inaccurate to say that Shelley condemned such ambition unconditionally. She refused to judge whether Walton's abandonment of the expedition in *Frankenstein* was good or ill-advised, and she refused again to pass a conclusive judgement on the men's desire for public action. Walton's ambition, though necessarily compared to Victor's in the novel, was not necessarily malevolent. He led his expedition in the true spirit of discovery, tempered by modest dreams of his subsequent fame. He also personified the spirit of scientific curiosity and the positive goals of demystification. As we discovered, the alternative to pursuing the voyage and risking the lives of his men, was to return to the barren life shared with his sister. Shelley herself never applauds his decision to abort his mission, nor are we clear that he has necessarily learned from Victor's lesson.

Likewise, as Lord Protector, Raymond does genuine, selfless good, despite the fact that the "selected passion of . . . (his) soul . . . was ambition" (p. 106). His affair with the destitute Evadne is characterized by compassion rather than desire. Shelley does not *blame* Raymond for his ambition; on the contrary, she seems to suggest that such ambition is a prerequisite for any successful activity. Personal ambition *may* lead to honest altruism, though, in the case of the cowardly Ryland, former Lord Protector, it may also succumb to self-preservation.

Yet families and happiness must necessarily be sacrificed for such action. In addition to Perdita's rejection of him, Raymond is personally punished for his negligent compassion towards Evadne. When Lionel discovers her dying on the battlefield, she is like one of the heroines of Byron's verse dramas come to life to turn upon her author. She is not prepared to die sweetly and heroically for love or for his welfare. Evadne curses Raymond's future and prophesies his doom:

> Many living deaths have I borne for thee, O Raymond, and now I expire, thy victim! – By my death I purchase thee – lo! the instruments of war, fire, the plague are my servitors. I dared, I conquered them all, till now! I have sold myself to death, with the sole condition that thou shouldst follow me – Fire, and war, and plague, unite for thy destruction – O my Raymond, there is no safety for thee! (p. 131)

Indeed, not long after Evadne's death, Raymond is killed by the collapsing walls of plague-ridden Constantinople.

But after the death of Perdita and Raymond in Greece and the arrival of the plague in England, the main characters once again create a refuge at Windsor:

> How unwise had the wanderers been, who had deserted its shelter, entangled themselves in the web of society, and entered on what men of the world call "life" . . . Who that knows what "life" is, would pine for this feverish species of existence? I have lived. I have spent days and nights of festivity; I have joined in ambitious hopes, and exulted in victory: now, – shut the door on the world, and build high the wall that is to separate me from the troubled scene enacted within its precincts. Let us live for each other and for happiness; let us seek peace in our dear home . . . Let us leave "life," that we may live. (p. 158)

Yet they do not isolate themselves like the selfish Ryland ("Every man for himself! the devil take the protectorship, say I, if it expose me to danger!" (p. 177)). On the contrary, they are animated by schemes for the local peasantry's good – their extended family after all. Like Euthanasia, they feel responsible for the people who depend on their protection. Shelley is very clear about the nature of such responsibility – "we have our duties, which we must string ourselves to fulfil: the duty of bestowing pleasure where we can, and by force of love, irradiating with rainbow hues the tempest of grief" (p. 311).

Yet Verney is anxious to the point of obsession that his own beloved Idris should not suffer any unhappiness. It is an anxiety that Verney exercises again and again:

> The plague is in London; the air of England is tainted, and her sons and daughters strew the unwholesome earth . . . This feeling of universal misery assumed concentration and shape, when I looked on my wife and children; and the thought of danger to them possessed my whole being with fear. How could I save them? I revolved a thousand and a thousand plans. They should not die – first I would be gathered to nothingness, ere infection should come anear these idols of my soul. I would walk barefoot through the world, to find an uninfected spot; I would build my home on some wave-tossed plank, drifted about on the barren, shoreless ocean. I would betake me with them to some wild beast's den, where a tyger's cubs, which I would slay, had been reared in health . . . no labour too great, no scheme too wild, if it promised life to them. O! ye heart-strings of mine, could ye be torn asunder, and my soul not spend itself in tears of blood for sorrow! (p. 180)

Later he confides, "I had vowed in my own heart never to shadow her countenance even with transient grief" (p. 185), something that PBS could never do for Shelley herself.

The retreat to Windsor, the shoring up of their diminished ranks, proves only a temporary success. The anxieties associated with the plague, and, more importantly, with Adrian's administration of the panic-stricken city and country, make the group aware of their ultimate vulnerability. Verney's family is devastated by the death of his son Alfred. When the Lord Protector decides to move the remnants of the British people to the glaciers of Switzerland in January 2098, and on to the balmy South, Idris dies. The survivors join together to form their own family. Eventually, only Evelyn, Clara, Adrian and Lionel remain in all the world. They adapt to a way of life characterized by constant travel, study and the leisurely enjoyment of luxurious landscape and surroundings. But passing a beautiful summer on Lake Como, they lose another of their tiny family: Evelyn succumbs not to the plague, but to typhus. Shelley's irony is cruel; the delicate boy escapes the pestilence only to fall victim to a banal but thoroughly realistic disease, the same in fact that killed William Shelley in 1819.

Only three remain, but enough potentially to begin to repopulate the earth (at least by Biblical reckoning). But Shelley's relentless annihilation persists. As the three adjust psychologically to form yet another family unit, Clara and Adrian are drowned. Lionel Verney is left the last man on earth. Each time that he enters an empty home or cottage, with a table set for the family meal, or the signs of domestic life arranged before him, he and the reader are reminded of the loss, and of the false security that the comfortable family offers. Each encounter with the intimate remnants of man is torture to the last man. He finds a cottage in the dark, on the road from Ravenna:

> [Its] neat entrance and trim garden reminded me of my own England . . . A kitchen first presented itself . . . Within this was a bed room; the couch was furnished with sheets of snowy whiteness; the wood piled on the hearth, and an array as for a meal, might almost have deceived me into the dear belief that I had here found what I had so long sought . . . I drew a chair to the table, and examined what the viands were of which I was to partake. In truth it was a death feast! The bread was blue and mouldy; the cheese lay a heap of dust. I did not dare examine the other dishes; a troop of ants passed in a double line across the table cloth; every utensil was covered with dust, with cobwebs, and myriads of dead flies . . . Tears rushed into my eyes; surely this was a wanton display of the power of the destroyer . . . Yet why complain more now than ever? This vacant cottage revealed no new sorrow – the world was empty; mankind was dead – I knew it well – why quarrel therefore with an acknowledged and stale truth? Yet . . . every new impression of the hard-cut reality on my soul brought with it a fresh pang . . . (p. 330)

All about him the last man is tormented by the ghost of the family; his own family and the family of man.

Set against Lionel's consistent anxiety for his family and the existence of the close domestic unit is the figure of the astronomer Merrival. Merrival, a friend to the Windsors, is so involved with his cosmological studies, that he is blind to the suffering of his numerous children, to the devotion of his over-worked wife, and finally, to their infection with the plague. Only at their death is his attention seized and his conscience pricked. He is also an embodied flaw in PBS's character; his ability to ignore the needs, both emotional and physical, of his own family. This episode in Merrival's life may also allude to the death of Clara Shelley in September 1818, a tragedy that Shelley may have blamed at least partially on her husband. The narrator observes:

> This old man . . . this visionary who had not seen starvation in the wasted forms of his wife and children, or plague in the horrible sights and sounds that surrounded him – this astronomer, apparently dead on earth, and living only in the motion of the spheres – loved his family with unapparent but intense affection. Through long habit they had become a part of himself . . . It was not till one of them died that he perceived their danger; one by one they were carried off by the pestilence; and his wife, his helpmate and supporter, more necessary to him than his own limbs and frame . . . closed her eyes in death. The old man felt the system of universal nature which he had so long studied and adored, slide from under him, and he stood among the dead, and lifted his voice in curses. (pp. 220–21)

Merrival dies in an agony of grief and madness, howling over the graves of his wife and children. Though perhaps responsible for some of his family's unhappiness – Clara's death, not to mention Shelley's pain at her husband's relationships with other women – PBS did not live to experience an agonizing grief. Shelley herself may have resented not just her husband's irresponsibility during his life, but her own permanent grief and her role as relict. She may have envied her husband's detachment in life and escape in death. Her devotion to and dependence on family and loved ones was a psychological burden, often at odds with her role as a professional author, that the poet was able to ignore and avoid.

Of all her novels, *The Last Man* is perhaps Shelley's most political; it considers the state of England, as well as the politics of her husband and father. It attempts to realize and debunk the variety of Utopian ideas imagined by her circle exemplified first in *Queen Mab* and later modified and developed in *Prometheus Unbound*. If Shelley is unfair in her attack – what political system *could* withstand the calamity of global scale that she portrays? – it is to show how her dark philosophy goes beyond politics for its answers. Initially however, Shelley's specific critique of England is aligned with PBS.

In the novel's first paragraph, a description of England, we are immediately informed of Shelley's theme; the power of fate and the helplessness of the individual. Mighty England, which held sway over the world at the beginning of the narrator's story, is reduced to an inconsequential speck:

> I am the native of a sea-surrounded nook, a cloud-enshadowed land, which, when the surface of the globe, with its shore-less ocean and trackless continents, presents itself to my mind, appears only as an inconsiderable speck in the immense whole; and yet, when balanced in the scale of mental power, far out-weighed countries of larger extent and more numerous popula-tion. So true it is, that man's mind alone was the creator of all that was good or great to man, and that Nature herself was only his first minister. England, seated far north in the turbid sea, now visits my dreams in the semblance of a vast and well-manned ship, which mastered the winds and rode proudly over the waves. In my boyish days she was the universe to me. When I stood on my native hills, and saw plain and mountain stretch out to the utmost limits of my vision, speckled by the dwellings of my countrymen, and subdued to fertility by their labours, the earth's very centre was fixed for me in that spot, and the rest of her orb was as a fable, to have forgotten which would have cost neither my imagination nor understanding an effort.
>
> My fortunes have been, from the beginning, an exemplification of the power that mutability may possess over the varied tenor of man's life. (p. 5)

Lionel Verney, the Last Man, begins his narration as if looking through the wrong end of a telescope. With the experience of global annihilation he looks back at what was once thought to be all-encompassing and commanding, now infinitely tiny and far away.

The narrator's later observations on England become increas-ingly dark, elegiac and, indeed, to Shelley's politically conservative contemporaries, strikingly subversive and unpatriotic. London is reduced to only one thousand inhabitants and as the diminished population prepare to leave for the continent, Verney and his family bid farewell to their home:

England, late birth-place of excellence and school of the wise,
thy children are gone, thy glory faded! Thou, England, wert the
triumph of man! Small favour was shewn thee by thy Creator,
thou Isle of the North . . .   So we must leave thee, thou marvel
of the world; we must bid farewell to thy clouds, and cold, and
scarcity for ever! Thy many hearts are still; thy tale of power and
liberty at its close! Bereft of man, O little isle! the ocean waves will
buffet thee, and the raven flap his wings over thee; thy soil will
be birth-place of weeds, thy sky will canopy barrenness . . . thy
children . . . are gone, and thou goest with them the oft trodden
path that leads to oblivion, –

> Farewell, sad Isle, farewell, thy fatal glory
> Is summed, cast up, and cancelled in this story.[12]
> (pp. 235–36)

Some pages later, the narrator urges himself on towards departure
with the invocation, "Yet let us go! England is in her shroud, – we
may not enchain ourselves to a corpse" (p. 237). Shelley's provocative, premature elegy for England becomes even more chilling –
"England remained, though England was dead – it was the ghost
of merry England that I beheld . . . " (p. 264).

Shelley's dramatic descriptions of the depopulated country of
course serve to heighten the atmosphere of darkness and foreboding
in the novel, but they also call attention to the England of her
own present, particularly in the light of the contemporaneity of
other references in the novel. The "death of England" surely also
suggests its conquest by an outside power. In Shelley's youth,
invasion by the French often seemed imminent and fear of the
mob, after the excesses of the Revolution, ran high. In the novel,
criminals and rabble-rousers from America and Ireland invade the
north of the country and Adrian must quell the panic that ensues.
The suggestion at such a sensitive time that England might suffer
a military invasion and defeat was a subversive notion.

The association with the French Revolution in the novel is further
suggested by Britain's isolation from the Continent. When the first
party of survivors leaves England for Paris, communication is
impossible. Information is limited to a vague sense of turmoil and
lawlessness. During the Terror and the wars that followed English
friends and relatives and refugee Frenchmen sought for information
about their loved ones across the Channel. In the novel

No vessel stemmed the flood that divided Calais from Dover; or if some melancholy voyager, wishing to assure himself of the life or death of his relatives, put from the French shore to return among us, often the greedy ocean swallowed his little craft . . . We were therefore to a great degree ignorant of the state of things on the continent . . . (p. 272)

Of course Shelley also points up England's isolation from the events in Europe which had suggested to her, and to PBS in particular, that reform and liberalization were imminent. England she implies, remains aloof and unimpressed.

Shelley alludes to the political situation of the Italy of her day, incorporating her circle's revolutionary dreams for the country. She echoes those political sentiments which, as discussed above, formed a theme in *Valperga*. Passing the Italian coast while returning from the ill-fated journey to Greece to find Raymond, Lionel contemplates the countryside where "fertility reposes" and the "free and happy peasant, unshackled by the Austrian, bears the double harvest to the garner; and the refined citizens rear without dread the long blighted tree of knowledge in this garden of the world" (p. 157). Later, describing the prevailing influence of good at work in the world before the advent of the plague, Adrian talks of Italy: the "favoured countries of the south will throw off the iron yoke of servitude" (p. 159). The Greek revolution that Raymond helps to lead in the twenty-first century, an idealized imitation of Byron's contribution to the Greek cause of his day, is itself an imitation of the same situation in the 1820s. Lee Sterrenburg has pointed out, that *The Last Man* "surveys intellectual expressions from the French Revolution of 1789 to Napoleon and the Greek Revolution of the 1820s, which was still in progress when she wrote her novel."[13] The slow destruction of England also suggests her mistreatment by a corrupt or incompetent government. Shelley was miserable in England while writing the novel and longed to return to Italy where she felt more closely connected to the countryside and its memories. England, especially its grim weather, was deeply disappointing to her and her fictional annihilation of it was no doubt gratifying.

Despite the contemporary political references in the novel, Shelley makes a point of playing with historical perspective, as we have seen from the novel's opening paragraph. In the introduction to *The Last Man* she explores the caves of the Cumean Sibyl, claiming to find Verney's record on the leaves scattered about the floor. Her task, in the present, is to preserve, arrange, and edit the leaves in order to give her readers a narrative of the future. Though her device is confusing – we must understand that though Verney's story is a record of his own past, it is overall the sibyl's prophecy for the twenty-first century – Shelley wishes us to reverse the Last Man's perspective and look into the distant future from the perspective of the past.

In fact, above and beyond party politics, Shelley was deeply interested in the random nature of fate and the fickleness of destiny. This is most pronounced in her fascination with the Italian city states of the middle ages and Renaissance which began with her research for *Valperga*. She became something of an expert on that period of Italian history and her extensive Italian biographies for *Lardner's Cabinet Cyclopaedia* between 1835 and 1839 are characterized by confidence and authority. The same fascination with mutability remains in her delineations of the baroque political machinations of the city states and the individuals caught up in them. It is interesting that one of the themes that dominates her fiction: precarious exist-ence, elusiveness, unfortunate change, also plays a role in Shelley's scholarly and journalistic work. Superimposed upon this relentless change and inconsistency is the pathetic activity of man, nowhere more apparent than in the political world.

Inevitably, Shelley's political discussions turn to a more personal critique of her husband's ideology. Many critics of *The Last Man* have proposed that Shelley's goals were simply biographical, that she wished to present the long-planned-for official biography of her husband that Sir Timothy had forbidden when he suppressed the *Posthumous Poems* in 1824. Hugh Luke, in his introduction to his 1965 edition of the novel writes: " . . . it is clear that Mary conceived *The Last Man* as a monument to the life and ideas of her husband".[14] Indeed, the figure of Adrian is a partial portrait of the poet. Shelley herself wrote to her friend John Bowring, editor of the *Westminster Review* and Honorary Secretary to the Greek Committee, on Febru-ary 25, 1826: " . . . I have endeavoured, but how inadequately to give some idea of him in my last published book – the sketch has pleased some of those who best loved him." Hogg was delighted with the character of Adrian as an accurate picture of PBS and Sir Timothy recognized his son in the anonymously published novel sufficient to temporarily cut his allowance to his daughter-in-law. Biography however was only an element of Shelley's project.

The Last Man may be a monument to PBS's life and ideas, but it is a critical one. Shelley's dynamic debate with the ideals of both her husband and father culminates in the novel, as does her own fight for intellectual independence. Politics and political figures, particularly in the first two volumes, are brought to the fore and Shelley uses the novel as a platform for arguing against some of the ideals of her husband, and against revolution and political idealism in particular. Sterrenburg has pointed out, for "Mary, all revolutionary experiments breed monsters. The monsterlike holocaust that descends upon the Greek revolution in *The Last Man* is a graphic fictional rebuttal of Percy's political views".[15] However, the 'portraits' of PBS which appear in the novel, primarily that of Adrian, almost unconditionally celebrate the *man*. Shelley's lover is much idealized, but through Adrian and Lionel she also celebrates the relationship that she and the poet shared. With Adrian's death the Last Man describes what their life-long friendship has meant:

> The best years of my life had been passed with him. All I had possessed of this world's goods, of happiness, knowledge, or virtue – I owed to him. He had, in his person, his intellect, and rare qualities, given a glory to my life, which without him it had never known. Beyond all other beings he had taught me, that goodness, pure and single, can be an attribute of man. (p. 328)

Shelley was grateful for their mutual intellectual dependency and, though she often felt remorse at her apparent coldness just prior to his death, and agreed privately with PBS's friends – her critics – that she disappointed the poet and provoked his emotional withdrawal from her, she was confident that they had remained kindred spirits, despite the independence of her ideas and their disagreement. She expressed this in a poem of 1832, printed in *The Keepsake for MDCCCXXXIII* and reprinted recently by Emily Sunstein in her biography. In "Stanzas" Shelley echoes the sentiments of the last man for his dead friend:

> I must forget thy dark eyes' love-fraught gaze,
>   Thy voice, that fill'd me with emotion bland,
> Thy vows, which lost me in this 'wild'ring maze,
>   The thrilling pressure of thy gentle hand;
> And, dearer yet, that interchange of thought,
>   That drew us nearer still to one another,

Till in two hearts one sole idea wrought,
And neither hoped nor fear'd but for the other.[16]

This sense of bitter-sweet regret regarding PBS persists in
Shelley's work, even beyond the fiction. In her biography of Mme.
de Sévigné for *Lardner's*, Shelley describes her subject's sorrow at
the death of her unfaithful but beloved husband:

The inconstancy of her husband did not diminish the widow's
grief: she had lived six happy years of a brilliant youth with
him . . . and, when he was lost to her for ever, she probably
looked on her jealousy in another light, and felt how trivial such
is when compared with the irreparable stroke of death.[17]

Yet Shelley's praise of PBS the man is not to be confused with
praise for his political and philosophical ideals. Even her apparent
approbation of the idea of perfectibility as she understood it, "that
goodness pure and single, can be an attribute of man", though it is
one of her most optimistic statements, does not acknowledge that
such goodness is *necessarily* present. In fact, her position suggests
that Adrian/PBS, as a kind of redeemer, is a unique and purely
fictional phenomenon, one not viable in reality. Shelley may have
had an erroneous understanding of perfectibility, but her negative
view of what she believed it to be implies disagreement nonetheless.
If PBS grew more sceptical about perfectibility as the years passed,
it is difficult to imagine that his generally optimistic belief in human
potential could ever have matched Shelley's certainty of humanity's
inevitable failure to achieve happiness or live up to an ideal. Having
stated her loyalty to PBS the man, she is free to criticize him (and
Godwin) politically throughout the novel.

Shelley establishes England at the beginning of the novel as a
republic with the Commons and House of Lords amalgamated.
She then exposes its considerable deficiencies, suggesting to both
Sterrenburg and Walling some inspiration from Burke's *Reflections*,
which indeed she quotes throughout the novel. The character of
Ryland, who rivals Lord Raymond for the Lord Protectorship is,
Walling believes

an adversary who clearly represents, in his over-all presentation,
both the virtues and limitations of the kind of mind . . . which

Mary thought likely to come into prominence in a republic. For
Ryland, although he is sincere in his championing of individual
liberty and the continuance of the republic, is himself a medio-
cre man, severely handicapped by his moral and philosophical
ignorance.[18]

Ryland panics when the plague reaches London, resigning his post
hurriedly to Adrian and fleeing to his country retreat in an attempt
to avoid contamination.

Shelley's narrator is clearly not ideologically opposed to the Burke
of the *Reflections*. In fact, he believes in the moral and even physical
superiority of aristocracy and royalty. When Adrian takes on the
Protectorship, he shows that the blood royal still courses through
his veins. His natural nobility in an automatic dedication to the
job is expressed as *noblesse oblige*: "To England and to Englishmen
I dedicate myself. If I can save one of her mighty spirits from the
deadly shaft; if I can ward disease from one of her smiling cottages,
I shall not have lived in vain" (p. 179). Shelley as narrator warms to
her theme. Following her paean to Eton as the training ground for
great men (no doubt prompted in part by PBS's education there) she
praises Adrian's innate skill to rule:

> Here was a youth, royally sprung, bred in luxury, by nature
> averse to the usual struggles of a public life, and now, in time
> of danger, at a period when to live was the utmost scope of the
> ambitious, he, the beloved and heroic Adrian, made, in sweet
> simplicity, an offer to sacrifice himself for the public good. The
> very idea was generous and noble . . . (p. 182)

Later, as Adrian, formerly introspective and frail, grows in vitality
and purpose he enthuses:

> This is my post: I was born for this – to rule England in anarchy,
> to save her in danger – to devote myself to her. The blood of my
> forefathers cries aloud in my veins, and bids me be first among
> my countrymen . . . my mother, the proud queen, instilled early
> into me a love of distinction, and all that, if the weakness of my
> physical nature and my peculiar opinions had not prevented such
> a design, might have made me long since struggle for the lost
> inheritance of my race. (p. 185)

Despite his republican ideals, Adrian's true and glorious nature is fundamentally influenced by his royal lineage. In some sense, Shelley is claiming back for her husband – unauthorized – the aristocratic background that his choice of political alignment rejected. It is also an opportunity for her to impose *her* intellectual ideals upon *him*.

In the debate leading up to the elections for the new Lord Protector, Ryland proposes a law to abolish "hereditary rank, and other feudal relics" (p. 160), a proposal which Lionel and his friends, former opponents in Raymond's time – and the nobility after all – do not support. In *Political Justice* Godwin addressed the question of "hereditary distinction" and made his views clear – "A principle deeply interwoven with both monarchy and aristocracy in their most flourishing state, but most deeply with the latter, is that of hereditary pre-eminence. No principle can present a deeper insult upon reason and justice" (*PJ*, Vol. II, p. 86). Though Shelley's narrator does not reject the idea outright, it is clear that abolition is not favoured. In fact, the narrator attacks the advocates of the scheme:

Yet could England indeed doff her lordly trappings, and be content with the democratic style of America? Were the pride of ancestry, the patrician spirit, the gentle courtesies and refined pursuits, splendid attributes of rank, to be erased among us? We were told that this would not be the case; that we were by nature a poetical people, a nation easily duped by words, ready to array clouds in splendour, and bestow honour on dust. This spirit we could never lose; and it was to diffuse this concentrated spirit of birth, that the new law was to be brought forward. We were assured that, when the name and title of Englishman was the sole patent of nobility, we should all be noble; that when no man born under English sway, felt another his superior in rank, courtesy and refinement would become the birth-right of all our countrymen. Let not England be so far disgraced, as to have it imagined that it can be without nobles, nature's true nobility, who bear their patent in their mien, who are from their cradle elevated above the rest of their species, because they are better than the rest. Among a race of independent, and generous, and well educated men, in a country where the imagination is empress of men's minds, there needs be no fear that we should want a perpetual succession of the high-born and lordly. That

party, however, could hardly yet be considered a minority in
the kingdom, who extolled the ornament of the column, "the
Corinthian capital of polished society;" they appealed to preju-
dices without number, to old attachments and young hopes; to
the expectation of thousands who might one day become peers;
they set up as a scarecrow, the spectre of all that was sordid,
mechanic and base in the commercial republics. (p. 161)

The narrator, with almost Burkean disgust, dismisses the tactics
of the campaigners for democracy as ignoble, distinctly without the
breeding that they erroneously claim is common to the national
character. In any case, Ryland is forced to give up the "dear
object of his ambition" (p. 170) when faced with the urgent need
to raise taxes from the landed aristocracy. With the relinquishing
of his plans, calm "was now restored to the metropolis, and to the
populous cities, before driven to desperation" (p. 170).

In addition to an obvious advocacy of *noblesse oblige* on the part
of the narrator and Adrian, the correspondingly natural loyalty of
the servant class is illustrated. Even after the plague has freed riches
and food stores sufficient so that no one need work for a living, the
royal family still manages to retain and indeed depend on servants.
Preparing to leave Windsor with the emigrating survivors Lionel
narrates: "Our escort had been directed to prepare our abode for the
night at the inn, opposite the ascent to the Castle" (p. 263) and the
same escort, with the attendants of the Countess of Windsor, proceed ahead of the family "to provide horses; finding them either in
the warm stables they instinctively sought . . . or standing shivering
in the bleak fields" (p. 266). Perhaps the most striking example of
such natural inclination to class submission occurs when the plague
reappears to wreak havoc among the few survivors making their
way across the Alps. Lionel describes various vignettes of death
about him, highlighting one for its particular poignancy in a style
reminiscent of Burke: "Here a servant, faithful to the last, though
dying, waited on one, who, though still erect with health, gazed
with gasping fear on the variety of woe around" (pp. 303–304).

The longed-for republic championed by PBS is not only inadequate, but a complete delusion. Shelley does not shrink from
very pointed criticism of PBS. Adrian, speaking like the poet of
Prometheus Unbound and the Godwin of *Political Justice*, remarks on
the coming of Spring and news of a universal cessation of military
conflict in the beginning of Volume II:

Let this [peace] last but twelve months . . . and earth will become
a Paradise. The energies of man were before directed to the
destruction of the species: they now aim at its liberation and
preservation. Man cannot repose, and his restless aspirations will
now bring forth good instead of evil. The favoured countries of
the south will throw off the iron yoke of servitude; poverty will
quit us, and with that, sickness. What may not the forces, never
before united, of liberty and peace achieve in this dwelling of
man? (p. 159)

But Adrian's rapturous idealism is first challenged by Ryland, and
then by news of the plague:

"Dreaming, forever dreaming Windsor!" said Ryland, the old
adversary of Raymond, and candidate for the Protectorship at
the ensuing election. "Be assured that the earth is not, nor ever
can be heaven, while the seeds of hell are natives of her soil. When
the seasons have become equal, when the air breeds no disorders,
when its surface is no longer liable to blights and droughts, then
sickness will cease; when men's passions are dead, poverty will
depart. When love is no longer akin to hate, then brotherhood
will exist: we are very far from that state at present." (p. 159)

Shelley herself speaks through Ryland's pessimism in a mordant
parody of *Political Justice* and of *Prometheus Unbound*. Shelley's
answer to the debate is offered by Lionel who follows the two
opposing views by informing those present that the "curse of God"
has fallen upon the conquered city of Constantinople, the winter has
not killed off the disease, and "every one who has ventured within
the walls has been tainted by the plague" (p. 159), and that the
pestilence is widening its grasp. The earthly heaven of Adrian's
rhapsody is replaced and mocked by an earthly hell. The "curse
of God" echoes the ravings of the fallen prophetess of *Valperga* and
her prophecy of the Ascendency of Evil is about to be born out in
The Last Man.

However, Lionel is not yet aware of the ultimate outcome, and can
still quote Burke when reflecting on the young hopefuls of nearby
Eton and the important role that his own son might someday fill:

It was not long since I was like one of those beardless aspirants;
when my boy shall have obtained the place I now hold, I shall

have tottered into a grey-headed, wrinkled old man. Strange system! riddle of the Sphynx, most awe-striking! that thus man remains, while we the individuals pass away. Such is, to borrow the words of an eloquent and philosophic writer, "the mode of existence decreed to a permanent body composed of transitory parts; wherein, by the disposition of a stupendous wisdom, moulding together the great mysterious incorporation of the human race, the whole, at one time, is never old, or middle-aged, or young, but, in a condition of unchangeable constancy, moves on through the varied tenour of perpetual decay, fall, renovation, and progression."

Willingly do I give place to thee, dear Alfred! advance, off-spring of tender love, child of our hopes; advance a soldier on the road to which I have been a pioneer! I will make way for thee. (p. 165)

Lionel, the sometime alter ego of Shelley herself, is still confident enough in the immortality of humanity to imagine a distant future. Of course, as the story progresses and Lionel loses not just Alfred but his youngest son Evelyn, Idris, and ultimately the rest of mankind, we see how hollow ring the words of both Burke and Adrian; criticism of the radical PBS did not necessarily mean the consequent celebration of conservative values on Shelley's part. They will have little to do with the reality of the novel once the plague takes hold in England and "Nature, our mother, and our friend, had turned on us a brow of menace" (p. 168).

Yet in the novel's greatest irony, the plague becomes not only the agent of annihilation but that of universal equality as well. Plague becomes the great leveller. As it takes hold in England there

was but one good and one evil in the world – life and death. The pomp of rank, the assumption of power, the possessions of wealth vanished like the morning mist. One living beggar had become of more worth than a national peerage of dead lords – alas the day! than of dead heroes, patriots, or men of genius . . . (p. 212)

The rate of death increases and Adrian's beleaguered government is hard-pressed to maintain old laws. The levelling of the classes continues:

As the rules of order and pressure of laws were lost, some began with hesitation and wonder to transgress the accustomed uses of society. Palaces were deserted, and the poor man dared at length, unreproved, intrude into the splendid apartments, whose very furniture and decorations were an unknown world to him. It was found, that, though at first the stop put to all circulation of property, had reduced those before supported by the factitious wants of society to sudden and hideous poverty, yet when the boundaries of private possession were thrown down, the products of human labour at present existing were more, far more, than the thinned generation could possibly consume. To some among the poor this was matter of exultation. We were all equal now; magnificent dwellings, luxurious carpets, and beds of down, were afforded to all. Carriages and horses, gardens, pictures, statues, and princely libraries, there were enough of these even to superfluity; and there was nothing to prevent each from assuming possession of his share. We were all equal now; but near at hand was an equality still more levelling, a state where beauty and strength, and wisdom, would be as vain as riches and birth. The grave yawned beneath us all, and its prospect prevented any of us from enjoying the ease and plenty which in so awful a manner was presented to us. (pp. 230–31)

Shelley outlines a grim and inevitable equality that seems to mock the lofty Godwinian view, as expressed in *Political Justice*, that equality would result as a natural by-product after the universal philosophical adoption of Reason. In Shelley's novel, Reason's role is taken by the Plague. As if to pour salt on the wounds, the people of England, despite the calamity that they face, do not alter their banal priorities: " . . . while the decree of population was abrogated, property remained sacred. It was a melancholy reflection; and in spite of the diminution of evil produced, it struck on the heart as a wretched mockery" (p. 220).

What is more, Shelley defies the censure of superstition central to the victory of Reason. Halted at the gates of the abandoned Constantinople Raymond's troops fear to enter the plague-ridden city – a "universal shudder and fearful whispering passed through the lines . . . " (p. 139). When Lionel relates the strange events to Perdita she exclaims, "How beyond the imagination of man . . . are the decrees of heaven, wondrous and inexplicable" (p. 140). Raymond replies angrily:

Foolish girl . . . are you like my valiant soldiers, panic-struck? What is there inexplicable, pray, tell me, in so very natural an occurrence? Does not the plague rage each year in Stamboul? What wonder, that this year, when as we are told, its virulence is unexampled in Asia, that it should have occasioned double havoc in that city? (p. 140)

If superstition is associated with the feminine, then Shelley is pointing out the exclusively masculine nature of Reason and its opposition to the intuitive, emotional female. Though Shelley championed the Enlightenment mission to abolish ignorance she nonetheless questioned the validity of monolithic male Reason and its necessary insistence on obliterating all other systems. She saw the radicals, despite their liberalities, as hostile to the feminine in this respect.

Of course, Perdita's superstitious fears are once again realized. Raymond defies – and mocks – a power stronger than that of rationality. The soldiers' superstitions are founded in a sensitivity to nature, to reality, that the supposedly enlightened Raymond does not share. His bravado, that of the (macho) Romantic over-reacher,[19] calls down the curse of the plague upon the world. Raymond is doomed and Romantic idealism is doomed for their rejection of alternative possibilities.

THE SELF-OBSCURING CAVE

Seeking always to separate herself from her appearance in public as an author, and from public criticism of members of her family, Shelley employed a device in *The Last Man* which enabled her, once again, to reject responsibility for the novel as a creation exclusively of her own imagination. The legacy of Beatrice is blasphemous in the extreme, but Shelley was careful to distance herself from it. She placed herself, decorously and with great cleverness, above reproach.

In her Author's Introduction to *The Last Man* Shelley describes a day's excursion from Naples on December 8, 1818. She and her "companion", whom we *and* her contemporary readers must take to be PBS, crossed the Bay of Naples to Baiae, site of the sunken, ruined Roman villas featured in "Ode to the West Wind". Their trip also included a visit to the Elysian Fields and

Avernus. These events are corroborated in actuality by her journal note for the same day: "Go to the sea with S. – Visit Cape Micaene – The Elysian fields – Avernus Solfatara – The Bay of Baiae is beautiful but we are disappointed by the various places we visit".

Shelley obviously referred back to her real experience to give her introduction authority as well as a clear distinction from the fantasy of the story which follows it. However, her investigation of the cave, reputed to be that of the Cumaean Sibyl, does not appear in the journal. At this point, despite the sustained tone of dispassionate relation of fact, we recognize the beginning of the fiction. Shelley's technique is to construct a fiction which bears the glint of reality. Just as the reader is drawn into Victor's story by his explainable acquisition of scientific knowledge, the reader of *The Last Man* is guided by the true facts of the Introduction. We must take the author at her word. The story that she is about to relate existed before her arrival on the scene. She and her companion find the cave floor scattered with leaves:

> On examination, we found that all the leaves, bark, and other substances, were traced with written characters. What appeared to us more astonishing, was that these writings were expressed in various languages: some unknown to my companion, ancient Chaldee, and Egyptian hieroglyphics, old as the Pyramids. Stranger still, some were in modern dialects, English and Italian. We could make out little by the dim light, but they seemed to contain prophecies, detailed relations of events but lately passed; names, now well known, but of modern date; and often exclamations of exultation or woe, of victory or defeat, were traced on their thin scant pages. This was certainly the Sibyl's Cave; not indeed exactly as Virgil describes it; but the whole of this land had been so convulsed by earthquake and volcano, that the change was not wonderful, though the traces of ruin were effaced by time; and we probably owed the preservation of these leaves, to the accident which had closed the mouth of the cavern, and the swift-growing vegetation which had rendered its sole opening impervious to the storm. We made a hasty selection of such of the leaves, whose writing one at least of us could understand . . . (p. 3)

Shelley's reference to geography, geology and climate again underline her factual objective. The leaves are collected on successive visits and the author arranges them into the story that follows.

Shelley maintains the factual fiction, as she does in her 1831 preface to *Frankenstein*, that the novel which follows her disclaimer was simply given to her, as a vision or as raw literary material, for her to impose order and shape a story. In 1826, she deployed another smokescreen, allowing the image of her private self to recede from the public view, obscured by her own device.

The cave of the Cumaean Sibyl also echoes Euthanasia's cave of the human mind, outlined in the previous chapter. Shelley's allegory is remarkably Freudian, anticipating the idea of the division of the mind into the three separate, sovereign but struggling regions of Ego, Superego and Id. The power of Conscience is limited in Shelley's scheme to the first part, or the vestibule of the cave. It holds no sway over the inner cavern where, among other things, "Poetry" and "Imagination" dwell. In the same chamber of the cave is "the habitation of the madman, when all the powers desert the vestibule, and he, finding no light, makes darkling, fantastic combinations, and lives among them. From thence there is a short path to hell . . . " (Vol. III, pp. 101–102). Beatrice confirms Euthanasia's fears about the perilous proximity of creativity to insanity and torment when she remarks, "No content of mind exists for me, no beauty of thought, or poetry; and, if imagination live, it is as a tyrant, armed with fire, and venomed darts, to drive me to despair" (Vol. III, p. 102).

Beatrice's dangerous, uncontrollable imagination, as we have already learned, contributed to her downfall and destruction. When Shelley, as herself, enters the cave of the Sybil to retrieve the materials for her novel, she is ransacking her own mind for its creative faculty, but at the same time, as if heeding her own advice (as delivered by Euthanasia), she is wary of the incursion into the dangerous part of the cave, the proximity of creative genius and madness. The familiar Romantic conceit, as exemplified by Coleridge's *Kubla Khan*, becomes a personal and very real concern. Shelley's dramatization of the artistic process schematized by Euthanasia's Cave of the Mind then enacted at the beginning of *The Last Man* in the cave of the Sibyl suggests a desire on her part to separate herself from her art and from her life as author. We are reminded of the author's vulnerability and of her desire to avoid the necessary publicity of authorship. It might also be suggested that Shelley actually believed that her grasp on "Content of Mind," or sanity, was tenuous – she was very much aware of her own moodiness, of what might be considered depression today

– and that engaging her imagination was courting psychological disaster. The reader need only consider the mad Beatrice's fear of the imagination and her belief that it is God's cruel joke. It is perhaps not coincidental that the last productive years of Shelley's life were also her most contented. From 1835–1839 she was engaged in strictly non-fictional work, preparing nearly seventy biographies of literary and scientific men for *Lardner's*. The biographies are amongst her finest work and several critics who find her fiction without merit, believe her reputation redeemed in the journalistic and historical work of her later career.

The constant grief that the characters of *The Last Man* suffer and their repeated exposure to calamity, culminating in the realization that the world's population will be completely wiped out, is the legacy of Beatrice in the novel. The evil and destruction that she prophesies in *Valperga* actually comes to pass. Her words of conviction in her speech to Euthanasia are echoed in the words of despair uttered by the characters who are her inheritors. However, as the last man assumes his solitary state and gives way to grief, he does not despair. His views on the God who destroyed the human race but selected him for life are inconclusive and, most interestingly, without bitterness. Lionel, who has at least as much reason as Beatrice to hate the author of his misery, looks for an explanation for that misery and, like the existential writers that followed Shelley more than a century later, discovers a reason for choosing life.

Beatrice's image of God is a simple inversion of her earliest beliefs. Where once He was benevolent, her brutal experiences and misguided training have taught her that He is purely malevolent:

> Look around. Is there not war, violation of treaties, and hard-hearted cruelty? Look at the societies of men; are not our fellow creatures tormented one by the other in an endless circle of pain? Some shut up in iron cages, starved and destroyed; cities float in blood, and the hopes of the husbandman are manured by his own mangled limbs . . . think of jealousy, midnight murders, envy, want of faith, calumny, ingratitude, cruelty, and all which man in his daily sport inflicts upon man. Think upon disease, plague, famine, leprosy, fever, and all the aching pains our limbs suffer withal. (Vol. III, pp. 44–45)

Beatrice's words are echoed in *The Last Man*, by Adrian's reminder of the reality of war and by Raymond's angry response to frustrated victory: "Am I for ever . . . to be the sport of fortune! Must man, the heaven-climber, be for ever the victim of the crawling reptiles of his species!" (p. 141). During the early ravages of the plague in England the true precarious position of the whole of the human race strikes Lionel for the first time. Again, as a victim subject to the whim of a greater power, he echoes Beatrice:

> What are we, the inhabitants of this globe, least among the many that people infinite space? Our minds embrace infinity; the visible mechanism of our being is subject to merest accident. Day by day we are forced to believe this. He whom a scratch has disorganized, he who disappears from apparent life under the influence of the hostile agency at work around us, had the same powers as I – I also am subject to the same laws. In the face of all this we call ourselves lords of the creation, wielders of the elements, masters of life and death, and we allege in excuse of this arrogance, that though the individual is destroyed, man continues for ever.
>
> Thus, losing our identity, that of which we are chiefly conscious, we glory in the continuity of our species, and learn to regard death without terror. But when any whole nation becomes the victim of the destructive powers of exterior agents, then indeed man shrinks into insignificance, he feels his tenure of life insecure, his inheritance on earth cut off. (p. 167)

Lionel repeats the sentiment later when he hears of the resurgence of the plague and the disappointment of their false hopes:

> A sense of degradation came over me. Did God create man, merely in the end to become dead earth in the midst of healthful vegetating nature? Was he of no more account to his Maker, than a field of corn blighted in the ear? Were our proud dreams thus to fade? Our name was written "a little lower than the angels;" and, behold, we were no better than ephemera. We had called ourselves the "paragon of animals," and, lo! we were a "quint-essence of dust." We repined that the pyramids had outlasted the embalmed body of their builder. Alas! the mere shepherd's hut of straw we passed on the road, contained in its structure the principle of greater longevity than the whole race of man. How reconcile this sad change to our past aspirations, to our apparent powers! (p. 290)

Yet despite the notion of a cruel or incomprehensible God that certain characters of *Valperga* and *The Last Man* share, Shelley's ideas had developed and matured with the later novel. The conclusion of *The Last Man* is indeed dark, but it does not hold out the complete and utter pessimism, indeed the annihilation, that we find in *Valperga*. Verney is the first of Shelley's principal characters to learn something from his experience. His thoughts on the nature of the supreme power do not drive him mad as they did Beatrice – he is an altogether more modern character. Likewise, he is more flexible and more responsive to change than Euthanasia, who snaps in the heavy wind of adversity. He comes to a conclusion regarding his fate and the workings of God, which, curiously, includes some ideas familiar to PBS. Anxious about new evidence of the resurgence of the plague Lionel again contemplates annihilation:

> Mother of the world! Servant of the Omnipotent! eternal, changeless Necessity! who with busy fingers sittest ever weaving the indissoluble chain of events! – I will not murmur at thy acts. If my human mind cannot acknowledge that all that is, is right; yet since what is, must be, I will sit amidst the ruins and smile. (pp. 290–91)

Alone on earth, without "love, without sympathy, without communion with any" (p. 337), Lionel addresses the question of suicide. He asks: "Why did I continue to live – why not throw off the weary weight of time, and with my own hand, let out the fluttering prisoner from my agonized breast?" (p. 337). Faced even with his horrifying experience, and the knowledge that, being the only individual to have contracted the plague and survived it, he is somehow immune to disease, Lionel chooses life emphatically. His experience, though similar in its suffering to Beatrice's, provokes a diametrically opposed reaction. Where she saw malevolence in God, Lionel perceives a reason, not for the destruction of humanity, but for his own exclusive survival:

> . . . death had a soothing sound accompanying it, that would easily entice me to enter its demesne. But this I would not do. I had, from the moment I had reasoned on the subject, instituted myself the subject to fate, and the servant of necessity, the visible laws of the invisible God – I believed that my obedience was the

result of sound reasoning, pure feeling, and an exalted sense of the true excellence and nobility of my nature. Could I have seen in this empty earth, in the seasons and their change, the hand of a blind power only, most willingly would I have placed my head on the sod, and closed my eyes on its loveliness for ever. But fate had administered life to me, when the plague had already seized on its prey . . .   By such miracles she had bought me for her own; I admitted her authority, and bowed to her decrees. If, after mature consideration, such was my resolve, it was doubly necessary that I should not lose the end of life, the improvement of my faculties, and poison its flow by repinings without end. (pp. 337–38)

Verney's resolve precludes suicide but it is not a consolation. It is simply a reason for going on with life and if we take into account Shelley's journal entry for October 1824 – "I never, in all my woes, understood the feelings that led to suicide till now", we understand that Verney's decision is in part a result of a very personal struggle on his author's part. His loneliness is profound, as Mary Shelley's must have been after the deaths of so many loved ones (including the suicides of Fanny Imlay and Harriet Shelley in 1816). Verney's loneliness increases as he discovers, after a year, that his faint hope of finding another living human being is a delusion. He decides to leave Rome and like the Wandering Jew, to travel around the world, finding purpose in activity; reading, exploring, facing danger and fear. He forms "no expectation of alteration for the better; but the monotonous present is intolerable" (p. 342).

Despite her preoccupation with the political throughout the novel, *The Last Man* remains a fundamentally *anti*-political book. Shelley systematically samples and rejects both conservative and radical political ideals. Again, as Sterrenburg observes, despite the obvious influences of Burke upon the novel, Shelley negates his theory as well. The great entity of society, that lives on despite individual death, is wiped out by the plague. And we have seen Shelley's relentless satire of the ideology of her family: "the plague . . . cancels out the Utopian rationality of Godwin as surely as it cancels out the conservative organicism of Edmund Burke".[20]

Shelley's view, if compared to that of her contemporaries, is undeniably pessimistic. But it does fall short of the obvious solution to utter despair – Lionel does, after all, choose life. In fact, *The Last Man* is less bleak than *Valperga* and offers a narrow path towards hope, found in Lionel's critical determination to live out an inquiring life.

The glimmer of hope at the conclusion of such a monumental catastrophe is Verney's determination to explore and to study. These were the very consolations that Shelley felt were on offer to her in her own profound loneliness – she adored and thrived on travel, and was dedicated to learning, still studying Greek long after PBS's death. But Verney's isolation is also a freedom – a freedom from emotional anxiety for his loved ones and from intellectual domination or distraction. Verney seems to have won the infinitely open intellectual space that Shelley surely craved during her life with men and family. In an expansion of the fantasy – Shelley's own fantasy – Verney's new life also includes ready access to all the libraries of the world.

Until the last few years of her life Shelley explored new intellectual horizons, turning her pen to a variety of subjects. This compulsion to learn, to push back the borders of one's knowledge, is an assertion of independent will. It is the same compulsion that initially motivates Victor Frankenstein, Walton, Raymond, and even to a certain extent, Castruccio. The egotistical desire to impose oneself and one's achievement onto the human scene is in fact a confirmation of life and a blow against death. It is ironic that the ambition so associated with destruction and evil in *Frankenstein* and the novels that followed is also represented as the very spark of life itself. Intellectual curiosity drove Victor to his doom, but so too does it drive the Last Man onward and provide him with a purpose *beyond* love, beyond domestic satisfaction. Thus, arriving at *The Last Man*, with its understanding of and indeed celebration of the human spirit as exemplified in ambition and curiosity, we can look back at *Frankenstein* with a new insight. Shelley's condemnation of Victor would not be so unqualified were she to have rewritten his story in maturity. In fact, the apparent "softening" and evasiveness of the message of the 1831 edition of the novel might have some bearing on this modification of her views. The new emphasis on Victor's crime as a straight-forward usurpation of God's role undercuts the earlier political and philosophical ambiguities of the first editions. However, if we assume that Shelley herself grew more sympathetic to Victor after writing *The Last Man* – his brazenness should to some extent be congratulated rather than censured – then she had to alter the nature of his transgression in order to maintain the menace and morality of the story. Thus, her changes in the text might not simply be the result of a growing rigidity and conservatism, but rather an adjustment to maintain the original power of the story *for herself;* Shelley had come to know her first character more intimately.

If Victor's crime was simply against God then Shelley, an avowedly religious person, could unconditionally condemn it. If his creative affront is against decorum, domesticity and responsibility, then she might now feel a sympathy beyond the experience of the writer of 1818. After the personal experience of excruciating loneliness, Shelley had discovered that she could survive without PBS after all. With *The Last Man* she laid her husband to rest emotionally. She could also continue to love him and to cherish his memory and to reconcile herself, like the Last Man, to her new life. In so doing she satisfied her need for intellectual independence; she formed a philosophy of her own, one unrelated to her husband's and not less appropriate to modern conditions or sympathetic to modern minds.

7
Creating a Literary Reputation

Shelley undertook many difficult literary and journalistic projects in addition to novel-writing, but the most taxing was her first edition of PBS's poetry. Though *Posthumous Poems* was no sooner published than Sir Timothy suppressed it, Shelley was determined to fulfill her pledge to immortalize her beloved husband's name. She produced the four-volume *Poetical Works of Percy Bysshe Shelley* in 1839.

With that effort the roles of the Shelleys were reversed. Mary had come full circle from the impressionable intellectual ingenue, directing her energies to the approbation of her husband, to the undisputed master of PBS's posthumous reputation. Shelley's 1839 edition was considered definitive at the time and though some criticized her handling of individual poems, her copious notes, with their authentic biographical detail, validated her status as foremost authority on the poet.

Modern critics have found fault with the edition and claim variously that she miscopied, misinterpreted, purposely obscured, and attempted to turn the poet into something that he was not. Arguable as these points are individually, the significance of Shelley's effort is unassailable. She created and presented a poet in a form usually reserved for the acknowledged greats, far exceeding PBS's popularity at the time. Like Athena, he sprang fully grown from Shelley's forehead. If she did manipulate his work, it was only to ensure his instant fame.

Immediately following his death in July 1822, Shelley began to assemble PBS's poetry, essays and letters for a collected edition of his works. She wrote to Peacock, Maria Gisborne and Godwin asking them all to retrieve the poet's papers from publisher Charles Ollier.[1] She began sifting through the mass of fragments, notebooks, scraps of paper, proofs and first editions that made up the body of PBS's uncollected, unfinished, published and unpublished work.

Later, she wrote to PBS's correspondents asking for his letters or their copies.

The task was monumental and Shelley was later to comment to friends that the effort required to make sense out of the chaos and to draw editorial conclusions from the confusing manuscripts sapped her energy for many years to come.[2] Her unswerving devotion to the task was in some respects therapeutic; she clearly enjoyed the work and seems to have found some relief from her depression. However, Shelley also had clear, professional reasons for her undertaking and a goal in mind which, it can be maintained, she achieved. In presenting PBS to the world in a series of volumes that, with a few exceptions, contained the entire range of his work – poetry, translations, fragments, essays and letters – Shelley was determined to establish his fame in her *own* lifetime.

Contrary to popular belief, PBS had received important, if very select, recognition while he was still alive. N. I. White points out that several of the prestigious journals found that his work merited their attention (but not unconditional praise). Barcus disputes this, pointing out that limited circulation, publishers' fears of prosecution and PBS's self-imposed exile, far from where the poems were printed and distributed, severely limited his contemporary success.[3] It remains true that PBS was more notorious for his personal habits and lifestyle than he was universally admired as a poet. Shelley sought to direct public attention to where it was due, and away from the scandal that so diverted it.

John Lockhart of *Blackwood's Edinburgh Magazine*, or *Maga*, was, for a time, PBS's defender. In its review of *Rosalind and Helen*, *Maga* apologized to its readers for providing so many extracts of the poem, " . . . but it is our anxious desire to bring the genius of this poet fairly before the public . . . ".[4] *Blackwood's* confidence in his genius (though not always his morality) was often emphatically expressed, despite its conservative bias, over the seven years that Shelley published. During his lifetime however, PBS's reputation was never positively or widely established. Those reviews which did not revile him for his objectionable political and religious views paid passing tribute to his "genius" and the richness of his imagery. However, the pattern set by the reception of the juvenilia – *Zastrozzi* (1810), *Original Poetry by Victor and Cazire* (1810), *St. Irvine* (1811) and *Queen Mab* (1813) – like later works such as *The Revolt of Islam* (1818) was for all intents and purposes unchanged during his life. Not surprisingly, the pirated re-issue of *Queen Mab* in 1821 did nothing to quell hostilities. According to Trelawny, PBS "could number his readers on his fingers. He said, 'I can only print my writing by stinting myself in food!'"[5]

The early efforts were reviewed and dismissed at best as laughable and at worst as blasphemous by organs such as *The Literary Panorama, The British Critic,* and *The Critical Review.* Only *The Gentleman's Magazine* found some merit in *Zastrozzi.*[6] And after the juvenilia, PBS's more mature work often received similarly damning criticism. As James Barcus has pointed out, "nearly all of the reviewers fear(ed) that *Queen Mab* undermin(ed) the very structure and fabric of all social institutions including marriage, religion, family, and the parliamentary system."[7]

Leigh Hunt fought for PBS (and also for Keats) in the pages of *The Examiner,* particularly in defense of *The Revolt of Islam* (1818) but, as Barcus again points out, "the lines were clearly drawn and not until after Shelley's death, when most of his proposals for reform were at least legal realities, would Shelley's reputation be restored".[8] What is more, PBS's close association with Hunt, perceived as a prominent radical and PBS's social inferior, did much to fan the flame of conservative ire against him.

In addition to generally poor reviews,[9] PBS's published work had only the most limited circulation. Though reviews in some of the lesser quarterlies and monthlies often printed extended passages of the poetry with only a passing commentary, exposure remained circumscribed. With the exception of the juvenilia, PBS published only ten books in his lifetime; *Queen Mab;* a *Philosophical Poem* (privately printed and circulated, 1813), *Alastor, or, the Spirit of Solitude and Other Poems* (1816), *Laon and Cythna; or The Revolution of the Golden City* (published in December 1817 then withdrawn and reissued after amendments as *The Revolt of Islam* in January 1818), *Rosalind and Helen: A Modern Eclogue; with Other Poems* (1819), *The Cenci: A Tragedy, in Five Acts* (1819), *Prometheus Unbound: A Lyrical Drama in Four Acts with Other Poems* (1820), *Oedipus Tyrannus; or, Swellfoot the Tyrant* (1820), *Epipsychidion* (1821), *Adonais* (1821) and *Hellas: A Lyrical Drama* (1822).

Queen Mab, Adonais (for which he paid himself), and *Alastor* each appeared in editions of 250 copies. No more than 20 copies of *Prometheus Unbound* were sold and only 100 copies of Epipsychidion were printed. *The Cenci* was of course attacked for its portrayal of incest, a theme which, as I have already suggested, surfaced repeatedly within the Shelley circle. But *The Cenci* was his only real contemporary success and went to a second printing after the original 250 copies were sold. The strong character of Beatrice and the gothic nature of the story, it has been suggested, were responsible for its modest popularity. Godwin remarked:

> I have read the Tragedy of the "Cenci" and am glad to see Shelley at last descending to what really passes among human creatures. The story is certainly an unfortunate one, but the execution gives me a new idea of Shelley's powers. There are passages of great strength, and the character of Beatrice is certainly excellent.[10]

Horace Smith preferred *The Cenci* to *Prometheus Unbound*, writing to PBS in September 1820:

> "Prometheus Unbound", which is certainly a most original, grand, and occasionally sublime work, evincing, in my opinion, a higher order of talent than any of your previous productions, and yet, contrary to your own estimation, I must say I prefer the "Cenci", because it contains a deep and sustained human interest, of which one feels a want in the other.[11]

Shelley was not alone in her admiration of the play. She believed it Shelley's best major work.

However, resident in Italy, it was nearly impossible for PBS to oversee, defend or promote his work in London. He asked for copies of reviews in letters to England, at the same time professing lack of interest in the opinions of professional critics. At his death, the twelve obituaries in the London journals varied between the more charitable which mourned the passing of a misguided and ethereal genius or great classicist, and the blatantly vindictive which, like *The John Bull*, saw his dramatic death as just recompense for an evil life. *The Courier* was the most vicious; "Shelley, the writer of some infidel poetry, has been drowned . . . *now* he knows whether there is a God or no."[12] It was this accumulation of prejudice and outrage that his wife sought to assuage and correct in 1824.

Posthumous Poems is made up in part of poems that had been published in single sheets, journals, small editions or fragments, but it also contained finished pieces that had never been seen by the public; "Stanzas Written in Dejection Near Naples", "When the Lamp is Shattered", *Julian and Maddalo*, *The Witch of Atlas* and *Mont Blanc*, *The Triumph of Life* and several translations from Homer, Euripides and Goethe. Charles Taylor believes that it is these poems, in addition to those published with *Prometheus Unbound* in 1820, that established PBS's nineteenth century reputation.

Only 300 of the 500 copies of *Posthumous Poems* were sold to the public before Sir Timothy Shelley ordered his agent to acquire the remaining volumes. Shelley was forbidden, at the pain of forfeiture of the small advance on the baronetcy's fortune that she received annually for her son's keep, to put her husband's name before the public. Not until 1839 did Sir Timothy finally relent and allow his son's widow to publish the collected works with the condition that no biography be included. Nonetheless, in February 1824 Shelley was able to write to Hunt, "Shelley has celebrity even popularity now – a winter ago greater interest would perhaps have been excited than now by this volume – but who knows what may happen before the next". She was right to feel optimistic. Much transpired in the intervening fifteen years to promote PBS's reputation and to create a political and cultural milieu that was eager to receive him. As Sunstein explains:

> *Posthumous Poems* accomplished what Mary Shelley intended: before it, Shelley's immorality, destructiveness, and incomprehensibility were legend, and he was largely unread; upon its publication there was a surge of interest as he seemed at once more accessible and admirable. Moreover, though she has been charged with initiating the legend of the ethereal Shelley, that legend evolved out of his projection of himself and a cultural shift from the Byronic ideal to one of pre-Victorian evangelism, dedication and earnestness. Besides, he grew to be a hero to radicals as well. The age would seize upon Shelley.[13]

The practical task that his widow undertook was anything but straightforward. The papers that Shelley had to work from were very difficult to read, fragmentary, uncorrected and largely unpunctuated in any final, authoritative sense. While living in Italy PBS usually left the correction and modification of the printer's copy to Peacock, his designated agent in London. After the gift of one third of the Shelley papers to the Bodleian Library by Lady Jane Shelley in 1893, C. D. Locock produced *An Examination of the Shelley Manuscripts in the Bodleian Library* (1903) one of the earliest examinations of the material that Shelley had worked from, and again highlighted the extraordinary complexity of her task. Though Neville Rogers' conviction that Locock's work, "established that [PBS's] manuscripts, while important as a guide to editorial judgement, can never be more than a guide to it"[14] is certainly far-fetched, critics of Shelley's editions have perhaps been unaware of the greater than normal objective judgement and decision that a coherent and satisfactory reading of the texts necessarily required. As Kelvin Everest has pointed out, though Shelley's edition has its limitations:

> Mary Shelley's efforts in the volume of 1824 were truly remark-able. In the face of appalling difficulties, and under the most distressing personal circumstances, she produced a large number of readable texts out of what must have at first seemed irredeem-able chaos.[15]

Shelley was scrupulous in the preparation of the 1824 edition. An errata slip with some 24 corrections appeared in some volumes of *Posthumous Poems* and testifies to the meticulous manner in which she undertook the project; she obviously detected her own oversights or mistakes after the volume had gone to print and was determined that the alterations be noted and registered in subsequent editions. Of course, *Posthumous Poems* was not her final word on the poet; her corrections were also noted for the benefit of a later and more comprehensive collection. But *Posthumous Poems* itself never went to a second printing and the errata sheet was never properly incorporated. In fact, according to Taylor, Shelley evidently did not have the slip available during her preparation of the 1839 volumes.

Instead, Shelley worked from two of the four pirated editions of PBS's poetry that appeared in Britain and France between 1826 and 1836. She even contributed her services to Galignani's Paris edition *The Poetical Works of Coleridge, Shelley and Keats* (1829), eager to exercise her thwarted intentions after Sir Timothy forbade her own official publication. This action on Shelley's part, giving aid to a project from which she stood to gain neither credit, payment or control, is further testimony to her determination to establish PBS's professional reputation on the broadest possible base and as quickly as possible.

However, in her preparation of the 1839 volumes, when Shelley turned to the pirated editions, she assumed that they had taken careful note of her errata slip. Taylor maintains that the edition prepared by John Ascham, *Works of Percy Bysshe Shelley, With his Life* (1834), was used by Shelley as the chief printer's copy for volumes One, Three and Four of her 1839 edition.[16] The Galignani edition, he continues, was evidently used in the printing of volume Two. Though Ascham did apparently make careful use of the errata slip, he nonetheless left out some of Shelley's corrections. Then in turn, claims Taylor, Shelley recorded those same errors in 1839. Taylor criticizes Shelley for working from inferior copy when she should have used the best possible printer's copy for "an edition purporting to have textual value".[17] She was, he concedes, exhausted by her work on *Posthumous Poems* and believed that she could take a short cut, having worked initially from originals and manuscripts. Indeed, Everest and Matthews have pointed out that as sources the pirated editions were useless to an editor: "None of these is here regarded as possessing any textual significance".[18]

It is more important to recognize, as few critics of Shelley's project have, that her primary goal was not simply to create an incontrovertible text. It was to establish the poet's reputation before his memory was lost to the public. In attacking her, Shelley's contemporary and present-day critics misunderstood her overriding editorial concern, that of presenting PBS to the world in the most popular form possible. It was important to her that the poet be accepted widely, that he be read by men of letters as well as ladies of leisure, and secure his rightful place in the poetic pantheon. She worked against time and her own deteriorating health, approaching the editing of the poems with integrity and with the best of her abilities.

Shelley knew what the public wanted but she refused to include details of the poet's private life that didn't relate specifically to the poetry. She stated in the Preface:

> I abstain from any remark on the occurrences of his private life; except in as much as the passions which they engendered, inspired his poetry. This is not the time to relate the truth; and I should reject any colouring of the truth. No account of these events has ever been given at all approaching reality in their details, either as regards himself or others . . . [19]

Shelley was determined to separate the life from the work, to quash gossip and speculation and to offer the poetry unencumbered, only illuminated by the poet's thoughts on his subject. Her editorial aims and principles are set out at the very beginning of the Preface:

> . . . I hasten to fulfill an important duty, – that of giving the productions of a sublime genius to the world, with all the correctness possible, and of, at the same time, detailing the history of those productions, as they sprung, living and warm, from his heart and brain.[20]

Shelley's concern in presenting the poetry was not so much scholarly or academic, that is to say, rooted methodologically in the critical assessment of variations and alternative readings of the text, but points to a larger and more difficult objective; that of offering formally, completely and comprehensively the whole oeuvre of a relatively unknown poet; Shelley packaged and presented PBS as a major voice. Modern critics who find her textually lazy or indeed find fault with her commentary are applying their own analytical and textual methods and fashions anachronistically. They misunderstand the project and have failed to appreciate Shelley's terms and objectives. In one of the few essays that treats the body of Shelley's work in some detail, William Walling has said, " . . . by twentieth-century standards, she was woefully remiss as an editor"[21] but, he continues:

> Mary should be judged as an editor by a standard somewhat broader than that of today's academic "perfection". By her own lights – and the editorial lights of her generation – she was often conscientious to a praiseworthy degree. Often, too, her distortions and suppression apparently grew out of nothing more sinister than a desire that Shelley's writings be as "popular" as possible. Indeed, one of the least attractive things about some of her critics is their inability to remember that at the time of Mary's most strenuous editorial labours – on the *Posthumous Poems* – there were few people in England who believed Shelley worthy of any trouble at all.[22]

Shelley had to present not only her husband's material but to put the case for his *greatness* as well. Indeed, she may have felt defensive on this point. Joseph Raben claims of PBS that his "reputation, even in 1839, did not warrant the production of a scholarly edition with all the banished readings and false starts".[23] For Shelley, the 'Truth' about events in the poet's life and argument over textual variation could come later and from another source. Furthermore, as Bennett has pointed out, her

> achievement was not merely the work of a wife seeking post-humous fame for the writings of a beloved husband, as has been suggested or implied by many critics; she approached her commitment as a professional, deliberate editor, capable of making the most difficult kinds of editorial decisions.[24]

Shelley's vexed preparation of *Queen Mab* for the edition of 1839 is a good example of the obstacles that she faced, from friends *and* critics, in achieving the goals that she set herself in establishing PBS's fame.

In the preparation of *Queen Mab* Shelley took great pains to acquire one of the few original editions and wrote to everyone who might have received a copy when PBS circulated them privately in 1814. The manuscript and her own copy had been left behind at Marlow in 1817 and along with their other belongings had been held by the former landlord claiming arrears in rent. Shelley wrote to Thomas Moore (who evidently never received a copy), Charles Ollier, T. J. Hogg, Peacock and Leigh Hunt.

Queen Mab still presented other and greater problems. The publisher Edward Moxon who agreed to handle Shelley's project at the end of 1838 had profound reservations about publishing the notorious poem; the public was in some degree familiar with *Queen Mab* after its pirate circulation in 1821. That unauthorized publication was distributed widely enough to receive nine reviews, and not all of them critical. In 1838 Shelley was at great pains to present the poem correctly, but she had to please a nervous publisher, fulfill Shelley's own directions about the poem's publication, satisfy eager friends and her own integrity. She sought the advice of Hunt, Peacock and Hogg, emphasizing her natural reluctance to "mutilate" the work, and they advised her to proceed with what she believed PBS had intended.

In fact, PBS himself had not been adverse to altering the poem. In 1816 he published sections 1 and 2 as "The Daemon of the World", as part of the *Alastor* volume. Hunt had himself suppressed some of the material that PBS had sent him from Italy, such as an indignant public letter condemning the government for its harsh treatment (prosecution, imprisonment, fine) of Richard Carlile and his wife for publishing Paine's *Age of Reason* and Palmer's *Principles of Nature* in 1819. Hunt also attempted to protect PBS by withholding publication (for ten years) of the *Masque of Anarchy*, an expression of the poet's outrage at the Peterloo Massacre and the repressive government that had sanctioned it. White has pointed out that it "cannot be doubted that as an experienced and courageous radical Hunt had cogent and justifiable reasons for such suppressions",[25] though PBS was certainly frustrated with his friend for not publishing several of his works at this time. Though Hunt's radical integrity and loyalty has never been questioned, Shelley herself has received often vicious criticism for handling some of the poet's material in similar ways.

Shelley was aware of PBS's own change in feelings about *Queen Mab*. That it was never intended for the general public is well known. PBS evidently told Shelley, when news of the pirated edition of 1821 reached the couple in Italy, that he preferred the poem in its unauthorized form; without the dedication to Harriet and with some of the more shocking passages removed. Yet Timothy Webb argues that despite his desire to alter the poem, and his public letter disassociating himself from the pirate edition, PBS's fundamental views of religion and politics had not changed.[26]

However, 1821 was also the first year that Lockhart and *Blackwoods* turned on PBS unreservedly. In the same year that saw a scathing attack on *Adonais* (PBS's own thrust at the critics), PBS was left without a champion and the reappearance of *Queen Mab* and his clear association with Hunt and Byron in the public's eye was fatal. His defenders gave up and *The Cenci* was met by *Maga* and the other reviews with implacable hostility.

Shelley was not prepared to provoke a similar response in late January 1839 with the first official presentation of *Queen Mab* in twenty five years in the first of the volumes of collected poetical works. In her preparation of the one-volume edition of the poems and prose later in the year, Shelley was equally anxious about publishing the essay, "On the Devil and Devils", "for", she wrote to Hunt on October 6, 1839, "so many of the religious particularly like Shelley". Four days later she was soliciting Hunt's advice again, this time on the problems of presenting PBS's translation of Plato's treatise on love. She was deeply concerned about PBS's intentions and her own position regarding the delicate nature of the essay's subject.

Shelley responded to the anxiety of her publisher, her own judge-ment and her understanding of PBS's feelings; she altered *Queen Mab*. She was immediately attacked by her friends. Trelawny even sent his complimentary volume back to Moxon with an insulting letter. He and Hogg called her a traitor to the radical cause and more hurtfully, maintained that she had never been a suitable partner for the angelic poet (both men would go on to create a greatly mythologized PBS in their respective biographies). They accused her too of jealousy of Harriet's memory and claimed that vanity had led her to remove the poem's dedication to her.[27] Under this onslaught, Shelley reconsidered the poem. In the one-volume edition the poem was published in its entirety and Moxon, as he feared, was prosecuted and found guilty of blasphemous libel in June 1841.[28] He did not go to jail but it is clear that Shelley's original judgement had not been ill-founded.[29] She explained to the beleaguered Moxon from Paris exactly why she had gone ahead with publication of the complete poem:

> I being prompted so to do from being assured on all sides that in these days there was no fear of <mutilation> prosecution – that it seemed to me a mark of disrespect to my husband's Memory {Memory}, under these circumstances, to keep them back & that in short being written at the age of 18 they would be regarded by those who admired him with reverence due to his genius – by all with curiosity – without awakening the malice of <those> any. (November 30, 1840)

How had the poet's reputation developed in the years between *Posthumous Poems* and 1839? Shelley's four-volume edition came out as soon as possible after Sir Timothy's long-awaited consent, by which time the heat of PBS's notoriety had cooled. In the perceptive introduction to his *Bibliography of Shelley Studies*, Clement Dunbar has pointed out how the political climate in England, by the time *The Works* were published, had become more liberal. Many of the hoped-for changes that PBS's poems specifically addressed had come to pass.

The great Tory ascendency was already on the wane, having reached its climax in the Peterloo Massacre on August 16, 1819, and the Cato Street Conspiracy on February 23, 1820.[30] PBS had been deeply affected by these events back in England and he responded emphatically with the *Masque of Anarchy*. But only after his death did the political atmosphere begin to change. In the decade that led up to the Great Reform Bill of 1832, the governmental anxiety about imminent, bloody revolution that had coincided with and coloured PBS's career gradually dissipated. The steady liberalizing that followed Castlereagh's death in 1822 (just one month after the poet's) was reflected in the easing of the Corn Laws, the Catholic Emancipation Act of 1829, the abolition of slavery and Peel's reform of the Criminal Code, as well as other progressive legislation.[31]

With the supremacy of the Whigs in 1830 many of PBS's fondest hopes were realized and his prophetic views may well have been appreciated by the eager as "Christian", consequently nullifying the religious outrage that had greeted *Posthumous Poems* in 1824. Indeed, Victorian readers seemed eager to co-opt PBS as a Christian poet and with remarkable ease he became a favourite of the religious, as Shelley pointed out to Hunt. Contrary to what many modern critics believe, the dilution of PBS into a Christian did not originate with Shelley. However, even taking into account the *Essay on Christianity*, where PBS expresses sympathy to certain aspects of the religion, principally the figure of Jesus, it is impossible to deny his consistent atheism. The Christianity that the Victorians found in PBS was of their own devising.

Nonetheless, the figure of PBS had, especially in comparison to Byron, already become sympathetic and even sentimentalized. Before Shelley's often effusive notes on his personality, PBS had been romanticized by Medwin, Hunt and Hogg. This counters Herbert Read's accusation that Shelley was

> . . . the villain of the piece . . . who, however difficult she may have found her husband in life, did nothing but sentimentalize him in death. It was she who, in the notes she affixed to the posthumous editions of his Poems, created the image of a whimsy Ariel which has ever since been so dear to superficial critics and romantic biographers.[32]

Evidently, Read never read the gushing biographies of the poet written by his friends.

Medwin's *Journal of the Conversations with Lord Byron: Noted During a Residence with His Lordship at Pisa, in the Years 1821 and 1822* (1824), contained a 10-page footnote on PBS, as well as 35 additional pages of biographical material. In 1832 he wrote a series of memoirs for *The Athenaeum* which also included several unpublished poems. The following year those poems, papers and articles were collected into a book.

Also in 1832, Hogg wrote a series of articles, "Percy Shelley at Oxford" for *The New Monthly Magazine*, taking advantage of their university friendship. He portrayed PBS as beautiful and brilliant but impulsive, weak and dependent. In *Lord Byron and Some of His Contemporaries* (1828), Hunt damned Byron and praised PBS for over seventy pages. He contrasted the rich lord's stinginess with the impoverished PBS's selflessness and generosity. Hunt's extravagant portrayal of the poet continued in his edition of *The Masque of Anarchy*, published in 1832. Its long preface included much biographical material, adding to the shining portrait that Shelley had given in her own short preface to *Posthumous Poems*. For the most part the biographies painted a very subjective picture of the poet – he became all things to all people.

Disraeli's *Venetia* (1837) further popularized PBS's image and through the character of a misunderstood but noble idealist, tried to explain the motives behind PBS's ostensibly offensive behaviour. In the same novel the character of Byron was likewise rehabilitated and, ironically his fidelity and even chastity lionized. Also during this period PBS's poetry was discovered at Cambridge by a group of undergraduates, most notably, Tennyson, Arthur Hallam and Richard Milnes (also a champion of Keats). The "Apostles'" enthusiasm and subsequent influence helped to advance Shelley's reputation and prepare the ground for the first *Collected Works* of 1839.

Thus, England and indeed America were ripe to receive PBS favourably and Shelley, as the living authority closest to the poet during his adult life, was understandably deemed the definitive editor and biographer. The religious and political developments of the preceding decade had warmed the public's heart to the poet but Shelley alone held his reputation, an entirely posthumous reputation, within her command. Just as PBS encouraged her early ideals and ambitions, she was now free to interpret and 'influence' him.

THE INTELLECTUAL AUTONOMY OF THE EDITOR

Yet Shelley's interpretation of her husband's work gives us further evidence that from very early on, certainly by the time she began *Valperga*, Shelley's views differed greatly from her husband's. However, the criticism that she has received, for supposedly capitulating to conventionality and wilfully blunting PBS's sharp radical attack, as Raben has claimed, is erroneous. She herself did not shrink from presenting the poetry that had so outraged the politically oppressed England of the first two decades of the nineteenth century.

Another criticism of Shelley's editing is that she suppressed those poems which gave evidence of emotional problems between her and the poet, or suggested that he had been infatuated with other women, Jane Williams and Emilia Viviani, to name two. In fact, Shelley acted bravely. *Posthumous Poems* contains poems that reveal something of the poet and his wife's intimate relationship, compositions and fragments that Shelley must have found distressing. She read many of these for the first time after discovering them among her husband's papers.

In 1839, in addition to the dedication to Harriet restored to *Queen Mab*, Shelley expressed her sense of guilt in the notes to the poems of 1818, a period of depression for the poet: "One looks back with unspeakable regret and gnawing remorse to such periods; fancying that had one been more alive to the nature of his feelings, and more attentive to soothe them, such would not have existed".[33] She also included two fragments about her own unhappiness and withdrawal from her husband:

VI

The world is dreary,
And I am weary
Of wandering on without thee, Mary;
A joy was erewhile
In thy voice and thy smile,
And 'tis gone, when I should be gone too, Mary.

VII

My dearest Mary, wherefore hast thou gone,
And left me in this dreary world alone!
Thy form is here indeed – a lovely one –
But thou art fled, gone down the dreary road,
That leads to Sorrow's most obscure abode;
Thou sittest in the hearth of pale despair,
    Where
For thine own sake I cannot follow thee.[34]

Both fragments are dated July 1819, immediately following the death of three-year-old William on June 7. She was similarly depressed in the weeks leading up to her husband's death and she remained ashamed and regretful of her emotional abandonment of him throughout her life. Her inclusion of poems referring to those painful episodes – her own weakness and his pursuit of other women for emotional support, particularly passionate in *Epipsychidion* – is testimony to her professionalism in producing *Posthumous Poems* and *The Works of Percy Bysshe Shelley*.

Written in 1820, the dedication to Mary from "The Witch of Atlas" appeared for the first time in 1824. Here, Shelley has chosen to reveal PBS's disappointment in her:

To Mary
(On Her Objecting to the Following Poem,
Upon the score of its Containing No Human Interest)

> How, my dear Mary, are you critic-bitten
> (For vipers kill, though dead) by some review,
> That you condemn these verses I have written
> Because they tell no story, false or true?
> What, though no mice are caught by a young kitten,
> May it not leap and play as grown cats do,
> Till its claws come? Prithee, for this one time,
> Content thee with a visionary rhyme.

(1–8)

PBS's tone is reproachful, even angry. He was not only responding to her judgement of "The Witch of Atlas", but probably to her enthusiastic encouragement of 'successful' projects like *The Cenci*. He resented her desire that he write more popularly. Shelley had criticisms of the poetry even during PBS's life, but at the same time, she did not shrink from acknowledging the fact that PBS may have found her insensitive and, worse, not able to appreciate his art. We are offered a painful self-revelation. Further, she published two of the "Jane Williams" poems, "The Invitation" and "The Recollection", when gossip about the poet's love affairs were no doubt still current. For her own part, Jane Williams encouraged the stories and mentally tortured Shelley on her unhappy return to England in 1823 by spreading the rumour that she herself was the poet's only solace before his death.

THE NOTES TO THE POEMS

The notes and prefaces have become the battleground upon which critics have fought for and against Shelley's integrity and loyalty in regard to her supposed beliefs and those of her husband. Sylva Norman maintains that Shelley's commentary was her greatest achievement. Her praise is somewhat backhanded however, as she continues, " . . . we should honour her not only for performing it, but for submerging her own literary egotism while she did so, in the recognition that it could be more valuable to edit that to create".[35] Beginning with *Queen Mab* we can see that Shelley's reluctance to publish it in its entirety was not simply due to fears of stirring up old animosity, but that in her professional opinion, the poem was not entirely worthy of the poet and what is more, that the poet did not really appreciate what he was doing. This is put down to extreme youth and enthusiasm, but Shelley includes PBS's own notes to the poem:

> . . . not because they are models of reasoning or lessons of truth; but because Shelley wrote them. And that all that a man, at once so distinguished and so excellent, ever did, deserves to be preserved. The alteration his opinions underwent ought to be recorded, for they form his history.[36]

Shelley attempts to diffuse the outrage that *Queen Mab* might still cause – it is after all, a vehement statement of atheism. By treating it as an historical relic, of interest from a purely academic view, she emphasized PBS's ultimate modification of the beliefs that he had expressed therein. She did this not to protect herself in 1839 from public condemnation, but rather to explain how one who was so vilified and feared for his ideas less than two decades before could now be safely appreciated and even admired. Shelley points out that PBS "never intended to publish *Queen Mab* as it stands".[37] At the same time she deems its complete inclusion necessary for a full understanding of the poet and his work; a modern, scholarly approach. She finds *Queen Mab* important because it represents the first comprehensive and unrefined expression of his vocation, "too beautiful in itself, and far too remarkable as the production of a boy of eighteen, to allow of its being passed over".[38] Shelley maintains that PBS's ideals of reform were noble, sincere, honest and compassionate and that his experience and rejection of oppression (refusing to fag at Eton!) led him to an understanding of universal tyranny and that he "saw, in a fervent call on his fellow-creatures to share alike the blessings of the creation, to love and serve each other, the noblest work that life and time permitted him. In this spirit he composed *Queen Mab*."[39]

All that might be construed as objectionable in the poem is put down to the fervency of his youthful zeal. Shelley nonetheless felt compelled to defend her edition of the poem. To answer the hostile critics of her earlier edition of *Queen Mab* she included in the second edition PBS's letter to the editor of the *Examiner* (June 22, 1821) which denied his intention of ever publishing the poem for the general public. At the same time she cannot be accused of trying to obscure PBS's true radicalism as he stated in the letter, "I am a devoted enemy to religious, political, and domestic oppression; and I regret this publication not so much from literary vanity, as because I fear it is better fitted to injure than to serve the sacred cause of freedom . . . ".[40]

Shelley contrasts the ardour and impulsiveness of *Queen Mab* with the poem that follows it in her edition, *Alastor; or the Spirit of Solitude*, explaining that none "of Shelley's poems is more characteristic than this".[41] Alastor, Shelley believed, reflected the poet's pain-wracked and disappointed hopes. It does not have the exuberance of *Queen Mab*, she states, because it is a reflection of personal suffering and therefore of personal feeling. But she prefers *Alastor*. It is she says, "the broodings of a poet's heart in solitude – the mingling of the exulting joy which the various aspect of the visible universe inspires . . . ".[42] By this time, she makes it clear, PBS had suffered personal loss and disappointment and consequently speaks with a mature voice. The two poems are offered together as a contrast: *Queen Mab* represents the experimental, primary articulation of the poet's beliefs, *Alastor* demonstrates the maturation of the voice and its effectiveness, and not just in the "the sacred cause of freedom".

In the notes to *The Revolt of Islam*, Shelley explains those features of PBS's character which had exercised his critics from the time of his first offerings: the fascination with both metaphysics and poetry. According to Shelley, PBS made a conscious choice between the two and having decided on poetry, pursued his studies in that direction with conviction. However, his love of philosophy did not disappear and many early complaints against his poems were directed against its intrusion into otherwise pleasing verse. According to Trelawny, Byron said of PBS, "If he cast off the slough of his mystifying metaphysics, he would want no puffing".[43] Although critics came to accept that to separate the philosophy from the poetry (a technique that Matthew Arnold suggested one might effectively employ in reading Wordsworth), would be absurd in PBS's case, Shelley herself remained (albeit with a measure of guilt) convinced that her husband was better employed in writing more 'human' poetry, inspired by his emotions and passions. In his biography Walling criticizes this attitude and evinces disappointment at Shelley's inability to appreciate her husband's greatest poetry. He suggests that she was only able to understand the lesser poetry and that her encouragement of PBS to write more popularly was the result of her own intellectual limitation. He does not take into account the principal goal of Shelley's edition of 1839 nor does he himself appreciate the necessity of accessible poetry to her cause. Her discussion of the troublesome dichotomy between poetry and philosophy begins in the notes to *The Revolt of Islam* and she carries this theme throughout her commentary, hoping to convince a doubtful public of the poet's and the poetry's moral and artistic beauty.

Her notes often act as annotations to guide the reader through difficult territory, reassuring and cajoling them along the way. For example, to emphasize his humanity, Shelley maintains that PBS was supersensitive to "exterior circumstances"[44] and that much of his work was directly inspired by the injustice that he saw around him, *The Revolt* no exception to this rule. Thus she was able to highlight and to praise unreservedly his altruistic objectives and deftly obscure the awkward question of his philosophy.

Shelley even suggests that during the summer of 1816 PBS and Byron improved their respective powers by absorbing something of the style of the other. She wrote of her husband:

> Perhaps during this summer his genius was checked by association with another poet whose nature was utterly dissimilar to his own, yet who, in the poem he wrote at that time, gave tokens that he shared for a period the more abstract and etherialised inspiration of Shelley.[45]

Byron tempered PBS's abstraction (to his wife's taste) and Byron was himself influenced. Shelley shows us that her husband could and would adapt and at the same time that the difficult, abstract part of his nature could be turned to some practical use. It is interesting to note that, though many critics have discussed PBS's relationship with Byron in detail, and in particular, the mutual effects of their different political perspectives, Shelley has emphasized an actual *stylistic* exchange.

Girded with Byron's robust influence and the recent disappointments of his own life, the loss of Harriet's children in Chancery, PBS wrote *The Revolt*. Shelley thus claims a human and passionate inspiration for the poem, emphasizing the poet's overwhelming desire (greater even than that for philosophy or poetry, she suggests) to do good for others in a non-partisan way. She offers an excuse for his radical, once offensive actions:

> He chose therefore for his hero a youth nourished in dreams of liberty, some of whose actions are in direct opposition to the opinions of the world; but who is animated throughout by an ardent love of virtue, and a resolution to confer the boons of political and intellectual freedom on his fellow-creatures.[46]

Finally, if her defence were not enough, Shelley gives us the poet's letter to Godwin (Marlow, December 11, 1817) which is his own defence of the piece, and of his powers, against Godwin's criticism. If she could not wholeheartedly embrace his singleminded idealism, she could understand and praise his desire, transformed by her pen to saintly rather than treasonable behaviour, to help the unfortunate.

In her notes to *Prometheus Unbound*, Shelley discusses the poet's concept of evil in humanity. Though more obscure champions of PBS in the years between 1824 and 1839 had tried to show that the poet was, after all, expressing his true Christianity, Shelley herself suggested parallels between the two systems. Again we see the sort of incidental compromise that she felt obliged to make in order to promote the book and to make clear her own judgement:

> The prominent feature of Shelley's theory of the destiny of the human species was, that evil is not inherent in the system of the creation, but an accident that might be expelled. This also forms a portion of Christianity; God made earth and man perfect, till he, by his fall, "Brought death into the world and all our woe".[47]

Shelley does not force Christianity onto the poet but rather attempts to show his system in its least blasphemous light, by suggesting its points of contact with conventional structures of belief. She emphasizes a dialogue between the two systems, rather than an out and out rejection of Christianity on PBS's part and follows on the same page: "Shelley believed that mankind had only to will that there should be no evil, and there would be none". She soothes the wary conscience of the Christian reader, while distancing herself from the debate and putting PBS's beliefs as objectively as possible:

> It is not my part in these notes to notice the arguments that have been urged against this opinion, but to mention the fact that he entertained it, and was indeed attached to it with fervent enthusiasm. That man could be so perfectionized as to be able to expel evil from his own nature, and from the greater part of the creation, was the cardinal point of his system.

In fact, as this study has attempted to show, the evidence from her work suggests that it is this cardinal point which Shelley herself rejected outright. She believed that evil was an invincible and inevitable fact of life, a theme that we have seen reiterated in her best novels and stories and significantly removed from those that boiled the pot. The "ascendency of evil" carries the action of *Valperga* and becomes an almost palpable antagonist. In an analogous fashion, as she describes it in the notes, the battle between good, or the "One" and evil, or the "Evil Principle", forms the dynamic of "The Revolt of Islam" and "a more idealized image of the same subject"[48] is the theme of *Prometheus Unbound*. This is how she chose to read the poems.

Yet again Shelley points out the difficulties that the poet's interest in philosophy, coupled with his remarkable imagination, might cause the reader: "[PBS] develops, more particularly in the lyrics of this drama, his abstruse and imaginative theories with regard to the Creation. It requires a mind as subtle and penetrating as his own to understand the mystic meanings scattered throughout the poem".[49] On the same page Shelley addresses the complaints of some of the poet's earliest supporters in *Blackwood's*; that though the poetry was commendable, the fantastical and vague metaphysics were intrusive and misguided. Anticipating similar criticism from readers of 1839, she explains that his theories

> . . . elude the ordinary reader by their abstraction and delicacy of distinction, but they are far from vague. It was his design to

write prose metaphysical essays on the nature of Man, which would have served to explain much of what is obscure in his poetry; a few scattered fragments of observations and remarks alone remain. He considered these philosophical views of mind and nature to be instinct with the intensest spirit of poetry.

If we are to believe her it seems clear that the poet himself must have recognized that his theories, images and philosophies, if not vague, were simply too difficult for the readers that he hoped to reach to glean from his poetry. To make his philosophy understood, he felt compelled to back poetry up with prose. If the poet was prepared to admit himself that his poems could be obscure, then it is surely unreasonable of Walling and others to accuse Shelley of not understanding or appreciating the important poems (while of course implying that they do themselves).

Shelley goes on to a more specific discussion of the imagery, modelled, she says, on Sophocles. She defends PBS, claiming that more "popular poets clothe the ideal with familiar and sensible imagery. Shelley loved to idealize the real – to gift the mechanism of the material universe with a soul and a voice, and to bestow such also on the most delicate and abstract emotions and thoughts of the mind".[50] Thus, despite what might earlier be read as criticism, Shelley finds that PBS's greatness, his extraordinary powers, are to be found precisely in the complexity, originality and subtlety of his imagery. Those modern critics who claim that she preferred the lesser poetry and mistakenly urged her husband to write popular verse have misinterpreted her role. She was determined, even before his death, to exact the fame for which he was due and to draw attention first to his easier work, but without disguising her contempt for those "popular poets" whose imagery is facile, overworn and sentimental.

However, Shelley again makes it clear that she did not share the poet's political convictions without qualification, in a footnote which continues the comparison of *Prometheus* to *The Revolt of Islam*. The later poem, she obviously believed, needed some explanation:

> While correcting the proof-sheets . . . it struck me that the Poet had indulged in an exaggerated view of the evils of restored despotism, which, however injurious and degrading, were less openly sanguinary than the triumph of anarchy, such as it appeared in France at the close of the last century.

But at this time a book, "Scenes of Spanish Life", . . . fell
into my hands. The account of the triumph of the priests
and the serviles, after the French invasion of Spain in 1823,
bears a strong and frightful resemblance to some of the
descriptions of the massacre of the patriots in the Revolt of
Islam.[51]

Shelley's anticipation of readers' objections to PBS's violent anti-
monarchism of course testifies to her own original doubts and
fears.[52] Her notes echo sentiments first expressed in the "History
of the Jews" and later developed in *The Last Man*, where governmental proposals against the aristocracy are condemned and where
even the war of independence is of questionable morality. But she
reassures the readers of 1839 that the poet was not exaggerating his
description of oppression after all. She is not attempting to soften
PBS's objectives, but to make the nature of his provocations and
the pureness of his convictions clear. Nonetheless, she does express
her dissatisfaction with the earlier poem, in contrast to *Prometheus
Unbound* whose achievements she illuminates. What is missing from
The Revolt is present in *Prometheus*, a theme which figures largely in
Shelley's own art: "Through the whole Poem there reigns a sort of
calm and holy spirit of love; it soothes the tortured, and is hope to
the expectant, till the prophecy is fulfilled, and Love, untainted by
any evil, becomes the law of the world".[53] Though Shelley never
offered love as a panacea in the same way that Godwin had
offered Reason in *Political Justice*, it was, she believed, the only
real anaesthetic available.

In her commentary Shelley appears most enamoured of *The Cenci*
(1819), but she also makes it clear that the medium of the drama was
one which PBS found the most difficult and artistically unnatural. It
is ironic that *The Cenci* represented his greatest commercial success,
such as it was. PBS was also sufficiently satisfied with the piece
to desire its production. He instructed Peacock that he wished it
to be staged at Covent Garden and the principal role be taken by
Kean. After his initial reluctance to begin the project it appears
that with Shelley's encouragement, the poet gained confidence. It
is likewise not impossible that PBS's recent reunion with Byron, coupled with Shelley's enthusiasm for Byron's dramas, was powerfully
persuasive.

In the same letter to Peacock (July 1819) that gave instructions
for the production of *The Cenci*, and which appears in Shelley's

commentary, PBS sheds more light on the vexed question of his imagination and imagery. In a marked contrast to his attack on "critic-bitten" Mary in the following year, PBS acknowledges (by implication) the wisdom of her advice:

> I have taken some pains to make my play fit for represen-
> tation, & those who have already seen it judge favourably.
> It is written without any of the peculiar feelings & opinions
> which characterise my other compositions; I having [attended]
> simply to the impartial development of such characters as it
> is probable the persons represented really were, together with
> the greatest degree of popular effect to be produced by such a
> development.[54]

PBS reassures Peacock, who, familiar with his work, would no doubt be uncertain about its popular or dramatic appeal. The poet's assurances that the piece is not like his other works, as well as his desire to remain anonymous, as " . . . essential, deeply essential to its success", makes clear that he understood just how badly his work was received. He did not wish potential audiences to stay away because of their prejudice against his poetry on moral and aesthetic grounds: " . . . there is nothing beyond what the multitude are contended to believe that they can understand, either in imagery, opinion, or sentiment". In a similar way he offered the copyright of *Charles the First* to Ollier:

> . . . My reason for selling it, to speak frankly, is, that the
> Bookseller should have sufficient interest in its success to give
> it a fair chance . . . I ought to say that the Tragedy promises to
> be good, as Tragedies go; and that it is not coloured by the party
> spirit of the author . . . [55]

Shelley describes how the drama project was initiated as a test of the poet's talents, and at the same time outlines the specific charges that she was to hold against the poetry in general:

> He asserted that he was too metaphysical and abstract – too fond
> of the theoretical and the ideal, to succeed as a tragedian. It
> perhaps is not strange that I shared this opinion with himself, for
> he had hitherto shown no inclination for, nor given any specimen

of his powers in framing and supporting the interest of a story, either in prose or verse.[56]

Despite these obstacles the play was completed and to make her point Shelley maintains that universal "approbation soon stamped The Cenci as the best tragedy of modern times . . . The Fifth Act is a masterpiece. It is the finest thing he ever wrote, and may claim proud comparison not only with any contemporary, but preceding poet".[57]

Shelley thus makes the case to her public, first that her husband's talents were extraordinary and not limited to one particular style; and secondly, that he acknowledged her influence and was grateful for it, believing as she did, that he had talent as a popular dramatist and that he was not compromising his poetic powers. Indeed, the centrality of incest in the play testifies to the poet's determination *not* to accommodate the delicate tastes of the public. And, in the notes to the poems of 1821, Shelley shows nothing but approbation for the "lofty scorn" which PBS expressed towards Keats's critics – implicitly his own as well – in *Adonais*.

Shelley addressed the anticipated criticisms of her edition from opposite quarters and attempted to diffuse the attacks. Radical friends could not argue with the play's success or PBS's satisfaction with it. Hostile readers could not fault the poet for being too abstract. PBS could satisfy many tastes and was accessible to a wide public. She 'sells' the poet, with *The Cenci*, in much the same way that PBS himself 'sold' the play to Peacock.[58] Shelley did not back down from her advocacy of such work nor, even at the distance of two decades, find that she was wrong to have done so. In the notes to the poems of 1820 she says of *The Witch of Atlas*:

> The surpassing excellence of The Cenci had made me greatly desire that Shelley should increase his popularity, by adopting subjects that would more suit the popular taste, than a poem conceived in the abstract and dreamy spirit of the Witch of Atlas. It was not only that I wished him to acquire popularity as redounding to his fame; but I believed that he would obtain a greater mastery over his own powers, and greater happiness in his mind, if public applause crowned his endeavours. The few stanzas that precede the poem were addressed to me on my representing these ideas to him. Even now I believe that I was in the right.[59]

Shelley hoped to influence the poet during his lifetime in order to bring him the credit that he was due. All her subsequent professional editing for Trelawny, Godwin and others testifies to her canny knowledge of the publishing business. She simply carried on this process in *The Poetical Works*:

> I had not the most distant wish that he should truckle in opinion, or submit his lofty aspirations for the human race to the low ambition and pride of the many, but I felt sure, that if his poems were more addressed to the common feeling of men, his proper rank among the writers of the day would be acknowledged; and that popularity as a poet would enable his countrymen to do justice to his character and virtues . . . [60]

Shelley saw PBS's poems as falling into two broad categories, those which were "purely imaginative" and those that "sprung from the emotions of his heart", appealing to the "emotions common to us all".[61] Shelley held up Byron as a brilliant proponent of the latter form. Greatly admired too by PBS, Byron could express his commitment to political and spiritual reform in a manner that was true to his natural style and self-image but which was consistently popular. Shelley saw that Byron spoke to many while preserving his integrity and art. Byron's proximity, and Shelley's unqualified praise of his art (if not of his person) must have had a profound effect on PBS at this time.

In her notes to *Hellas*, Shelley takes the opportunity to advertise enthusiastically the poet's commitment to liberty. In the events that she narrates, the various rebellions in Italy against occupying forces, she was aware that her own and PBS's approbation of the Italian struggle for independence could not be met with anything but praise by the public of 1839. Indeed, she prefaces her explanation, we "have seen the rise and progress of reform".[62] Shelley speaks unreservedly to a sympathetic audience, and with the knowledge that at least as far as this issue is concerned, she and PBS had been simply ahead of their time.

What is more, his association with the Greek cause was another activity in PBS's favour. Byron himself was morally rehabilitated almost solely on the publicity surrounding his financial and personal contributions to the Greek war against the Turks. He had become a martyrized hero by the time his preserved body returned to England and was processed through London. With *Hellas*, PBS could share in that glory without the previously customary repudiation of his anti-Christian views.

Her notes to *Swellfoot the Tyrant* represent Shelley's practiced technique for opening the minds of her readers to the 'questionable' poetry and easing their potential disquiet about PBS's unpatriotic sentiments. She explains the absurd uproar over Queen Caroline's supposed misconduct some twenty years earlier. As the event itself was both ridiculous and perhaps trivial, PBS's poem about it may also be seen in this light, she implies. She maintains that she and the poet considered it a frivolity. What is more, she thought so little of the satire that hesitation

> . . . of whether it would do honour to Shelley prevented my publishing it at first; but . . . each word is fraught with the peculiar views and sentiments which he believed to be beneficial to the human race; and the bright light of poetry irradiates every thought . . . This drama, however, must not be judged for more than was meant. It is a mere plaything of the imagination . . . But, like everything he wrote, it breathes that deep sympathy for the sorrows of humanity, and indignation against its oppressors, which make it worthy of his name.[63]

Shelley allays the fears of her readers first by explaining her own doubts about the poem, and emphasizing its harmlessness. Finally, she aggrandizes the poet by reminding readers of the vital importance of his every effort and his unswerving commitment to humanity.

NOTES TO THE PROSE

It is in *Essays, Letters From Abroad and Fragments* that Shelley's praise for PBS becomes extravagant and her image of him as an ethereal being the most vivid; she loses the measured tone of the notes to the poetry. In the Preface she preaches to the converted, to the readers of the poetry who wish to know more of the man and his motivations:

> Let the lovers of Shelley's poetry – of his aspirations for a brotherhood of love, his tender bewailings springing from a too sensitive spirit – his sympathy with woe, his adoration of beauty,

as expressed in his poetry; turn to these pages to gather proof of sincerity, and to become acquainted with the form that such gentle sympathies and lofty aspirations work in private life.[64]

The essay on Love she maintains, "reveals the secrets of the most impassioned, and yet the purest and softest heart that ever yearned for sympathy, and was ready to give its own, in lavish measure, in return."[65] She also takes the opportunity again to make the case for PBS's general appeal when she highlights the 'Christian' features of his work:

> To me, death appears to be the gate of life; but my hopes of a hereafter would be pale and drooping, did I not expect to find that most perfect and beloved specimen of humanity on the other shore; and my belief is, that spiritual improvement in this life prepares the way to a higher existence. Traces of such a faith are found in several passages of Shelley's works.[66]

In the Preface she once again pre-empts criticism of PBS's vagueness. She uses the *Defence of Poetry* as an example of his clarity: "His Defence of Poetry is alone sufficient to prove that his views were, in every respect, defined and complete; his faith in good continued firm, and his respect for his fellow-creatures was unimpaired by the wrongs he suffered."[67]

In general, Shelley's comments on the prose lack the critical perspective that she displayed in her notes to the poetry. The prose that she chose to publish represents a small selection, though she reminds us that the *Defence of Poetry* is "the only entirely finished prose work [PBS] left".[68] Shelley's greatest effort went into the poetry. She was content to leave a comprehensive volume of the prose to another.

Though her treatment of the prose lacks discipline and objectivity, Bennett has shown through the letters that Shelley was nonetheless a dedicated professional. She did not simply retreat into conventionality after PBS's death but on the contrary was dedicated to her career, an unconventionally public one, and determined to maintain herself and her son independently. She provided Percy Florence with the best education that England could offer. She remained deeply interested in politics until the end of her life and took the trouble to write an enthusiastic letter of congratulations to Lafayette (whom she had met in Paris in the summer of 1828) on November

11, 1830. She hailed the "Hero of three Revolutions" and expressed her pleasure at the success of the liberals in the 28–29 July revolution and Louis Philippe's ascension. Furthermore, she complains of the failings of her own government, wishing that "England imitate your France in its moderation and heroism . . . for what course of measures can annihilate the debt? and so reduce the taxation, which corrodes the very vitals of the suffering population of this country". She shows that her original political sympathies are maintained in exactly the same way, with the same basis for their conviction, as during PBS's lifetime:

> I was the wife of a man who – held dear the opinions you espouse, to which you *were* the martyr and *are* the ornament; and to sympathize with successes which would have been matter of such delight to him, appears to me a sacred duty . . . I rejoice that the Cause to which Shelley's life was devoted, is crowned with triumph.

However, Shelley did not believe that personal involvement in politics was necessarily the only authentic expression of individual reason. Rather, she found that political activity and struggle for an elusive cause was often motivated by emotion and egoism. Thus Raymond of *The Last Man* returns to political life through sheer boredom and vanity and Louis, the eponymous Swiss Peasant of Shelley's short story (1831) is motivated to lead the revolutionaries from a personal jealousy towards the local aristocrat. Though she naturally supported her husband's genuine altruism and desire to do good, Shelley believed these to be qualities of his character and not necessarily transferable as a remedy for the ills of mankind.

Thus, contrary to her detractors' claims, Shelley did not suddenly or inexplicably embrace conservatism. Those who question her commitment to liberalism after PBS's death have failed to see that though Shelley supported PBS's political ideals, they were founded in her emotional attachment to him, and faith in his intellect. They were also a reflection of her affinity, indeed worship, of her mother's memory – her *memory*, it should be stressed, rather than to an unqualified celebration of her beliefs and teachings. But Shelley was not afraid to disagree with PBS, before and after his death. It is erroneous to believe that her original attachment to the radical cause had been exactly parallel to that of her husband and was then suddenly abandoned. It simply never became the central focus of her life as it had been for him. Though it is often quoted, critics misunderstand the significance of the famous journal entry of October 1838 where she attacks the hypocrisy of the proponents of the "Cause". Her anger seems directed not so much at the blame she received after PBS's death but at the failure of her friends to understand that she didn't and had never intended to take her husband's kind of radicalism as a personal ethos. By the 1830s and 40's she was at odds with the Liberals. In a letter to Moxon regarding his prosecution she wrote:

> I know not what to say to your refusal of compensati(o)n for all the expence which the Liberals have put you to. Since the evil sprung from them solely – I think you ought to let them repair it – not by a formal subscription – but by allowing them to take the fine &c on themselves. (July 14, 1841)

The message that Shelley tried to illustrate in her own art was different from her husband's and we see that from the beginning of her professional career.

Shelley disagreed with PBS on some issues, but at the same time the presentation of his views and beliefs to the world was solely in her hands. Her handling of this conflict was sensitive and as fair as possible. Those who claim that she systematically sanitized her radical husband's views have not read her commentary with the same thoroughness that they may have addressed to the poetry. Those interested in the poet, his wife, or their relationship, must read the notes and poetry as a collaborative effort, much like *Proserpine* and *Midas*. Bennett sums it up:

> . . . the letters show that even her most serious error, the failure to use first editions consistently as copy-text when manuscripts were not available, was not the result of amateurishness or indifference. In fact, Mary Shelley's letters reveal that her editorial principles, stated or implied, stand up well even by modern standards. As editor, Mary Shelley became Shelley's collaborator, returning more than in kind the guidance he had given her when she wrote *Frankenstein* and other early works. She gathered and preserved his writings. She brought the experience of a professional author to the editing of his works. Finally, biographers and critics agree that Mary Shelley's commitment to bring Shelley the notice she believed his works merited was the single, major force

that established Shelley's reputation as a poet during a period when he almost certainly would have faded from public view.[69]

Shelley more than paid her husband back for the love, instruction and guidance that he had offered to her, influencing her most keenly in her earliest youth. The circle is completed by *her* influence, posthumously, on him, in her middle age. Though they remained ideologically fundamentally different, they were united in their profound confidence in each other's talents, integrity and potential for greatness.

8

Conclusion

Shelley's artistic vision was deeply pessimistic and even in *The Last Man*, which offers a kind of existential hope, she proposed no redemption of any kind. Her best work was, by the standards of her time, blasphemous, indeed atheistic. Yet Shelley herself was none of these. She maintained a solid faith. In her own life she looked forward to a reunion with her "lost divinity" (*Journal*, November 10, 1822) after death.

Countless letters, journal entries, poems and her monumental editing of PBS's work testify to her belief in joining him after death, a belief from which she clearly took spiritual solace. In a letter to Jane Williams, December 5, 1822, she speaks of their common loss and consolation, "God has still one blessing for you & me – the hope – the belief of seeing *them* again, & may that blessing be as entirely yours as it is mine." A general Christian belief is also in evidence at this time: "I believe that we all live hereafter", she wrote in her journal on October 10, 1822. She was attending church regularly from as early as December 1821. She records her church-going on the 9th and 16th of December and again on February 24, 1822 and into March. She joked about her new interest in a letter to Maria Gisborne from Pisa:

> Yet though I go not to the house of feasting, I have gone to the house of prayer – In the piano sotto di nos there is a Reverend Divine who preaches and prays, and sent me so many messages that I now make one of his congregation . . . I went once, and then that I might not appear to despise his preaching, I went again and again . . . (January 18, 1822)

PBS's feelings about Shelley's church-going – perhaps her most potent defiance of him – are unrecorded, but she was surely the only member of their highly unconventional group-in-exile to recite prayers with the English community in Pisa.

But it was not only her religious belief that consoled Shelley. The act of writing itself became a source of relief and fulfilment. Her journals of the years following her husband's death are focused on her career and continued education. Still in Italy she wrote:

Study has become more necessary to me than the air I breathe. In the questioning and searching turn it gives to my thoughts, I find some relief to wild reverie; in the self-satisfaction I feel in commanding myself, I find present solace. (March 19, 1823)

Just after her return to England in June 1824 she was rewarded with creative inspiration:

I feel my powers again – & this is of itsself, happiness – the eclipse of winter is passing from my mind – I shall again feel the enthusiastic glow of composition . . . study & occupation will be a pleasure not a task. (June 8, 1824)

In her first positive observations for months, Shelley was obviously excited by her new-found energy. She was beginning to find her way and perhaps to see the advantages of widowhood.

Shelley's fiction therefore was not simply a crude reflection on the hardships of her own life. Her religion, in evidence before PBS's death, her trust in the therapeutic action of writing, her growing excitement about her career and her anticipation of an afterlife, kept her from adopting a personal philosophy continuous with the series of sterile apocalypses that she portrays in the fiction. Her worlds of destroyed faith, the ruined lives of the characters of *Valperga* and its prophesy of evil, the failure of love and cruel nature's mockery of the derelict world of *The Last Man* are at odds with her own fundamental spirituality.

Though Shelley's religiosity was not conventionally Anglican, it was markedly different from the spirituality of her husband and was surely a symptom of her disagreement with him on fundamental intellectual principles. Shelley's Christian faith and PBS's atheism, which later evolved into a kind of agnosticism, are not the only indicators of ideological difference between the two. In the first excitement of love Shelley impressed and no doubt flattered PBS with her passionate interest in his aspirations, both artistic and political. But Shelley's intellectual independence asserted itself remarkably quickly. Her love for PBS did not weaken but after much emotional struggle she was able to separate her own intellectual programme from his. She did this, as we saw in *Frankenstein*, by projecting her disquiet about radicalism into fiction, imaginatively illustrating the fallacies and shortcomings of certain precepts of *Political Justice* and of the radical system. In the same way she criticized the behaviour of radicals: Victor, Castruccio and Raymond represent different aspects of the radical character. At the same time she illustrated the consequences of radical behaviour with the creation of uniquely symbolic fictions; she projected her concerns onto the malevolent Monster, into the ruination and death of Beatrice and Euthanasia, and the incompetence of the republican government in *The Last Man*. Her pessimism about the future in her vision of global annihilation transcends mere literal representation.

Shelley's pessimistic fictions are not a reflection of her personal problems – as critics have implied, the fruits of a limited imagination. Rather, her dark visions reflect the vehemence of her intellectual rejection of a system that tried to swamp her, a system championed by those she loved most. Yet she presented her case: revolutions were of questionable moral and practical value, and blind advocacy of them was as dangerous as it was ignorant; the French Revolution had been a terrifying failure due to its abandonment by its ideological creators, and no political system, radical, conservative or otherwise, could answer all the needs of life or could be called into the service of art. Once she had addressed these issues to her own satisfaction in the early novels she abandoned such demanding themes to write in a mode more familiar to the novel-reading public and one more welcomed as the creation of a woman. Though the three novels that followed *The Last Man* have some interesting features, they are not ambitious or challenging. They embrace a world where the heroine is central and where love and marriage – and wealth – solve all her ills.

After PBS's death Shelley found her own way in the world without benefit of a guide. Perhaps her loneliness and isolation helped her to gain her autonomy. Even the editions of the poems are stamped with her identity; she made them into a true collaboration. She was very conscious of the fact, particularly from a business point of view, that her notes and prefaces would be of interest in themselves and could boost sales. Her skill at travel writing and biography was known and the notes function on these levels too, in addition to their more obvious purpose of illuminating the poetry. She also left her unmistakable mark on the edition in her attempt to 'humanize' the poems and make them accessible to a large audience. This is not philistinism, as some have implied, but rather shows her love of the poetry, her appreciation of its complexity, and her desire to share it with the world. In the last resort it has proved unhelpful to concentrate so much on her personal relations with the poet in evaluating her achievement as an editor. For, as an independent critic and thinker, she has her own manner of reading the poet and this in effect has been underrated by the persistent tendency to consider her role as principally that of a wife; she has not been considered as a professional in regard to PBS. Her problems with the poetry are no greater than many a modern critic's or editor's, as is shown by the variety of interpretation that the great poems – *Mont Blanc, Prometheus Unbound* and *The Triumph of Life* – have provoked.

Of course it is difficult to over-stress Shelley's love for PBS. In later years she had many admirers and it is clear that more than once she reciprocated with affection. Yet she never remarried or ever openly expressed a desire to do so. Her personal loyalty to PBS has been as much underrated as her need and ability, when necessary, to distance herself from him. She was emotionally conflicted, with a personality and career more difficult to resolve than critics have appreciated. She was demure in manner, but never complacent; she was driven to speak. For any who choose to listen, her distinctive voice of dissent rings out from as early as 1815, asserting its own pitch and timbre against Percy's great Shelleyan symphony.

Appendix A:
Manuscript Essay:
"A History of the Jews"

Editorial symbols:

1. < > – Words appearing between < > are those which Shelley crossed out.
2. [?] – Words appearing between brackets and preceded by "?" are uncertain readings.

The MS consists of sixteen quarto leaves and appears to have been loosely bound, perhaps in a notebook. The leaves are watermarked "J. Hall 1810".

All <the> ideas <that these people had formed> upon the creation of the world & upon <all> natural phenonoma formed by so illiterate a people were of course false <[?grose] and betrayed> at a time when even the <civilized> conceptions of the enlightened Greeks were rude & unformed no great proficiency in phisical knowledge could be expected from a herd of Arabian robbers-yet as Moses had <formed> received most of his opinions in Egypt then the most civilized country in the world-it appears <wonderful> extraordinary that his tenets should be in every respect those of the most unenlightened savage.

Thier notions of the sun and moon were of a greater & a lesser light placed in heaven. the one to rule the day the other the night. God they said had created the world in six days – before this time all was void & his spirit floated on the face of the waters – he had ordered light to be & there was light – he had ordered all animals & all plants to bring forth abundantly after their kind & to increase upon the face of the earth – on the sixth day he finished his labour & rested on the seventh –

He then <found> discovered that the earth still <wanted> needed

a being of superior intelligence who might superintend & adorn it –
he created man of the dust of the earth & blew into his nostrils the
breath of life – But man was alone and as unfortunately he was of a
sociable disposition – <of course> he could not be perfectly happy –
But God remedied this evil by <take> casting him into a deep sleep
and then taking out one of his ribs which he moulded <it> into a
woman – He placed this first pair in the beautiful garden of Eden
there to live happily & for ever if they touched not of the fruit of
the tree of Knowledge of Good & Evil.

This tree, the Jews affirmed, was the cause of all the unhappiness
that afterwards befell <till then crime & death was unkown upon
earth – but the spirit of this tree infused [? all] [ ] upon man> the
children of men – <for this man & woman> the blessed pair (named
Adam & Eve) disobeyed the command of God <they ate one of the
apples> for the <lady> woman being tempted by a serpent (who
like Asops foxes could speak in those days) ate <one> one of the
apples which grew on the tree and finding it of a fine flavour (a
quality not to be resisted <untempting> by a lady of the Jewish
race) she presented one to Adam who also ate – till this fatal deed
crime & death was unknown upon earth but the*[1] God <for this
misdemaenor> also enraged at their disobedience turned them out
of <t>his garden, took from them the gift of immortality & for their
sake cursed the earth so that it should not bring forth fruits without
cultivation. Women were also sentenced to <bring forth> bear their
children with pain to punish to all posterity the fault of the first
mother.

After their expulsion from Eden Eve had two sons – Cain a tiller
of the earth & Abel a <shepperd> guarder of flocks. God, for no
apparent reason was favourable to the youngest of these bretheren
while he refused the sacrafises of the other – the elder therefore,
Cain, conceived a jealousy towards his brother & one day slew him
with a club. This fraticide had a mark set on his forehead that all
might know him & be detered by a heavy curse from killing him –
he was condemned to be a wanderer & a vagabond on the face of the
earth – It appeared afterwards however that he dwelt very quietly
with his wife in the land of Hod <& had ma a child> – The Jewish
author does not mention who his wife was or indeed that Eve ever
had any daughters – <but> but as the earth was peopled solely from
<the first pair> Adam & Eve commentators agree the <first> men
must at first have married their sisters. Eve had afterwards another
son called Seth.

Section II

<The children of Cain are recorded to the 6th generation – one was an inventor of the harp & organ – another an artificer in brass & iron. The great grandson of the grandson of Cain was also a murderer but escaped <all> punishment by alledgeing that God would revenge <77 fold> him on his slayer seventy seven fold & the people of those days believed him.> The <from Seth down however> is the human race is descended from Seth – his children in a direct line to Noah were virtuous so that one Enoch was taken up into heaven. he had other descendants however who were the most wicked of the sons of man – so that it is affirmed that however the present race may haved erred from the paths of Righteousness thay cannot even in their minds form an idea of the crime that existed in those times.

Now the Jewish God we must suppose <could> did not foresee what kind of beings men would turn out to be else of course he <must> would have altered the whole plan of things from the beginning – but when he found that his creation which when he first made <it> he declared to be good disappointed his fond hopes in so cruel a manner it repented him that he had ever made man & he determined to destroy them & all other animals, who perhaps took after their masters in their way of life, from off the face of the earth.

But, while he was thus exasperated it was the good fortune of one Noah the only virtuous man & a descendant of Seth *to find grace in his sight*. <Noah was commanded to pre and as a last hope God commanded him to preach to his bretheren. This was however with him> God determined to save him & therefore ordered him to build a clumsy kind of machine called an ark, made of wood & to retire into it with his wife & his sons with their wives – he was to take with him seven of each sort of *clean* animal & two of the unclean with food for all this large company to last them forty days and nights – the ark was –

All ancient mythology has agreed in an account of a deluge which at one time drowned the world & its inhabitants – Deucalion & Pyrrha except that they are by far more amiable persons have a strong resemblance to Noah & his wife. <their being saved at the top of a high mountain> The Greek fable is, however, in much better taste than the Jewish. This concordance of circumstance renders it very probable that some great & unexampled flood did at once time destroy the inhabitants of <as> a part of Asia this might have been the violent eruption of the Mediteranean sea – but it impossible to form an thing but conjectures on such a subject. Be this as it may the Jewish historian continues to relate that God *opened the windows of heaven* and broke up *the fountain of the great deep* and overwhelmed the whole world with a frightful deluge of waters which lasted with such violence for forty days & nights that the tops of highest mountains were <destroyed> covered everything was destroyed but the Ark which floated on the surface of the waters – if any vessels <ships were built> existed in those days they were all wrecked. for God would show no mercy to any but Noah & his sons.

In forty days the rain ceased <as as the> & a great wind was sent from heaven to dry the earth – such were Jewish notions upon natural objects – if the water was thus evaporated we must suppose it to have been very cloudy weather for some time afterwards. Noah as he observed the flood to abate sent out a raven who did not come back he afterwards sent a dove who returned with a branch of olive in his beak – a good sign – accordingly in a very short time the ark rested on dry ground and God ordered its inhabitants to quit it & promised this favoured race as a peculiar mark of <favour> kindness that for their sake he would never more drown the earth <again> but when one day it must be again destroyed it should be by fire & but <only burn it> as a <sign> *token of this covenant with earth* he placed a rainbow in heaven (a proof that it had not entirely ceased raining) and told Noah that he might remember every time he looked at that his <might remember> God promised that he would never inflict such watry punishment on earth again. Noah in gratitude made a scarifice of one of every clean beast on an alter before the Lord. a rather imprudent action considering the scarcity of animals.

Section III

Now we may suppose that although Noah was very tolerably virtuous in comparison with his wicked fellow creatures he had not entirely escaped the contagion of their vices. Accordingly we soon find that (perhaps in his rapture at his deliverance) he having planted a vineyard *drank of the wine and was drunken* Such are the feelings of a Jew & befitting the father of their race but surely the sentiments of Deucalion & Pyrrha were of a much <softe gentler> milder and more amiable nature when they wept for the loss of their fellow creatures & companions. Soldiers are a brutal and unatural race of men but hard must be the heart of that man who could look with an unmoistened eye on a field after the day of battle who would not <sympathize> conjure in his imaginations a thousand ties of of affection snapt a thousand dreams of happiness blasted <in their very beginning> for ever. but ten thousand times harder than a rock of flint must that heart be whom a world destroyed a human race cut of for ever from the face of the earth would not lead to meditation & gentleness.

When <Noah was> the reason of Noah was destroyed in this disgraceful manner – he was, to use the historians own expression, uncovered in his tent. His son Ham who was also saved from the deluge on account of his virtue laughed at him & called his brothers to be witnesses – they had more decent feelings they took a garment & walking backwards covered their father. When Noah came to his senses and <found> learnt how it had all happened he did not punish Ham but according to the laudable custom of the Jews cursed his posterity to the latest generation with the curse of servitude. <This was>

The sons of Noah divided the descendants of Shem peopled Asia – those of Japhet Europe and Ham had Africa for his portion – perhaps it is the consequences of Noahs curse that renders the inhabitants of that <part> quarter of the globe so uncivilized even in present day. This curse also <must> must quiet the conciences of those traders in negroes who believe in the Jewish mythology.

America was not then discovered else of course Noah would have had a forth son –

Soon after the flood man again sinned murder and other crimes became frequent and such was their presumption that in a short time they agreed to build a high tower & by this means to scale the heavens the <pala> seat of God himself – this was a very bold attempt & not at all relished by the deity who the historian makes thus to address himself to the other inhabitants of Heaven – *Behold the people is one, & they have all one language; & this they begin to do: & now nothing will be restrained from them which they have immagined to do. Go to, let us go down, & there confound their language, that they may not understand one anothers speech* – this project was approved of & executed – it succeeded and the sons of man leaving their tower were scattered on the face of the earth

The origen of the Jews is <uncertain> doubtful. Nations must rise

<& play a distinguished part> to a certain degree of eminence before their fellow men will <deign to> trouble themselves with enquiries concerning their existence A nation must be possessed of a force capable <by its forces> of acting in a hostile manner <& by their numbers of opposing some boastful & murderous conqueror & then> it must have acquired a capacity for mischief and destruction before <historians can flourish> neighbouring <nations> states will take an interest in their history. It is true that the Jews were not a harmless & unoffending race the were warlike & sanguinary but there numbers were small and their depredations could only be committed on a few adjoining states too insignificant in themselves to become the historians of their troublesomes neighbours. The Jews were often slaves & always tributaries but their masters disdained a race who were only <eminent> distinguished <by their singular customs> by a preeminent cruelty of disposition their territory was as a speck in the mighty empires of the east & It was not till the Romans had taken an interrest in <these> their affairs that they immerged from obscurity. It was not till they had become rebels to this power that they excited any curiosity. Tacitus therefore is the first author who in recording the siege of their city[2] took some pains in his discovering their origen and early history <drew them into the observations of the ancients>

It is true that they have historians of their own but, the first part of their history more particularly is so interspersed or rather so entirely made up of fables that it requires the nicest discrimination to cull out the little truth that may by chance be scattered among the gross falsehoods & inconceivable absurdities of the Pentateuque.

<They themselves relate a strange story of their being captives in Egypt and in a short space of four hundred years that they here multiplied to such a degree in 400 years one family that from an inconsiderable number they outnumbered the natives of the soil.> Pharoah the King of Egypt frightened (as well he might be) at so prodigious an increase ordered all their male infants to be destroyed. this command was so faithfully executed that for a considerable period they were only able to save two brothers Moses & Aaron destined to be the deliveres of their race. for <stranger as it may appear> although according to their own account <although> they far exceeded the Egyptians in number they were held by this people in the most degrading <bond. bondag> servitude.

Moses when he grew up murdered an Egyptian & was obliged to abscond for some time <during> towards the conclusion of which period God bad him go to Pharoah and demand leave that the whole Jewish people might be permitted to go to keep a religious feast in the wilderness & <that they might by this excellently contrived stratagem> they might by these means contrive to steal off altogether from their masters. as a sign also of his being sent by a deity God told him that if he cast <down> his rod <crook> to the ground it should be turned into a serpent.

This plan did not however succeed for Pharoah had magicians at his court who could also change their rods into serpents and although the King heartily wished to get rid of the Jews the God of this nation wishing to make a display of his power hardened his heart so that he would not let them depart. <seven dreadful plagues did> Moses by the power he had acquired from Jehovah inflicted seven dreadful plagues upon the unfortunate Egyptians <seven times did> – Pharoah seven times indeavoured <strenuously> to give his consent – it was in vain – Jehovah hardened his heart – the productions of his kingdom <was> were devoured by locusts several times <were> the <poor> animals possessed by poor husbandmen were doomed & the country suffer death – Jehovah himself walked through <all> the country & destroyed the first born of all the Egyptians (taking care to have a mark placed on the doors of his favourite Jews for fear of a mistake) and at length <he> Pharoah was allowed to do what he most earnestly desired and the Jews <stealing & borrowing what ever> robbing the good natured Egyptians of whatever they could borrow from them departed much to the satisfaction of the king.

Jehovah however was not satisfied. should he <loose> part with his lawful prey – could he give over tormenting while he had power. he determined to try once more if he could not heap the already overflowing measure of his barbarities & utterly destroy the ill fated king of Egypt.

For this purpose he caused the Jews to turn their steps to the red sea which he divided so that the waters stood as a wall to the right and to the left and the Jews walked on dry ground. Poor Pharoah whose heart he had again hardened was drowned by the flowing of the waters back into their natural channel as he attempted to follow & bring back the favoured people of this merciless <God> deity.

But it is not my intention to trace the Jewish historian through his long maze of absurdities. I wish <merely> to give a credible account of this people. <mearly> adopting the facts that they relate & rejecting their fictions this is not an easy task as no light is cast on the subject of the history of any neighbouring nation – they were a band of robbers – hated by the lesser & despised by the greater powers that surrounded them – Tacitus gives only a superficial account & <in everything else> when we would enlarge upon that we must depend upon the history they give of themselves <follow in their account> in the pentateuque.

<According to the History their given> In this strange <history consisting merely of a> they relate that they remained forty years in the wilderness after their departure from Egypt – where their leader gave them laws & they practised all kinds of enormities – from <such extravagant accounts> from this record of deeds of the most abominable & sanguinary nature <here recorded> from <which> the extravagant account they give of their own cruelties which fortunately for the world at that time they were not in a condition to practise <we> turn with pleasure to Tacitus who gives the following

It is impossible to reconcile these contradictory statements Moses himself affirms (if we are to believe that he was the author of the Pentateuque <was written by him>) that he was never allowed to enter the promised land – yet he was their leader for many years giving them laws & endeavouring to <overcome> soften their singular & <abominable> sanguinary dispositions. It is very possible that although they entered Canaan they <were never> had not for a considerable period force sufficient to subdue a permanent resting place for themselves but lived as Arabians on rapine and <plunder> murder.

But no robber ever equalled them in barbarity. every prisoner that fell into their hands was most barbarously murdered neither sex or age was spared except in <some> few instances when their decrease of population rendered it politic to preserve some of their female captives.

Fortunately they were seldom victors. their defeats they record as punishments sent on them <from> by their <bloodthirsty God> jealous & revengeful deity – but they were numerous & [?signal] – often reduced to the most abject slavery they called in vain <upon> for succour from the God of their fathers upon that Jehovah who they affirmed had delivered them from out of the hands of the Egyptians.

During the life of Moses they were seldom successful & it does not appear that their attempts <more from force> extended beyond the providing themselves with necessary provisions & the pleasure of steeping their swords in the blood of their enemies. Joshua was the successor of Moses <they affirm> who with out the talent of his predecessor excelled him in cruelty of disposition and that unaccountable hatred towards all other nations which has <ev> been the characteristic of the Jews in all ages. His first exploit was the taking of the little town called Jerico. This paltry success seems to have surprised none so much as the Jews themselves they declared it to be miraculous – that the sun itself had stood still to afford light for the glorious enterprize – the walls they affirmed had been cast down <by> before them by the express command of God himself. But alas! they make but sorry fables <the sun did not need a command not to move> it is more than probable that there were never any walls to Jerico which was scarcely more than a village & it would have been altogether a much greater miracle if the sun and moved at the command of their leader & if if had it is probable it would have caused greater devastation than the destruction of a few sticks plastered with mud placed round a village whose name would have ever been unknown bu for the extroardinary popularity that the Jewish history has acquired of late years.

after the sack of Jerico & the murder of its inhabitants Joshua went against the Town of [?A]i – in the<ir> first attack the Jews <attempted they> were defeated with great loss but the next day Joshua employed a stratagem – he planted am ambush near the town – & then by a feigned flight they drew off the men of Ai from the immediate defense of their walls – on a signal given by him his soldiers in ambush entered the defenceless town fired it & then attacked their enemies in the rear who surprised & dismayed were dispersed & mascerkered with out mercy –

their King who fell into the hands of Joshua was hung & his body contemtuously cast among the ruins of his town.

These successes alarmed the little tribes of Palestine who, either wandered <about Palestine> or fixed in villages or encampments were harmless from their poverty & the smallness of their numbers. But <they> at the <Jews who wr alarmed> destruction of Jericho & Ai the <five> leaders of 5 different tribes leagued together against the common enemy – their first attempt was against the Gebeonites who had treacherously allied themselves with the bloodthirsty strangers. The Jews however called upon by their allies & led by Joshua overcame their enemies and persued them with an insatiable barbarity – <they destroyed> The tribes were dispersed & their leaders hung.

The Jews performed several other exploits of this kind among the neighbouring tribes & by these means possessed themselves of a small territory <which th> were they built themselves villages and established their law which was as yet in a very imperfect state. The priesthood was established which was ever of considerable importance in the Jewish history – for high priests taking advantage of the belief that Moses had instilled of the watchful eye of God being perpetually on them innovated on the power of their leaders till for a time they became the sole governors of the people. Joshua died in this interval of peace <he was a success>. & for a considerable time nothing more is recorded of the Jews than that they kept to the worship of their fathers & obeyed the laws of Moses.

as the number of the Jews encreased so they endeavoured to enlarge their territory by new conquests – nothing can be more uninterresting than the details of the warfare of this little people – the tribe of Judah possessed themselves of Jerusalem – which afterwards became the Capital of Judea – the <the other tribes> other tribes also <enlarged> took a few villages where they established themselves but the Historian expressly relates that they did not drive out the conquered natives but dwelt with them either on equal terms or <as> making the tributaries

This intercourse caused a change which Moses had always dreaded – and which he had endeavoured to provide against by many sanguinary laws – they no longer adhered to their own peculiar worship – but <either adoring the gods of the surrounding tribes or mixed> <or customs> insensibly mingled the idolatry of other nations <mixed> with their their purely deistical notions – <and> they gave gods of wood & of stone as companions to their powerful & immaterial Jehovah and violated the jewish law by worshipping the forms of animals <as> at this time they <were very unfortunate &> suffered numerous disastors in the chance of war often becoming tributaries <of> or slaves & the Jewish Historian represents them as the punishment of their God revenging his violated dignity. It is very probable that the customs of other nations mingling with their own they lost much of that ferocity & courage which so peculiarly characterised them in the times of Moses & Joshua. and each captivity doubtless diminished

the<ir> ideas they had formed of their own powers & that love of
lawless freedom which <is> the most irrisistable barrier against the
encroachments of a conqueror.

These several captivities did not each of them endure any great
length of time From time to time there arose to the aid of the people
some bold conspirator who delivered his countrymen from their
oppressors – murder & the violation of laws otherwise sacred was
in old times deemed pardonable in the avenger of his country and as
<sordid> the Jewish laws <which> peculiarly inculcated that hatred
and destruction of ones enemies so contrary to the theory yet so
consonant to the practice of the [?Morderns – <the means therefore
that> it is not to be supposed therefore that these barbarians spared
either bloodshed or treachery in the pursuit of <liberty> freedom.
<For what could be so dear to a rambling nation whose existen> Do
not let them be reprobated for this let us sympathise even with these
bloodthirsty robbers in an ardent lover of Liberty Let us admire the
daring assassin that entered the labour of the king of [?Moal] and
let us excuse the ungentle Deborah when she drove the nail into
the head of Sisera but while we approve of the murders of a petty
arrabian tribe shall we reprobate those acts performed by civilized
beings who horror struck even in the very deed shed the blood of
man for the benefit of man – who have commited unhallowed acts
for the love of their <Libert> country & who while their bosoms
panted for Liberty shrunk with human feelings from that deed
which was to ensure its blessings to so many fellow creatures.

But let us return to the Jews.

The Phoenicians or as they themselves stile them the Philistines
were always the most powerful enemies that the Jews had to
encounter – <after passing after> warfare was continually carried on
between them and <for a time> generally with manifest advantage
to the Philistines <who indeed held them> who in the first rise of the
Jews often held the unfortunate and barbarous people in captivity
for a long succession of years. <for the first of these captivity>

The first <bondages> time that the Jews submitted to them they
were continued in bondage for eighteen years before they endeavoured by any revolt to shake off their oppression. Jephthah was the
first chief who assembling some forces led the Israelites against the
enemy. I mention this particular revolt from a curious circumstance
connected with <which> it related by the Jewish historian <relates>
the truth of which no contradiction in the statement or manifest
falsehood leaves us room to doubt.

on the eve of the first battle Jephthah implored the assistance of his God – vowing in case of success to sacrifise at his alter the frist of his household who should come out to greet his return.

He was victorious <and I but> but to blast his triumph on his return his daughter hastening to welcome her fathers safe return was the first of his household who approached him <Jephthah>. the unfortunate man dared not break the vow which he had made to <his> the merciless deity whom he worshipped alas! my daughter he exclaimed do you also come to trouble me – I have vowed a vow to Jehovah and I must sacrifise my child – I dare not retract. The enemies of my country are overcome said the maid & Jehovah has <received your> accepted the sacrifise do my father as you have vowed – <Let me go to> I only entreat you to allow me to retire for two months to mourn my fate then will I present myself a willing sacrifise to our God. Jephthah consented for two months was she spared & then the unhappy & fanatic father sheathed his sword in the bosom of his child. a frightful <The Bible mentions no othe human sacrifise this seems> instance of the devastation a cruel and sanguinary religion commits on the affections of the heart. Could the man love that God at whose alter<s> he shed the life blood of his innocent child no – a cold shuddering fear must have frozen his feelings the Deity must have appeared a cruel & remorseless fiend whom he <dared not disobey> could most please by the offer of a human victim & whom he dared not disapoint of his promised prey – These are the genuine works of Religion. Mexitili – Jehovah – ye have have all of ye your worshippers – Religion is the triumphant & bloodstained emperor of the world – who with canting hipocrisy casts his <faults> crimes on superstition – a shadow – a name who acts <his> a part in hiding from the wellmeaning & credulous the enormities committed by <that> the daemon king.

The unfortunate Jews reaped little benefit from so horrid a sacrifise – for about thirty years no new <warfares> battles are recorded except a civil war which cut off according to the Jewish records 42 thousand of the vanquished party. at the end of that time the Israelites again became bondsmen of the Philistines. <which to their aid> Samson arose among them to their aid. He did them little permanent service & in short time fell into the hands of the enemy – He is however the Hercules of the Jews – God they said had himself descended from heaven to fortell his birth – he was invincible with his single & unarmed hand he slew multitudes. <In vain> he was in vain confined by bonds he burst all revenging himself an hundred fold upon his enemies – But like the Grecian demigod he at length fell a victim to female artifice. He married a Philistine of uncommon beauty – who took advantage of [?sucurity] & sleep to deliver him into the hands of her countrymen who deprived him of his eyesight & then employed him <in> as a slave in their public mills – how long he languished in this wretched state is uncertain – the Jews dignify the story of his death by the destruction of a Philistine Temple – but it is impossible to discover any semblance of truth in many of their fables – it may be supposed that their hero died in prison or perhaps he fell in endeavouring to revenge himself on his masters – However it may be his life thus wonderfully foretold by God – his strength thus miraculously vested in his unshorn locks availed little to ameliorate the condition of his unfortunate countrymen

Appendix B:
Shelley's Reply to Leslie's
Short and Easy Method

The text of this essay is taken from from *Proserpine and Midas: Two Unpublished Mythological Dramas*. Ed., A Koszul (London: Humphrey Milford, 1922).

The necessity of a Belief in the
Heathen Mythology

—

to a Christian

—

If two facts are related not contradictory of equal probability & with equal evidence, if we believe one we must believe the other.

1st. There is as good proof of the Heathen Mythology as of the Christian Religion.

2ly. that they [do] not contradict one another.

Con[clusion]. If a man believes in one he must believe in both.

Examination of the proofs of the Xtian religion – the Bible & its authors. The twelve stones that existed in the time of the writer prove the miraculous passage of the river Jordan. The immoveability of the Island of Delos proves the accouchemennt of Latona – the Bible of the Greek religion consists in Homer, Hesiod & the fragments of Orpheus &c. – All that came afterwards to be considered apocryphal – Ovid=Josephus – of each of these writers we may believe just what we cho[o]se.

To seel in these Poets for the creed & proofs of mythology which are as follows – Examination of these – 1st with regard to proof – 2 in contradiction or conformity to the Bible – various apparitions of God in that Book[–] Jupiter considered by himself – his attributes – disposition [–] acts – whether as God revealed himself as the Almighty to the Patriarchs & as Jehovah to the Jews he did not reveal himself as Jupiter to the Greeks – the possibility of various revelations – that he revealed himself to Cyrus.

The inferior deities – the sons of God & the Angels – the difficulty of Jupiter's children explaned away – the imaginaiton of the poets – of the prophets – whether the circumstance of the sons of God living with women being related in one sentence makes it more probable than the details of Greek – Various messages of the Angels – of the deities – Abraham, Lot or Tobit. Raphael [—] Mercury to Priam – Calypso & Ulysses – the angel w^d then play the better part of the two whereas he now plays the worse. The ass of Balaam – Oracles – Prophets. The revelation of God as Jupiter to the Greeks – a more successful revelation than that as Jehovah to the Jews – Power, wisdom, beauty, & obedience of the Greeks – greater & of longer continuance – than those of the Jews. Jehovah's promises worse kept than Jupiter's – the Jews or Prophets had not a more consistent or decided notion concerning after life & the Judgements of God than the Greeks [—] Angels disappear at one time in the Bible & afterwards appear again. The revelation to the Greeks more complete than to the Jews – prophesies of Christ by the heathens more incontrovertible than those of the Jews. The coming of X. a confirmation of both religions. The cessation of oracles a proof of this. The Xtians better off than any but the Jews as blind as the Heathens – Much more conformable to an idea of [the] goodness of God that he should have revealed himself to the Greeks than that he left them in ignorance. Vergil & Ovid not truth of the heathen Mythology, but the interpretation of a heathen – as Milton's Paradise Lost is the interpretation of a Christian religion of the Bible. The interpretation of the mythology of Vergil & the interpretation of the Bible by Milton compared – whether one is more inconsistent than the other – In what they are contradictory. Prometheus desmotes quoted by Paul [–] all religion false except that which is revealed – revelation depends upon a certain degree of civilization – writing necessary – no oral traditon to be a part of faith – the worship of the Sun no revelation – Having lost the books [of] the Egyptians we have no knowledge of their peculiar revelations. If the revelation of God to the Jews on Mt Sinai had been more peculiar & impressive than some of those to the Greeks they w^d not immediately have worshiped a calf – A latitude in revelation – How to judge of prophets – the proof [of] the Jewish Prophets being prophets.

The only public revelation that Jehovah ever made of himself was on Mt Sinai – Every other depended upon the testimony of a very few & usually of a single individual – We will first therefore consider the revelation of Mount Sinai. Taking the fact plainly it happened thus. The Jews were told by a man whom they believed to have supernatural powers that they were to prepare for that God wd reveal himself in three days on the mountain at the sound of a trumpet. On the 3rd day there was a cloud & lightening on the mountain & the voice of a trumpet extremely loud. The people were ordered to stand round the foot of the mountain & not on pain of death to infringe upon the bounds – The man in whom they confided went up the mountain & came down again bringing them word

Appendix C:
The Byron Manuscripts

Mary Shelley's first 'official' work for Byron was on the two poems "Ode on Venice" and *Mazeppa*, published together on June 28, 1819. Of the first piece, a poem of 160 lines, McGann has found only Byron's intermediate draft, dated July 26, 1818 – July 27, 1818 (Morgan Library) and Mary Shelley's fair copy with Byron's corrections (John Murray) which was used as the copy text for the first edition. He maintains that all these corrections, save one, are of Mary's miscopying from the intermediate draft. However, there are a number of small changes which Shelley undertook in the fair copy and which Byron allowed to remain. We find that in nineteen cases, Shelley replaced Byron's capitalization of a noun with the lower case. In four cases she attempted a similar change but Byron changed it back. She also reversed this process in three cases which Byron also allowed. However, he did not permit similar liberties with whole words; Shelley attempted to substitute a total of six words for those of the poet's originals, either mistakenly or intentionally, which he did not allow.

However, with the punctuation of the poem, we see a very different pattern. Including the elimination of end-of-line dashes, the addition of internal dashes, commas and full stops, Shelley made 54 changes which Byron evidently approved. What is more, in *Mazeppa* Shelley removed 244 of the original 417 end of line dashes, and also made 19 additional punctuation changes and additions (including the insertion of quotation marks in the relevent places). This evidence suggests that Byron allowed Shelley to "tidy-up" the drafts and to perform the same sort of service, vis à vis punctuation, that PBS often left to his various agents in London. However, there is also evidence that Byron came to trust Shelley's judgement further after her copying of the "Ode on Venice".

In *Mazeppa* we find some changes in the corresponding fair copy (the Library of the University of Leeds) and rough draft (Morgan Library) that though still small, represent a significant enlargement of Shelley's responsibility. Though it may be unattributable specifically to Shelley's earlier alterations, Byron's draft shows relatively far fewer arbitrary capitalizations of nouns than in the "Ode to Venice". If he altered his style, or simply addressed himself to *Mazeppa* with greater grammatical discipline, one may speculate that he was influenced by Shelley's regularization of this propensity in her treatment of the first poem. Byron often complained of the difficulty of finding an efficient amanuensis who could decipher his "scrawl". Shelley evidently fitted the bill and her later work on the confusing PBS manuscripts must be further testimony to her particular skill in this area.

But *Mazeppa* shows some more interesting evidence. At line 57 Byron begins a description of Mazeppa, the "Cossack Prince" caring for his tired horse at the end of the day. Before he provides food and bedding for himself, he sees to the needs of his "courser". This episode is very important, a foreshadow to the doomed man's relationship with another horse which makes up the central narrative of the poem. Byron draws Mazeppa's treatment of his animal with extreme care. Thus, it is particularly interesting to see how Shelley not only understands the dynamic of the poem, but improves upon Byron's thought. The change is quite simple. At line 63, of the horse, the draft reads, that Mazeppa " . . . joyed to hear how well he fed". Shelley changes this to, " . . . and joyed to *see* how well he fed" (italics mine), thus underscoring Mazeppa's personal care of his horse – he makes certain that he sees with his own eyes, rather than hearing from a servant, that the exhausted horse is fit enough to eat heartily. Mazeppa is seen even more sympathetically and, we will later discover a further echo: the wild horse that bears the young Mazeppa strapped to his back eventually dies of exhaustion and hunger. Mazeppa's cruel lesson has made him a more kind and sensitive man. Byron lets this change stand and it was published as such.

At line 301 Shelley clarifies Byron's sense by adding an internal dash and a plural. The draft reads, "My days & night were nothing all/ Except that hour – which doth recall/In the long lapse from youth to age". Shelley modifies the line slightly, "My days and nights were nothing – all/Except that hour, which doth recall . . . ". The first correction is almost certainly an oversight on Byron's part but Shelley's insertion of a dash highlights the exception – the exception that is *Mazeppa*'s tale – and signals the beginning of his terrible story. When Shelley changes Byron's "But" to "And" eight lines later and again improves the sense, the poet also lets it stand.

In a more complicated modification, at line 475 of the draft and

395 of the fair copy, Shelley offers Byron: " . . . Which clings fast like stiffened gore" instead of his original: "Which clings to it like stiffened gore". She also appears to suggest "stains it then . . . ", but this insertion, above the line, could refer to line 394 above which she had copied accurately as "And stains it with a lifeless red". This Byron crossed out and replaced with "Discoloured". He likewise crosses out the two alternatives for the following line ("clings fast" and "stains it then") and inserts "Which stains thereon". Though he did not accept Shelley's alternatives for the line, he did not return to his original version and recognized, as she did, that this first thought was inferior. She was able to coax a better line by pointing out to the poet the inadequacy of the first.[1]

Shelley's last, non-grammatical change is found at line 828 (fair copy). She replaces Byron's "But those she called had not awoke" to " . . . were not awake . . . ". Byron recognized this improvement and let it stand. Shelley's fair copy was not used as the copy text. Though they are not extant, McGann maintains that Byron corrected proofs for *Mazeppa* and returned them to Murray with the first and second canto proofs of *Don Juan* in May 1818.

Werner

Written between December 1821 and January 1822, during the interruption of the composition of *Don Juan*. (Resumed *DJ* with Canto VI.) Published November 23, 1822. Draft at Morgan Library, Shelley fair copy at Murray.

Werner was the last large assignment which Shelley completed before taking up her commission on *Don Juan*. Unlike her other fair copies, Byron's corrections show far more insistence on the details of his draft. He changed back to upper case many of the first letters of nouns that Shelley had adjusted in the fair copy and which had almost always been approved in *Mazeppa* and would be approved in *Don Juan*. Though she was allowed to make nearly 400 changes from Byron's upper case to lower case (in a poem of over 3000 lines), Byron restored to upper case over 140 of Shelley's changes. Shelley also attempted to change isolated words, reorder some words, insert or remove definite articles, prepositions and some punctuation. Of the 41 changes that Shelley introduced (a few almost certainly simple mistakes on her part), and not taking into account end-of-line dashes, Byron allowed only 9 to stand.

However, Byron seems to have taken Shelley's advice in regard to the stage directions. Shelley regularizes the directions by taking them out of the margins and incorporating them, where she deemed appropriate, into the body of the text. She also neatened it and simplified; Byron's first stage direction in Act III reads, "Scene The same Hall in the same palace-from whence the secret passage leads-which is mentioned in Act first-" and Shelley improves with,

"Scene I
A Hall in the same palace. from whence the secret passage leads."

She even added an original stage direction when she has Ida reply "Peevishly to Rodolph" in Act IV. Byron allowed this addition to remain.

One can only speculate as to why Byron exhibited such attention to detail in his review of the fair copies in the case of *Werner*. He did not object to the improvement of the stage directions because they were superior to his first thoughts. However, he did not let Shelley get away with the usual number of minor changes. If Byron had offered her the *Werner* commission as a fair-copyist's test before taking up the remainder of *Don Juan* (from Canto 6 onwards) then he was naturally being vigilant in his corrections with a view to learning Shelley's habits and perhaps teaching her his desired copying technique, as her former work for him had been undertaken nearly four years previously. If this is so – that Shelley was being auditioned for the job – it is clear that Byron took the role of copyist very seriously, if only for his important work to come. It also becomes clear that though he was watching carefully, Byron was not uniformly against Shelley's offer of improvements. On the contrary, she persevered quite forcefully, as we shall see in *Don Juan*, in offering her own thoughts despite Byron's initial, stringent test.

Don Juan

Shelley's largest and most important project for Byron was of course the fair-copying of *Don Juan*. Byron had copied the first five cantos himself. No doubt he was much relieved to employ Shelley and the generosity that many have read into his offer of work to the poor widow was almost certainly balanced by self-interest. He had used Shelley before and he trusted her. She worked quickly and accurately (she received Cantos VI,VII,VIII and IX at the end of August/beginning of September 1822 and returned them to Byron with the fair copies on the 7th and 10th of September) and she was not afraid to point out his mistakes. Indeed, Shelley offered editorial advice to the poet freely. Years later, when she was editing and seeing through the press Trelawny's *Adventures of a Younger Son*, she cautioned him against retaining episodes and expressions that might offend women readers – " . . . I have named all the objectionable passages, & I beseech you to let me deal with them as I would with Ld Byrons Don Juan – when I omitted all that hurt my taste . . . " (December 27, 1830).

Unfortunately only the fair copies of Cantos VI through VIII are extant so that comparison between the poet's original and Shelley's work is limited to those three. It is possible that the additional omissions referred to in the letter to Trelawny were made in the later cantos, after Shelley had won Byron's trust and regard completely. We can only speculate as to the exact nature of those particular changes. However, even in these earlier cantos McGann maintains that "Mary Shelley plainly felt free to introduce minor alterations in the text on her own authority. The MSS. also show that Byron sometimes accepted her alterations, but at other times restored the original work".[2] What is more, before his departure to Greece, Byron authorized Shelley's fair copy of the last completed Canto (XVI) to be used as printer's copy.

Canto 6 (119 stanzas)

As with *Mazeppa* and the "Ode to Venice", Shelley regularizes Byron's punctuation and spelling. She removes a set of parentheses and many of the end of line and internal dashes, replacing them with commas as required. She also replaces the majority of the capitalized nouns with the lower case and only rarely does the poet correct her copy to his original spelling. However, from around stanza 48, he becomes more meticulous and allows approximately half of Shelley's lower-cases to remain. But as anticipated, there is more definite evidence of a greater responsibility on Shelley's part.

Immediately following stanza 2, Byron has offered two alternate couplets, each preceded by the centred word "or". Byron seems to be offering Shelley three possible endings to the stanza. The first, as original to the stanza: "Men with their heads reflect on this and that – /But women with their hearts or Heaven knows what!" is followed by:

or

Man with his head reflects – (as <   > tells –)
But Women with the heart – or something else. –

or

Man's pensive part is (now & then) the head –
Woman's the heart – or anything instead. –

As the second two alternatives do not appear in the fair copy, it seems clear that Shelley chose the original (and less risqué couplet) and Byron accepted her decision and it was published as such.

Shelley encountered the same kind of choice at stanza 19. She again chooses the original, "And no one Virtue yet, except starvation/Could stop that worst of vices, propagation", over the alternative (which is nearly identical to the lines crossed out by Byron and over-scored by the couplet above) – "And Nothing ever heard of save starvation/Could stop the tendency to propagation."

There are further examples of direct editorial contribution. At stanza 14, Shelley changes the order of Byron's list from "kisses, embraces, sweet words & – all that" to "kisses – sweet words, embraces and all that". She does the same at stanza 22 changing the original, " . . . is Mind or Soul . . . " to " . . . is soul or mind . . . ". Likewise, at stanza 29 she changes "Yet he at times could not . . . " to "Yet he could not at times . . . ", the poet allows all three alterations to stand and it was published as such.

At stanza 15 Shelley improves the sense of the concluding couplet by rearranging Byron's underlining. Reading originally as "A sincere Woman's breast, for *over* Warm/Or Over cold annihilates the charm.", Shelley underlines "warm" and "cold" and removes the underline from "over", thus underscoring the poet's joke in the representation of romantic extremes. Shelley does this a second time at stanza 54 (stanza 55 as published). Reading originally, " . . . *not* what was/But what was not . . . ", Shelley underlines "was not" thereby emphasizing the second line's function as counterpoint to the first. In both cases the published version reflects Shelley's changes.

As I have suggested, it is also clear that Shelley considered herself an editorial censor. In addition to her letter to Trelawny, one finds evidence in the fair copy which points to her role as guardian of taste. Three separate times, at stanzas 15, 66 and 86, Shelley attempted to substitute "heart" for Byron's chosen word "breast". Though Byron did not allow these particular changes to stand, it seems clear that Shelley must have found "breast" rather more anatomical than metaphorical. She did win her point at stanza 91 however. In the description of the reign of Catherine of Russia, Byron refers to the " . . . Greatest of all Sovereigns and Whores". Shelley refuses to spell out the word and writes "w – res" instead. Byron allows this delicacy, wise in the face of potentially outraged women readers, to stand, in the fair copy and in print. Only the newest editions of the poem restore the full spelling. He may have seen that Shelley was not simply prudish, but had the poem's commercial success in mind, a goal similar to that in her editing of the PBS poetry.

Canto 7 (87 stanzas)

It is clear that Byron checked the fair copies very carefully, though with the exception of Canto 16 none were used as printer's copy. It is impossible to say whether he physically compared the fair copies to his originals, but where his corrections become more persistent and trivial, it may be supposed that he was working with both copies. Nevertheless, his examination of Shelley's work was thorough – he consistently corrects her erratic spelling – and he doubtless considered her contributions with care. Those that he did allow to stand were recognized, clearly, as improvements, just as those that he did not approve were considered before being rejected. It is also important to understand that Shelley knew that she had the poet's trust and felt free to make the many small alterations that she did and that she persevered in the expression of her own judgement despite the rejection of a portion of her 'advice'.

Canto 7 appears to be the most carefully read of the three fair copies. In it Byron is most insistent on retaining the capitalization of nouns. Shelley successfully removes two sets of parentheses, changes the order of " . . . not only cuts up branch.." in stanza 41 to "cuts up not only branch . . . ". She also substitutes a number of individual words; "Mongst these" is changed to "Mongst them" in stanza 18, "erected" to "contracted" in stanza 51 (where the published version does not reflect Shelley's change) and "how'er" to "where'er" in stanza 62.

Over all, Shelley was allowed few changes in Canto 7. However, Byron's trust had not diminished. He still offers an alternative couplet ending to his amanuensis and at stanza 54 Shelley chooses it over the original. Thus, "For some were thinking of their wives and families/And others of themselves (as poet Samuel is)" is exchanged for "For some were thinking of their homes and friends/And others of themselves and latter ends". Shelley chooses the less controversial of the two couplets, avoiding the gentle send-up of a contemporary, probably Samuel Rogers (1763–1855), whom Byron actually admired. The first part of Roger's collection of verse tales, *Italy*, appeared in 1822. But " . . . thinking of themselves . . . " perhaps refers to his 1792 work, *The Pleasures of Memory*, in which the poet reflects on his childhood. Shelley's modified version of the couplet was that which was eventually published.

Canto 8 (141 stanzas)

With Canto 8 Shelley once again successfully changes the majority of Byron's capitalized nouns to the lower case. It appears that in this, the longest of the three copied cantos, Byron was not so concerned with the minute changes that had caught his attention in the comparatively short Canto 7. He is content to allow the spelling changes as well as the tidying of punctuation.

As in Cantos 6 and 7, Shelley attempted a few substitutions that Byron did not allow and some minor changes or word reordering that he did. What characterizes Shelley's editorial contribution to Canto 8 is of a higher order. As consistent with the preceding two cantos, Byron offers three alternate ending lines at stanza 87 (stanza 86 as published). Shelley chooses the second, "Which Satan angles with <for> Souls like flies", over "Which most of all doth Man characterize" or "The twigs that Satan [?lines] for with human <sh – >." Again, at stanza 123, Byron offers an alternative couplet ending instead of the very obscured and much crossed original. Shelley takes the second option. She chooses "Of burning streets like Moonlight on the water/Was imag<ed> back in blood, like the Sea of Slaughter" over "Of burning Cities, those full Moon<s> of Slaughter/Was imaged back in blood instead of Water" and it was published as such.

Yet in Canto 8 Shelley goes still further, providing Byron with the moral restraint that the public demanded. Thus, in stanza 77 she

modifies Byron's obscene and, more importantly, personally rele-
vant joke into an impersonal satire. Byron's draft reads, "Then being
taken by the tail – a taking/Fatal to warriors and to women . . . ",
a reference not only to sodomy but to the rumours that surrounded
the separation scandal. This self-destructive defiance on Byron's
part is changed by Shelley to, " . . . a taking/Fatal to bishops as
to soldiers . . . ", equally obscene one might argue but at least
open to alternative interpretation and removing Byron personally
from the fray. Byron no doubt realized that his original lines were
unpublishable – Shelley's version was wildly improper but has been
maintained in print. Byron no doubt anticipated Shelley's veto. He
may also have included the offending lines to tease his squeamish
editor, never intending to publish, but to share the joke – and the
self-mockery – with Shelley alone.

Shelley may have been amused by the poet's familiarity, but at
stanza 131 she balked at copying one of the poem's most objectionable passages. Byron had to fair-copy the missing lines himself –
"But six old damsels each of seventy years/Were all deflowered by
different grenadiers".

It is impossible to say whether Shelley was shown Byron's corrections of her fair copies and where he rejected her substitutions. It is
equally difficult to know whether she saw the printer's proofs made
from her copies that were sent to Byron from England. It is clear that
she was not restrained in her advice and corrections of the original
drafts. Her involvment in the entire project, and Byron's evident
trust and dependence on her services, make it not unlikely that he
paid her the courtesy of informing her of his alterations during the
publication process, rather than let her see them in print for the first
time.

Byron of course had other women copyists during his career. Teresa
Guiccioli acted for him, but objected strongly to *Don Juan* and even
succeeded in forcing a promise that he would abandon the poem
(for a period). Claire Clairmont copied Canto III of *Childe Harold*,
during the Geneva summer and it was used as printer's copy.
Byron's opinions of Claire are well known and his relations with
her, even during that summer, were strained.

Lady Byron also worked for her husband for a time and her
fair-copying of the *Hebrew Melodies* represents the only compete
body of work that is in any way analogous to Shelley's work on *Don
Juan*. Lady Byron's modifications on the fair copies of the individual

poems are so minute as to represent no change at all. "Saul", "Song of Saul", "All is Vanity", "When Coldness Wraps this suffering clay", "Were my bosom as false", "Herod's Lament" and "The Rout of Semnacherib" were compared, draft to fair copy, and no significant changes were found. Byron's drafts are in the Lovelace Deposit, Bodleian Library and Lady Byron's fair copies are at John Murray.

Appendix D:
The Late Novels: *Perkin Warbeck, Lodore* and *Falkner*

Shelley wrote three novels after *The Last Man*. Though none of these share the complexity, scope and ambition of the first three, they nonetheless feature certain themes and issues raised earlier in *Frankenstein, Valperga* and *The Last Man*. Though these novels portray Byronic characters and offer partial portraits of PBS and others of the familiar group, they are not as obsessively biographical. The personalities that so influenced Shelley's thoughts and fiction in her youth appear to grow less imaginatively potent. Four years passed between the composition of *The Last Man* (begun in 1824) and that of *Perkin Warbeck* in 1828. Shelley was thirty and the misery that she had suffered since PBS's death and her return to England in 1823 had somewhat abated. Percy Florence had become heir to the Shelley estates with the death of Harriet's son Charles, her allowance from Sir Timothy had been doubled and despite the discovery of her betrayal by her beloved friend Jane Williams, Shelley settled into a more comfortable life as a well-known woman of letters. She began to write short stories for the lucrative Annual market – expensively produced magazines such as *The Keepsake* and *The Bijou* designed as Christmas gifts. Her tortured sense of guilt, loss and intellectual resentment always inseparable from her feelings for PBS is missing from the late novels, making for more straight-forward story-telling and highlighting of themes, but also a corresponding loss of creative power.

The Fortunes of Perkin Warbeck (1830), is an historical romance in the popular and lucrative style of Walter Scott (though Shelley only received one hundred and fifty pounds from her publisher Henry Colburn for it). Shelley believed her eponymous hero to be the true Duke of York, rightful heir to the English throne and not the Dutch impostor who confessed all before his execution. Having escaped the same fate as his older brother – murdered by Richard III – Richard of York (Perkin) rallies support for his doomed cause and struggles for his throne and the White Rose against Henry VII. With the support of his noble followers, Richard's nomadic court moves across Europe, aided and encouraged by all those whose interest lies in Henry's downfall. Various Irish chieftains, the passionate Yorkist Lady Brampton, Richard's aunt Margaret of Burgundy, and James IV of Scotland offer him refuge, respect and armies; he even marries James' cousin Katherine Gordon in order to solidify his claim. Monina, a young Spaniard and childhood companion (a fictional character), inspired by a loyal fervour mixed with love, acts as a spy for his cause and like Evadne of *The Last Man*, devotes herself, with a 'man's' determination, to his struggle.

York is portrayed as outstandingly noble, immediately recognizable as a royal prince whose claim to the throne is instantly proven by his character and bearing; he is unequivocally heroic. But the novel, on the whole well constructed and simply told – Spark praises the rigorous research behind the novel as well as Shelley's unique and clever support of her theory[1] – has a serious issue at its centre, one raised in the earlier works. Richard has a just and noble cause, and his saint-like character shines in comparison to Henry's corruption, cruelty and greed. Nonetheless, Shelley still condemns the inevitable war and destruction that must result from Richard's pursuit of his claim. She recognizes the sanctity of the peace that the evil Henry's rule has brought to England and confronts Richard with his responsibility for its disruption. We hear Shelley's own voice and her familiar pacifism when Lord Surrey summons up the courage to speak his mind to the Duke of York:

My lord, the Roses contended in a long and sanguinary war, and many thousand of our countrymen fell in sad conflict. The executioner's axe accomplished what the murderous sword spared, and poor England became a wide, wide grave. The green-wood glade, the cultivated fields, noble castles, and smiling villages were changed to churchyard and tomb: want, famine, and hate ravaged the fated land. My lord, I love not Tudor, but I love my country: and now that I see plenty and peace reign over this fair isle, even though Lancaster be their unworthy viceregent, shall I cast forth these friends of man, to bring back the deadly horrors of unholy civil war? By the God that made me, I cannot? (sic) I have a dear wife and lovely children, sisters, friends, and all the sacred ties of humanity, that cling round my heart, and feed it with delight; these I might sacrifice at the call of honour, but the misery I must then endure I will not inflict on others; I will not people my country with widows and orphans; nor spread the plague of death from the eastern to the western sea.[2]

Surrey's plea is denied by the ambitious prince. It is not until his beloved wife Katherine expresses her similar view, and her contentment with a humble life as exile by his side, that Richard finally realizes that he might have chosen a different life. When he is finally captured and immured in the Tower to await execution, he is willing to sacrifice his pride to be reunited with his beloved wife. Again, we see Shelley's frustration with inflexible idealism; her portrayal of a hero prepared to sacrifice all that he believes in for a woman's protective love and the promise of a tranquil life together represents at least to some extent a pattern of behaviour that Shelley had searched eagerly for in PBS.

In this sentiment Shelley herself identifies with Katherine. Indeed the concluding chapter, devoted to Katherine's life at the court of Henry VII, is Shelley's apologia to her critics: PBS's friends. Accused by the loyal Edmund Plantagenet, a ruined man mourning a lost cause, of forsaking the memory of her noble husband to live in luxury in the household of his enemy, Katherine responds:

In my father's house – and when I wandered with my beloved outcast, I had no difficulty in perceiving, nor – God was so gracious to me – in fulfilling my duties. For in childhood I was cherished and favoured by all; and when I became a wife, it was no wonder that I should love and idolize the most single-hearted, generous, and kindly being that ever trod the earth. To give myself away to him – to be a part of him – to feel that we were an harmonious one in this discordant world, was a happiness that falls to the lot of few: – defeat, chains, imprisonment – all these were but shows; the reality was deep in our hearts, invulnerable by any tyrant less remorseless than death. If this life were the sum and boundary our being, I had possessed the consummation and fulfilment of happiness . . . . He was lost to me, my glory, and my good! Little could I avail to him now . . . I was forced to feel that I was alone: and as to me, to love is to exist; so in that dark hour, in the gaspings of my agony, I felt that I must die, if for ever divided from him who possessed my affections.

Years have passed since then. If grief kills us not, we kill it. Not that I cease to grieve; for each hour, revealing to me how excelling and matchless the being was who once was mine, but renews the pang with which I deplore my alien state upon earth. But such is God's will; I am doomed to a divided existence, and I submit . . . I must love and be loved. I must feel that my dear and chosen friends are happier through me. When I have wandered out of myself in my endeavour to shed pleasure around, I must again return laden with the gathered sweets on which I feed and live. Permit this to be, unblamed – permit a heart whose sufferings have been, and are, so many and so bitter, to reap what joy it can from the strong necessity it feels to be sympathized with – to love.[3]

Katherine's memories and her emotional needs are Shelley's. Fated to go on living without her husband, Shelley, like Katherine, also found herself dependent on a world that she had outraged in her carefree youth, when, with PBS's support, she had flouted convention. To alleviate her suffering, Shelley too had to carve out her niche of comfort, cultivate friends and intimacies and raise her son in an alien world. That she was able to succeed, and even excel in that world, irritated the self-dramatizing holders of PBS's flame.

But *Perkin Warbeck* did not bring the financial reward that Shelley had calculated on. Reviews were on the most part favourable, but the book did not sell, doomed perhaps, as Sunstein has pointed out, by the pre-empting of her story with the publication of a competing novel about the Pretender immediately before hers.

Lodore (1835), a novel of contemporary fashionable life, followed five years later. It is a more developed and certainly more socially acceptable version of *Mathilda*, but focuses nonetheless on a perilously close relationship between father and daughter – the heroine "inspired her father with more than a father's fondness" we are told.[4] Rupert Fitzhenry, Lord Lodore, removes his daughter Ethel from his vain and socially ambitious young wife and raises her in solitude in the wilds of America. He educates her to complete obedience, to be the perfect wife that has eluded him. His instruction of Ethel – in their isolated wilderness – is not unlike the education that Miranda receives from Prospero:

He taught her to scorn pain, but to shrink with excessive timidity from anything that intrenched on the barrier of womanly reserve which he raised about her. Nothing was dreaded, indeed, by her, except his disapprobation; and a word or look from him made

> her, with all her childish vivacity and thoughtlessness, turn as with a silken string, and bend at once to his will . . . she was always ready to give her soul away: to please her father was the unsleeping law of all her actions . . . [5]

Ethel returns to England following her father's death in a duel and falls in love with Edward Villiers, cousin of Horatio Saville, beloved of Ethel's mother, Cornelia Lodore. Cornelia meanwhile becomes more thoughtful and self-sacrificing, freed from the corrupting influence of her own grasping mother. After Edward and Ethel's marriage, the Villiers' financial problems reach a crisis and despite Ethel's inability to travel alone or to understand the use of money, she remains resolutely loyal to her idealistic husband. The pair evade duns and creditors and like Shelley and PBS's life following their return to London after the elopement, are hounded from lodging to lodging, the pair meeting only on Sundays, day of amnesty for the debtor. Eventually sent to a debtor's prison, Ethel and Edward are finally saved from their poverty by the intervention of Cornelia, who morally redeems herself sufficiently to win back the esteem of Saville whose Italian wife, married in the interim following Cornelia's coquettish jilting of him, conveniently dies.

Shelley highlights the fashionable ideal of the weak, dependent woman, particularly in contrast to the character of Fanny Derham, daughter of a childhood friend of Lodore. Fanny is bold and independent, devoted to books and learning with a "Superiority of intellect, joined to acquisitions beyond those usual even to men".[6] Her father, we are told, "contemplated the duties and objects befitting an immortal soul, and had educated his child for the performance of them."[7] By contrast "Ethel had received, so to speak, a sexual education. Lord Lodore had formed his ideal of what a wife ought to be, of what he had wished to find his wife, and sought to mould his daughter accordingly."[8] Cornelia is likewise crippled, the

> necessity of so conducting herself as to prevent the shadow of slander from visiting her, had continued this state of dependence during all her married life. She had never stept across the street without attendance; nor put on her gloves, but as brought to her by a servant.[9]

But it is Ethel and Cornelia who receive palpable reward in the novel. Ethel's loyalty is repaid by a return to comfortable protection and Cornelia's sacrifice of her fortune to her daughter's benefit (she secretly pays off Villier's debts) wins her the love and position of Horatio Saville, Viscount Maristow. By contrast, the independent but stolidly unglamourous Fanny Derham, is rewarded by nothing more than the author's commendation of her as a role model for young readers:

> Fanny Derham [can] be presented as a useful lesson, at once to teach what goodness and genius can achieve in palliating the woes of life, and to encourage those, who would in any way imitate her, by an example of calumny refuted by patience, errors rectified by charity, and the passions of our nature purified and ennobled by an undeviating observance of those moral laws on which all human excellence is founded – a love of truth in ourselves, and a sincere sympathy with our fellow-creatures.[10]

Ethel and Cornelia are Shelley's new women, not Fanny; they were probably more palatable to the popular market that she was aiming for. They are unthreatening – a far cry from Beatrice, Perdita or the Duchess of Windsor, and unhampered by the rigid principles and profound intelligence of the tragic Euthanasia. The woman of power and learning is no longer a romantic heroine.

The novel *Falkner* (1837) was Shelley's last, strikingly similar in plot and characterization to the one that preceded it. The novel presents a Byronic protagonist (not unlike the character of Falkland in *Caleb Williams*) though once again with a measure of Trelawny, tortured, appropriately, by a crime committed in the name of love. Having inadvertently caused the death of his beloved Alithea Rivers, since married to a cold and abusive husband, Falkner attempts suicide, but his hand is stayed by the "infant" Elizabeth Raby. He adopts the orphaned girl and raises her as his daughter. Coincidentally, Elizabeth meets and falls in love with Gerard Neville, distinctly reminiscent of PBS, whose life-long quest has been to find the agent of his mother's destruction, solve the mystery of her "flight" and disappearance and clear her beloved name of the charge of marital infidelity. The reader learns early on that Neville is the son of the wronged Alithea and the remainder of the novel's 1000 pages is devoted to the revelations that strike the various characters. Elizabeth may remain loyal to her father only at the cost of her lover; Neville discovers Falkner's "innocent" part in his mother's death, and the young couple devise a means of marrying despite the obvious moral complications.

The novel is replete with praise for the variety of entirely conventional womanly virtue already delineated in *Lodore*. Alithea, her mother, Elizabeth and her mother are praised for their timidity, docility, obedience and most significantly, fidelity to a man. They are all angelic, sensitive to an overwhelming degree, and completely in thrall – by choice – to the men that control their lives. "The divine stamp on woman is her maternal character".[11] Shelley's new women are raised onto a Victorian pedestal of dizzying height. Falkner is a keen worshipper of womanly virtue:

> To me there was something sacred in a woman's very shadow. Was she evil, I regarded her with the pious regret with which I might view a shrine desecrated by sacrilegious hands – the odour of sanctity still floated around the rifled altar; I never could regard them as mere fellow-creatures – They were beings of a better species, sometimes gone astray in the world's wilderness, but always elevated above the best among us.[12]

Falkner's paean is anticipated by Richard, Duke of York's praise for the loyal Monina; " . . . his heart whispered to him what a wondrous creation woman was – weak, frail, complaining when she suffers for herself; heroic fortitude and untired self-devotion are hers, when she sacrifices for him she loves".[13]

Shelley highlights such womanly virtues and their significance for her new type of heroine – new in Shelley's art but familiar to the romantic novel-reading public. Falkner finds a sterling governess and teacher for Elizabeth who does not simply impart the "masculine studies" of history and language, but teaches the importance of "needlework . . . as well as the careful inculcation of habits of neatness and order".[14] Thus, "Elizabeth escaped for ever the danger she had hitherto run of wanting those feminine qualities without which every woman must be unhappy – and, to a certain degree, unsexed".[15]

Elizabeth's crowning virtue is her devotion to Falkner and any fortitude that she possesses is exercised only in that devotion. Her identity is formed only in relationship to men, first Falkner, then Neville. Indeed, when the difficulties of her marriage to Neville are resolved, her adopted father writes to his future son-in-law,

"Come here, take her at my hand . . . you must be father as well as husband".[16] She is passed from the careful protection of one man to the next, her new relationship, supposedly mature, is little changed from the former.

Shelley's late fictions are unquestionably formulaic genre novels. Though Shelley found these novels the easiest to write, she was no longer striving to express new or complex ideas. She had resolved her paradoxical relationship to her father and husband with *The Last Man*. Though she continued to write fiction, in the shape of short stories, and contributed five volumes to *Lardner's*, she never entered the ideological-political fray again. She remained interested in politics in general (as her letters show) and her views were fundamentally liberal but such matters no longer engaged her passionately. She was finished with the intellectual and emotional struggle that had characterized all her previous work and she settled into an artistically unchallenging, but emotionally tranquil life.

Notes

CHAPTER 1: INTRODUCTION

1. Written in 1819, *Mathilda* was not published during Shelley's lifetime, and not until Elizabeth Nitchie's 1959 edition. It has been most recently published in *The Mary Shelley Reader*, eds, Betty T. Bennett and Charles E. Robinson (Oxford: Oxford University Press, 1990), pp. 175–246.
2. Charles E. Robinson's *Mary Shelley: Collected Tales and Stories*, 1976, has recently been reprinted as *Mary Shelley: Collected Tales and Stories, With Original Engravings* (Baltimore: Johns Hopkins University Press, 1990). In 1985 Hogarth Press republished *The Last Man*.
3. Helen Moore, *Mary Wollstonecraft Shelley* (Philadelphia: Lippincott, 1886), p. 286.
4. Safaa el-Shatar, *The Novels of Mary Shelley*, Salzburg Studies in English Literature: Romantic Reassessment, Vol. 59, ed., James Hogg (Salzburg: Institut für Englische und Literatur Universität Salzburg, 1977), p. 2.
5. Frederick L. Jones, ed., *The Letters of Mary Wollstonecraft Shelley* (Norman, Oklahoma: University of Oklahoma Press, 1945), Vol. I, p. xxx.
6. Mary Shelley, *The Last Man*, ed., Hugh Luke (Lincoln: University of Nebraska Press, 1965).
7. Jones, p. xxix.
8. Edith Birkhead, *Tale of Terror: a Study of Gothic Romance* (London: Constable and Co., 1921), p. 116.
9. Brendan Hennessey, *The Gothic Novel* (Essex: Longman Group, Ltd., 1978), p. 21.
10. Don Locke, *A Fantasy of Reason: The Life and Thought of William Godwin* (London: Routledge and Kegan Paul, 1980), p. 281.
11. Robert Kiely, *The Romantic Novel in England* (Cambridge, Mass.: Harvard University Press, 1972), p. 156.
12. Searles *et al.*, *A Reader's Guide to Science Fiction* (New York: Facts on File Inc., 1979), p. 131.
13. Muriel Spark, "Mary Shelley: a Prophetic Novelist", *The Listener*, 45 (1951), 305–306.
14. Sandra M. Gilbert and Susan Gubar, *The Madwoman in the Attic; The Woman Writer and the Nineteenth-Century Literary Imagination* (New Haven: Yale University Press, 1979), pp. 61–62.
15. Don Locke, p. 279.
16. Not surprisingly, these experiences are reflected in her work and critics such as Ellen Moers, Barbara Johnson and Anne Mellor have made much of it, by examining elements of the "birth trauma" and post partum depression in *Frankenstein*. Others, for example William

224

Veeder, have examined the psychological implications of the novel. Ellen Moers, *Literary Women*, (London: W. H. Allen, 1977), pp. 92–99. Barbara Johnson, "My Monster/My Self", in *A World of Difference* (Baltimore: Johns Hopkins University Press, 1987), pp. 144–54. Anne Mellor, *Mary Shelley: Her Life, Her Fiction, Her Monsters*, (London: Routledge, 1988). William Veeder, *Mary Shelley and Frankenstein*, (London: University of Chicago Press, 1986).

17.   Kenneth Neill Cameron, *The Young Shelley: Genesis of a Radical*, (London: Victor Gollancz, 1951), p. 62.

18.   William St. Clair, *The Godwins and the Shelleys* (London: Faber and Faber, 1989), p. 318.

19.   Cameron, p. 69.

20.   Shelley's fraught and clearly passionate relationship with her difficult father was perhaps the model for her novella *Mathilda*, with its themes of incest, guilt and death. Though *Mathilda* is interesting from a psychological point of view, it will not be discussed at length in this study for a number of reasons, in addition to that of limited space.

    Mathilda does not rank as one of Shelley's important novels; it is remarkably slim compared to her customary three-volume works of fiction. She herself, at Godwin's suggestion, decided not to publish the book – indeed, I would suggest that publication was not a serious original consideration. *Mathilda* is devoid of the professionalism which characterizes Shelley's important novels – it is undisciplined and uncomfortably personal. Most importantly, it rather deserves the evaluation that has customarily and erroneously been applied to *Frankenstein*; *Mathilda* is an uncontrolled, certainly therapeutic purge of psychological tensions and anxieties surrounding Shelley's relationship with her father. Shelley herself came to see how inappropriate it was for public consumption, unworthy to follow the distinguished *Frankenstein*.

    In some sense *Mathilda* provides that which is missing from the journals; it has the raw feelings and unbridled emotional expression that one would expect to find in an author's private writings – especially one as emotionally complex as Shelley – and which don't appear, except in a limited way after PBS's death, in Shelley's daily record.

21.   Mary Shelley, *Valperga: or, the Life and Adventures of Castruccio Prince of Lucca* (London: G. and W.B. Whittaker, 1823), Vol. III, p. 53. Hereafter, page references will be included within the body of the text.

CHAPTER 2: EARLY INFLUENCES: "A HISTORY OF THE JEWS"

1.   Frederick L. Jones, ed., *The Letters of Percy Bysshe Shelley* (Oxford: Oxford University Press, 1964), Vol. I, p. 413.

2.   See Appendix A.

3. *Queen Mab*, Canto IV, 82–83. *The Poems of Shelley*, eds, G. Matthews and K. Everest (London: Longman, 1989). Matthews and Everest point out that this is an image common to Radical literature and cite examples from Paine and Holbach, p. 301n.

This edition is used for the discussion of *Queen Mab* throughout this chapter and where possible, for PBS's poetry throughout the book. Line references will hereafter be included within the body of the text.

4. Frederick L. Jones, ed., *Mary Shelley's Journals* (Norman, Oklahoma: University of Oklahoma Press, 1947), p. 89.

5. Shelley would later record the German ghost stories that he told to the group in Geneva in 1816.

6. Robert Southey, *Poems of Robert Southey*, ed., Maurice H. Fitzgerald (Oxford: Oxford University Press, 1909), p. 58.

7. Ibid., p. 117.

8. Roger Ingpen and Walter Peck, eds, *The Complete Works of Percy Bysshe Shelley* (Oxford: Oxford University Press, 1929), Vol. VI, p. 33.

9. David Lee Clark, ed., *Shelley's Prose* (London: 1954; rpt. Fourth Estate, 1988), p. 196.

10. Southey, p. 608.

11. Marilyn Butler, *Romantics, Rebels and Reactionaries* (Oxford: Oxford University Press, 1981), p. 136.

12. Ibid.

13. Mary Shelley, *Proserpine and Midas: Two Unpublished Mythological Dramas*, ed., A. L. Koszul (London: Humphrey Milford, 1922), p. viii.

14. Mary Shelley, *Mary Shelley: Collected Tales and Stories*, ed., Charles E. Robinson (London: Johns Hopkins Press, 1976), p. 335.

15. PBS's unfinished essay was published by Claude Brew as "Miracles and Christian Doctrines" in "A New Shelley Text: Essay on Miracles and Christian Doctrines", *Keats-Shelley Memorial Bulletin*, 27 (1977), 10–28. Emily Sunstein has placed its composition sometime between late November 1820 and April 1821 in "Shelley's Answer to Leslie's *Short and Easy Method with the Deists* and Mary Shelley's Answer, "The Necessity of a Belief in the Heathen Mythology to a Christian'", *Keats-Shelley Memorial Bulletin*, 32 (1981), 49–54. The manuscript essay was published in full by A. L. Koszul in his introduction to *Proserpine and Midas* and is found here in Appendix B.

16. Ibid., p. 52.

17. Ibid., p. 51.

18. Matthews and Everest have established that *Queen Mab* was composed between April 1812 and February 1813, when PBS was 19–20 years old. The notes were written just before printing in May 1813. *Queen Mab* was first privately circulated, then published for the general public in a pirated edition in 1821.

19. At about this time Byron chose to celebrate the Jews as noble fighters for freedom in the *Hebrew Melodies* (1815), where their stubborn adherence to their faith and their martial nature is praised.

20. As further evidence of Shelley's unfamiliarity with the Bible at this time, Jephthah's campaign was waged against the Ammonites, not the Philistines.
21. Appendix B, p. 203. I have left Shelley's erratic spelling and punctuation uncorrected and unregularized to maintain the impression of the speed with which the essay was written down.
22. Lionel's feelings of regret and self-disgust are those that Shelley condemns the drunken Noah for not sharing in the "History of the Jews".
23. Jean de Palacio, *Mary Shelley dans son oeuvre* (Paris: Editions Klincksieck, 1969), p. 203.
24. Ibid.
25. Jones, *The Letters of PBS*, Vol. I., p. 261.
26. Ibid, Vol. I., pp. 269–70.
27. Constantin Francois de Chasseboeuf, comte de Volney, *The Ruins, or a Survey of the Revolutions of Empire* (London: J. Johnson, 1796), p. 37.
28. Voltaire, *La Bible enfin expliqué par Plusieurs Aumoniers (de Sa Majeste Le Roi De Prusse)* (Londres (Geneve): n.pub., 1777).
29. She also records that PBS read aloud Tacitus's description of the siege of Jerusalem on August 24, 1814, a source mentioned in the essay. Though PBS's fragmentary translation of Tacitus does not mention the Siege, it does include comment on the fierce nationalistic tendencies of the ancient Jews, a characteristic that Shelley highlights in the essay.
30. Edward Gibbon, *The History of the Decline and Fall of the Roman Empire*, ed., J. B. Bury (London: Metheun and Co., 1896), Vol. 2, pp. 2–3.
31. Jerome McGann, "The Idea of an Indeterminate Text: Blake's Bible of Hell and Dr. Alexander Geddes", *Studies in Romanticism*, 25 (Fall 1986), pp. 303–24.
32. Ibid., p. 311.
33. Alexander Geddes, ed., *The Holy Bible, or the Books Accounted Sacred by Jews and Christians; Otherwise Called the Books of the Old and New Covenants* (London: R. Faulder and J. Johnson, 1792), Vol. I, 1792, p. xix.
34. Geddes, Vol. I., p. xi.
35. Volney, p. 229.
36. Shelley does *attempt* to universalize the Hebrew stories as myth, but mars the exercise through excessive sarcasm. See Appendix A.
37. It could also be argued that this style of humour had its origins in Shelley's writings for children which Emily Sunstein has discovered in her new biography of Mary Shelley (Boston: Little, Brown and Co., 1989). Sunstein identifies "Mrs. Caroline Barnard" as a pseudonym that Shelley used to contribute children's stories to Godwin's *Juvenile Library*. Sunstein attributes (though not positively) three stories to Shelley/Mrs. Barnard. The first, *The Parent's Offering; or, Tales for Children*, she dates 1813. The other stories are from 1817 and 1819. Though Godwin's children's press was known to be of a radical

bent, the raw radicalism of the "History of the Jews" would have been too pungent for Godwin's essentially commercial project.

38. The cruelty of the God of the Hebrew Testament to his people was a theme much favoured by Byron in poems such as *Cain* (1821) and *Heaven and Earth* (1822). It also held great imaginative appeal for Mark Twain. With "Byronic" humour, Twain's nineteenth century *Letters From the Earth* satirizes Christianity as invented by man in perverse opposition to his mistaken idea of God and God's laws of nature.

39. Volney, p. 64.

40. Geddes, Vol. I, p. xvii.

41. Ibid., Vol. I, p. xviii.

42. This suggests parallels to PBS's and Peacock's fascination with the ancient Greek religion and its emphasis on life and the natural world.

43. Mary Shelley, *The Journals of Mary Shelley*, 1814–1844, eds, Paula R. Feldman and Diana Scott-Kilvert (Oxford: Oxford University Press, 1987). This edition is used throughout; hereafter, dates will be the only reference and will be included within the body of the text.

44. Shelley refers to the Israelites a number of times as "Arrabians" or "Arab" robbers. Historically of course, the Israelites were not Arabs but a separate population. In the preparation of *Valperga* and all her subsequent articles, novels and biographies Shelley's research was vast and meticulous. By the 1820s she appears to delight in accurate historical detail, which also points to the essay's early composition and her lack of dedication to its purpose.

45. Geddes, Vol. I, p. xvii.

46. " . . . A murderer heard/ His voice in Egypt, one whose gifts and arts/ Had raised him to his eminence in power,/ Accomplice of omnipotence in crime,/ And confidant of the all-knowing one." (*QM* VII, 100–104).

47. Volney, p. 29. It is interesting to note that during a time when racial prejudice was the norm, Volney identified such institutionalized ignorance as a contributing factor to the destruction of empires. The exceptional stance of Byron's *Hebrew Melodies* has already been noted. Maria Edgeworth's literary treatment of Jews in the caricature of an avaricious coachbuilder in *The Absentee* (1812) was later atoned for in her study of the irrational sources of racial prejudice in *Harrington* (1817).

48. It is worth noting however that G. Matthews has maintained that "many features of *Queen Mab* have a continuous development throughout (PBS's) subsequent work [most notable in *Laon and Cythna and Prometheus Unbound*]. Human society is always seen in a cosmic setting, and human history as inseparable from the history of stars and insects." Matthews and Everest, headnote, p. 268.

49. The principle sources for *Queen Mab* are Paine and the French materialists, particularly Holbach. Godwin's influence is rather less important. Matthews and Everest, headnote, p. 268.

CHAPTER 3: *FRANKENSTEIN* AND THE "GOOD CAUSE"

1. Christopher Small, *Ariel Like a Harpy* (London: Victor Gollancz, 1972), p. 100.
2. Mary Shelley, *Frankenstein, or, the Modern Prometheus*, ed., James Rieger (New York: Bobbs-Merrill, 1974), p. xliv.
3. Marilyn Butler, *Jane Austen and the War of Ideas* (Oxford: Clarendon Press, 1975).
4. *The Necessity of Atheism* was not inspired specifically by Godwin, rather, its origins were Hume and the French *philosophes*.
5. Gary Kelly, *The English Jacobin Novel*, 1780–1805 (Oxford: The Clarendon Press, 1976), p. 180.
6. William Godwin, *Things as They Are, or, the Adventures of Caleb Williams*, ed., David McCracken (1970; rpt, Oxford; Oxford University Press, 1982), p. viii. Hereafter the novel will be cited as *CW* and with the page reference, will be included within the body of the text.
7. Critics argue that *Caleb Williams* was also an opportunity for Godwin to modify some of his views of the preceding year.
8. William Godwin, *Enquiry Concerning Political Justice and its Influence on Morals and Happiness*, 3 vols, ed., F. E. L. Priestley (Toronto: University of Toronto Press, 1946), Vol. II., pp. 210–11. Hereafter the book will be cited as *PJ* and with the page reference, will be included within the body of the text.
9. Ronald Paulson, "Gothic Fiction and the French Revolution", *Journal of English Literary History*, 48 (1981), pp. 532–53, using a Freudian model, maintains that as a Jacobin novel, *Frankenstein* examines the implications of revolution, the French Revolution in particular. He describes the "Frankenstein syndrome" as the usurpation of the divine role of creator, the destruction of the family, property and life. He sees the novel as an allegory of the contemporaneous revolution in its focus on reason, Godwinian reason, as the single source of creation, ignoring the paternal and maternal.
10. Burton R. Pollin, "Philosophical and Literary Sources of *Frankenstein*", *Comparative Literature*, 17 (1965), pp. 97–108.
11. *Edinburgh Magazine*, 2nd Series, 2 (March 1818), 249–53.
12. Percy Bysshe Shelley, "On *Frankenstein; or the Modern Prometheus*" in *The Works of Percy Bysshe Shelley*, eds, Roger Ingpen and Walter E. Peck, (London: Ernest Benn Ltd., 1929), Vol. VI, p. 264.
13. Ibid., p. 172. More recent analysis of *Frankenstein* has addressed the particular problem of Shelley's prose style. Devon Hodges, in "*Frankenstein* and the Feminine Subversion of the Novel", *Tulsa Studies in Women's Literature*, 2 (1983), 155–64, has suggested that Shelley's problematic style is a deliberate "violation of the literary propriety" (p. 157) in an attempt to find a new feminine voice within the context of male language and literature. The stilted and patched-together nature of Shelley's prose is seen as analogous to the patched-together Monster, assembled from the pilfered segments of other bodies. Mellor on the other hand attributes some of the

inelegancies of the prose to PBS's not always superior alterations to the manuscript.

14. Don Locke, p. 280.

15. Ibid.

16. Ibid., pp. 280–81.

17. A. D. Harvey, "*Frankenstein* and *Caleb Williams*", *Keats-Shelley Journal* 29 (1980), pp. 21–27.

18. Mary Shelley, *Frankenstein, or, the Modern Prometheus*, ed., M. K. Joseph (1969; rpt, Oxford: Oxford University Press, 1984), pp. 166–67. This edition is used throughout. Hereafter, page references will appear within the body of the text. I have chosen this text for reasons of availability. The use of the 1818 text is not crucial to my purposes; where it is called for, I have indicated differences in the two texts.

19. Franco Moretti, "Dialectic of Fear" in *Signs Taken for Wonders, Essays in the Sociology of Literary Forms* (London: Verso Editions and NLB, 1983).

20. Mary Shelley and Percy Bysshe Shelley, *History of a Six Weeks' Tour through a Part of France, Switzerland, Germany, and Holland: with Letters Descriptive of a Sail round the Lake of Geneva, and of the Glaciers of Chamouni* (London: T. Hookham, Jr. and C. and J. Ollier, 1817). PBS was co-author but most of the volume was excerpted from Shelley's journal and letters.

21. Pierre Berton, *The Arctic Grail. The Quest for the North West Passage and the North Pole, 1818–1909* (New York: Viking, 1988), p. 20.

22. Shelley mentions reading *The Tempest* on October 6, 1818, nine months after *Frankenstein*'s publication. However, she apparently read "Shakespeare's works" in 1814, 15, 16 and 19 and was no doubt familiar with the play during the novel's composition.

23. Shelley and Godwin also went to visit the tomb of John Hampden in Oxford in October 1817 while *Frankenstein* was being prepared for the press.

24. As related in a letter to Hobhouse, July 29, 1810, Byron met Francis Darwin, Erasmus' son, on passage from Athens to Smyrna in March 1810. Leslie Marchand, ed., *Byron's Letters and Journals* (London: John Murray, 1973–1980), Vol. 2, p. 7.

25. *The Marriage of Heaven and Hell*, plates 5–6.

26. In his article, "Milton, Mary Shelley and Patriarchy", *Bucknell Review*, 28 (1983), 19–47, Burton Hatlen seeks to show how *Frankenstein*, as a radical text, uncovers and exposes the true radicalism of Milton's epic and strips it of the conservative interpretations that it had acquired. He maintains that the Romantics seized on *Paradise Lost* as a fundamental rejection of patriarchal power and that "*Frankenstein* represents . . . both a powerful synthesis of the responses to Milton . . . and an important step forward in the dialogue (a dialogue centred upon the themes of authority and equality) between the Romantics and Milton" (p. 24).

27. Percy Bysshe Shelley, *Zastrozzi, A Romance* (Oxford: Oxford University Press, 1986), p. 3.

28. *Lord Byron: The Complete Poetical Works*, 5 vols, ed., Jerome J. McGann

(Oxford: Clarendon Press, 1980–1986). This edition will be used throughout in discussion of all Byron's published poetry.

29. Paul Cantor, *Creature and Creator: Myth-Making and English Romanticism* (Cambridge: Cambridge University Press, 1984).

30. Ibid., p. 111.

31. Ibid., p. 117.

32. Ellen Moers, *Literary Women* (London: The Women's Press Ltd., 1978), pp. 91–92.

33. Mellor regards *Frankenstein* as a critique of revolutionary ideology, though she does not carry this line of argument into a discussion of the subsequent novels.

34. Iain Crawford, "Wading Through Slaughter: John Hampden, Thomas Gray, and Mary Shelley's *Frankenstein*", *Studies in the Novel*, 3 (Fall), 1988, 249–61.

35. After *Frankenstein* was completed and published and the Shelleys had left England for Italy, PBS urged Shelley to write a drama about Charles I. In the end, he took up the project in 1820–21, but never finished it.

36. Brown's heroine also suggests an origin for PBS's "Constantia" poems to Claire Clairmont.

37. Charles Brockden Brown, *Ormond*, ed., Ernest Marchand (London: Hafner Publishing Co., 1937), p. 148.

38. Victor's sinful presumption against God is highlighted in the editon of 1831.

39. Victor's crime is even a sin against the spirit of scientific research. His investigation began with a solution in sight. He never designed and tested hypothesis. His research was prejudiced from its inception and corrupted with his desire for its preconceived outcome.

40. St. Clair, p. 317.

41. Mary Shelley, ed., *The Works of Percy Bysshe Shelley* comprised of *The Poetical Works of Percy Bysshe Shelley* and *Essays, Letters From Abroad, Translations and Fragments* (London: Edward Moxon, 1854). Hereafter referred to as *The Poetical Works* and *Essays*

42. PBS would have added "Love" to Reason and Truth. He meant not just romantic and sexual love, but "the bond and the sanction which connects not only man with man but with everything which exists." From *Essay on Love* in *Shelley's Prose*, pp. 169–71.

43. Mellor, pp. 82–83.

44. Ibid., p. 82.

45. Readers may think of the name "Victor" as a purposeful echo of PBS's juvenile poem *Victor and Cazire* (1810), yet Shelley's selection of her protagonist's name is perhaps more sophisticated. The irony of "victor", in the context of the great failure at the heart of the novel, seems more likely and shows something of Shelley's mordant humour.

46. One is reminded of Wordsworth's 1802 Preface to *Lyrical Ballads* with its concern for the separation of the emotions and the creative-intellectual faculty, another example of the Romantic fear of the imagination, as Sandra Gilbert and Susan Gubar might point out.

47. In Shelley's short story, *The Mortal Immortal* (1834), the hero is punished for drinking the *elixir vitae* and retaining his youth while his beloved wife grows old, foolish and resentful.
48. Kiely, p. 170.
49. Cantor, p. 109.
50. Percy Bysshe Shelley, *Essay on Christianity* in *Shelley's Prose, pp. 196–214.*

CHAPTER 4: "CONNECTED IN A THOUSAND WAYS": MARY SHELLEY AND LORD BYRON

1.   Betty T. Bennett, ed., *The Letters of Mary Wollstonecraft Shelley* (London: The Johns Hopkins University Press, 1980–1988), 3 vols. All the Mary Shelley letters that I quote from or refer to are taken from this edition. Hereafter references – the date of the letter only – will be included within the body of the text.
2.   K. N. Cameron, ed., *Shelley and His Circle* (London: Oxford University Press, 1970), Vol. III, p. 408.
3.   Marchand, *Byrons Letters and Journals*, Vol. 5, p. 162
4.   Cameron., p. 401.
5.   Ibid., p. 410.
6.   Edward Trelawny (1792–1881), the Cornish adventurer and would-be Byronic corsair, who joined the Shelley circle in 1822, was fascinated by Byron's early romantic work. His own stories, which he offered as true, were so far-fetched as to be for the most part unbelievable. However, his stories were appreciated. Shelley herself was delighted with Trelawny and revelled in his curious, self-created persona for its artistic possibilities. Trelawny was also unreservedly generous to the impoverished widow and his noble behaviour and action at PBS's death, cremation and burial earned him her lifelong gratitude.
7.   Ernest Lovell, "Byron and Mary Shelley", *The Keats-Shelley Journal*, 2 (1953), 35–49.
8.   Byron's fragment was published at the end of *Mazeppa* in 1819.
9.   *Mary Shelley: Collected Tales and Stories*, p. 92.
10. It is perhaps interesting to note that Euthanasia resembles Byron's Haidée. Both have hair that nearly reaches the ground, both are associated with the radiance of dawn, and both (during the frequent extended absences of Haidée's father) represent the sole power in their respective domains.
11. Hunt's *The Story of Rimini* was published in 1816.
12. Marchand, *Byron's Letters and Journals*, Vol. 10, p. 34.
13. Iris Origo has pointed out that by 1823 however, Byron was fond of his increased wealth and confessed half-jokingly to Douglas Kinnaird, "I loves lucre". *The Last Attachment* (1949; rpt, London: John Murray, 1971), p. 328.
14. Lady Jane Shelley, ed., *Shelley and Mary* (London: Privately Printed, 1882), Vol. IV, p. 1046.

15. Shelley's Letter to Trelawny, July 28, 1824.
16. "Prince" was a courtesy title bestowed by the Turks upon a Greek who had been in their service as a local ruler in Wallachia and Moldavia, points out Marchand. *Byron's Letters and Journals*, Vol. 11, pp. 215–16.
17. Origo, p. 357.
18. Lady Jane Shelley, Vol. III, p. 601.
19. Marchand, *Byron's Letters and Journals*, Vol. 10, p. 199.
20. Butler, p. 128
21. Ibid., p. 129
22. Paula R. Feldman and Diana Scott-Kilvert, eds, *The Journals of Mary Shelley* (Oxford: Clarendon Press, 1987), Vol. I, pp. 383–84. All quotes from Mary Shelley's journal are taken from this edition. Hereafter, all references to the journal – the date of the entry – will be included within the body of the text.
23. William St. Clair, *Trelawny, the Incurable Romancer* (London: John Murray, 1977), p. 91.
24. See Appendix C.
25. Marchand, *Byron's Letters and Journals*, Vol. VI, p. 68.
26. See Appendix C.
27. Jerome McGann, *Lord Byron. The Complete Poetical Works* (Oxford: The Clarendon Press, 1986), Vol. V, p. xxii.
28. Shelley had been writing the short story *A Tale of the Passions* for the second number of the *Liberal*, January 1823, where Byron's *Heaven and Earth* also appeared.

CHAPTER 5: "THAT MASTERPIECE OF HIS MALICE": *VALPERGA*

1. The Carbonari were closely related to the Freemasons.
2. Kenneth N. Cameron, *Shelley: the Golden Years* (Harvard University Press: Cambridge, 1974), p. 116.
3. Byron's poem "Euthanasia" (1811 or 1812) may have inspired this unusual name.
4. Marilyn Butler, *Peacock Displayed* (London: Routledge and Kegan Paul, 1979), pp. 63–64.
5. To remind the reader of the presence of Dante in the book, Castruccio visits Florence as a youth and witnesses a pageant and masque depicting scenes from *The Inferno*.
6. Jones, *The Letters of PBS*, Vol. II, p. 592.
7. Godwin's letter appears as a footnote in Bennett, *Letters*, Vol. I, p. 323.
8. The Bodleian Library's Abinger Deposit contains a notebook (Dep. e. 274) of facts which Shelley collected for *Valperga*. The notes consist of military and political movements among the Italian city states for each of the years from 1282–1328. Also recorded are customs and domestic habits of the Italian aristocracy, from governmental

practices to furnishings and the details of food preparation. Shelley notes the details of the "morgincah or morning gift", presented to the bride by her husband, a tradition that figures in the breakdown of Euthanasia and Castruccio's betrothal. The volume also contains a note on the Paterins and Wilhelmina the Heretic, who becomes Beatrice's mother in the novel.

9.   On September 9, 1819, Godwin wrote a condolence letter to Shelley for the death of William. He complained that her excessive grief had caused her to forget her duty to him and his straightened finances, that she had dishonoured her name, that "You have all the goods of fortune, all the means of being useful to others . . . But . . . all is nothing, because a child of three years old is dead". Sunstein, *Mary Shelley*, p. 174.

10. Bonnie Rayford Neumann, *The Lonely Muse: A Critical Biography of Mary Wollstonecraft Shelley* Salzburg Studies in English Literature: Romantic Reassessment, Vol. 85., ed., James Hogg (Salzburg: Institut für Englische und Literatur Universität Salzburg, 1977), p. 126.

11. Jones, *The Letters of PBS*, Vol. II, p. 353.

12. Elizabeth Nitchie, *Mary Shelley, Author of Frankenstein* (Rutgers, New Jersey: Rutgers University Press, 1950), p. 110.

13. Mellor has offered an interesting discussion of fate and predestination in *Frankenstein*. She sees significant change from the edition of 1818 to 1831, predominantly in the latter's confirmation of Victor's actions as the result of fate, destiny or a greater power. By 1831 he has become a victim, rather than the author of his own evil actions.

14. It was during this Geneva summer that PBS persuaded Byron to read and appreciate Wordsworth.

15. Neumann, p. 131.

16. It is very important to note that in 1822 and 23, during the composition of *Valperga*, Shelley still identified PBS with the beliefs that he expressed in *Julian and Maddalo* (and possibly even those in *Queen Mab*). In any case, by 1819 PBS's optimism may have been somewhat modified, but it was still firm enough to oppose Byronic fatalism.

17. Thomas Moore, *Lalla Rookh* (London: George Routledge and Sons, 1891), p. 27.

18. Ibid., p. 45.

19. Mary Shelley and PBS, *History of a Six Weeks' Tour*, p. 19.

20. Percy Bysshe Shelley, *A Philosophical View of Reform* ed., T. W. Rolleston (London: Humphrey Milford, Oxford University Press, 1920), pp. 89–90.

21. Mary Shelley, *The Last Man* ed., Brian Aldiss (London: Hogarth Press, 1985), p. 116. This edition is used throughout. Hereafter page references will be included within the body of the text.

22. Once again I must stress that it is the Godwin of the earliest editions of *Political Justice* (and PBS of *Queen Mab*) that PBS is associated with in Shelley's mind. PBS modified his radical views, but not as swiftly or as extremely as Godwin.

23. William Veeder maintains that the two were fundamentally incompatible and that their relationship had begun to deteriorate as early

as 1818. He asserts, "All in all, the Shelley's marriage even before 1818 subverts Grylls' piety that 'in essentials Mary and [Percy] were at one' . . . Essentials is just where the Shelleys were at odds". *Mary Shelley and Frankenstein* (London: University of Chicago Press, 1986), p. 16.

24. Mellor, p. 208.

25. Perdita, the sister of Lionel Verney in Shelley's subsequent novel *The Last Man*, seems to occupy a character position somewhere between Euthanasia and Beatrice. She begins life as a primitive and isolated "visionary" and is gradually, but only partially cultivated and sensitized. Aware of her deficiencies, especially after the disruption of her marriage, she pushes herself, in a strikingly modern way, to grow and develop further.

26. *Blackwood's Edinburgh Magazine*, 13 (March 1823), p. 290.

27. *Shelley's Poetry and Prose*, p. 240.

28. Beatrice may also be another version of the (Percy) Shelleyan Wandering Jew. Where PBS's Ahasuerus hurls his curse back at a cruel and inflexible God, Shelley's tainted innocent, an aggressive and corrupt Ianthe, makes God himself the active creator of evil and herself the prophet and interpreter of that God.

29. The author has been identified as Cousin de Grainville.

30. Though the opening conceit is similar, the earlier novel progresses along biblical lines towards a classic apocalyptic scene and a Day of Judgement, events which never accompany Shelley's vision of the end of humanity.

31. Barbara Rigney and Gilbert and Gubar have demonstrated convincingly the Nineteenth century woman writer's pre-occupation with disease, and more especially madness. Barbara Rigney, *Madness and Sexual Politics in the Feminist Novel* (Madison, Wisconsin: University of Wisconsin Press, 1978), p. 7. Gilbert and Gubar, p. 57.

CHAPTER 6: "THIS EARTH IS NOT, NOR EVER CAN BE HEAVEN": *THE LAST MAN*

1. Mellor, p. 16.

2. Letter to Leigh Hunt, September 9, 1823.

3. Elizabeth Nitchie has remarked on the "prophetic" nature of Shelley's choice of name for the royal family.

4. Thomas Campbell, *The Poetical Works of Thomas Campbell*, ed., W. A. Hill (London: Routledge, Warne, and Routledge, 1863), p. 150.

5. Thomas Lovell Beddoes, *Plays and Poems of Thomas Lovell Beddoes*, ed., H. W. Donner (London: Routledge and Kegan Paul Ltd., 1950), p. xii.

6. Ibid., p. 116.

7. Thomas Hood, *The Complete Poetical Works Of Thomas Hood*, ed., Walter Jerrold (London: Henry Frowde, 1906), p. 42.

8. Ibid.

9. Anonymous, *The Last Man, or Omegarus and Syderia, A Romance in Futurity* (London: R. Dutton, 1806), p. 38.
10. Ibid., p. 113.
11. Emily Sunstein has pointed out that Perdita's cottage is modelled exactly on the Shelleys' home at Bishopgate near the entrance to Windsor Great Park, that they inhabited from March 1817 to January 1818. Shelley wrote to Howard Payne on September 27, 1825, "Windsor – Eton &c is the only spot of English ground for which I have an affection."
12. "Cleveland's Poems"; Mary Shelley's footnote, p. 236.
13. Lee Sterrenburg, "*The Last Man*: Anatomy of Failed Revolutions", *Nineteenth Century Fiction*, 33 (1978), p. 344.
14. Luke, p. viii.
15. Sterrenburg, p. 345.
16. Sunstein, *Mary Shelley*, p. 407.
17. Mary Shelley, *Lives of the Most Eminent Literary and Scientific Men of France*, ed., Dionysius Lardner, *The Cabinet Cyclopaedia*, Vol. 102 (London: Longman, Orme, Brown, Green, & Longman, 1838–1839), Vol. I, p. 218.
18. William Walling, *Mary Shelley* (New York: Twayne, 1972), p. 84.
19. Raymond is in this respect remarkably like the dangerously curious, ultimately foolish antiquaries of M. R. James' stories who, though their insensitivity and gauche scepticism, unleash some vengeful supernatural force.
20. Sterrenburg, p. 335.

CHAPTER 7:   CREATING A LITERARY REPUTATION

1. Godwin scolded her in a letter of November 1822 for charging too many friends with the task, leading to an embarrassing confusion. *Shelley and Mary*, Vol. III, p. 904.
2. Irving Massey's article "The First Editions of Shelley's *Poetical Works* (1839): Some MS Sources" *Keats-Shelley Journal*, 16 (1967), 29–38, illustrates clearly the difficulty of establishing definitive original sources for the poems. Kelvin Everest, in Volume I of *The Poems of Shelley* (1989), has likewise explained and demonstrated the considerable difficulty of arriving at a definitive edition of a given poem. Introduction, xii–xxxii.
3. James Barcus, ed., *Shelley: The Critical Heritage* (London: Routledge and Kegan Paul, 1975), pp. 3–4.
4. Newman Ivey White, *The Unextinguished Hearth; Shelley and His Contemporary Critics* (New York: Octagon Books, 1966), p. 162.
5. Edward John Trelawny, *Records of Shelley, Byron and the Author* (1973; rpt, Harmondsworth, Middlesex: Penguin, 1982), p. 102.
6. *The Gentleman's Magazine*, 80 (Sept. 1810), 258. "A short, but well-told tale of horror, and, if we do not mistake, not from an ordinary pen. The story is so artfully conducted that the reader cannot easily anticipate the denouement, which is conducted on the principles of

moral justice: and by placing the scene on the Continent, the Author
has availed himself of characters and vices which, however useful in
narratives of this description, thank God, are not to be found in this
country."

7. Barcus, p. 11.
8. Ibid., p. 18.
9. Reviews of some of the later works did receive favourable notices.
    While PBS's politics were condemned, his skill and imagination were
    sometimes praised.
10. *Shelley and Mary* (March 30, 1820) Vol. III., p. 488B.
11. Ibid., Vol. III., pp. 535–36.
12. White, p. 335.
13. Sunstein, *Mary Shelley*, p. 257.
14. *The Complete Poetical Works of PBS*, ed. Neville Rogers (Oxford: The
    Clarendon Press, 1972), p. xxvi.
15. Matthews and Everest, Vol. I., p. xvi.
16. *The Poetical Works of Percy Bysshe Shelley* was published in four
    volumes in 1839. Later in the same year, a single-volume "enlarged"
    edition was published. Completed in the same year, but dated
    1840, Moxon published the two-volume *Essays, Letters from Abroad,
    Translations and Fragments*.
17. Charles H. Taylor, *The Early Collected Editions of Shelley's Poems* (New
    Haven: Yale University Press, 1958), p. 45.
18. Matthews and Everest, Vol. I., p. xvii
19. *The Poetical Works*, p. v.
20. Ibid.
21. Walling, p. 133.
22. Ibid., p. 136
23. Joseph Raben, "Shelley's 'Invocation to Misery': An Expanded Text"
    Journal of English and German Philology, 65 (1966), 65–74.
24. Bennett, *Letters*, Vol.2, p. xvii.
25. White, p. 9.
26. Webb, p. 87.
27. Shelley's feelings about Harriet's death are a vexed issue. Sunstein
    believes that Shelley's feelings of guilt in relation to Harriet's suicide
    motivated all of her work and behaviour after the poet's death. Mark
    Twain, in his essay, "A Defense of Harriet Shelley" claims that a
    conspiracy on the part of the Shelley family contrived to blacken
    Harriet's name and justify the poet's desertion of her in 1814. Harriet
    Westbrook remained a sensitive subject to the Shelleys for both of
    their lives.
28. Bennett, *Letters*, Vol.2, p. 311.
29. The suit against the highly respected publisher was instigated by
    radical bookman Henry Hetherington who was forcing a principle
    in regard to discrimination against the radical press. The following
    passages of *Queen Mab* were cited in court; Canto 4, Lines 208–21,
    Canto 7, lines 84–97, 100–115, and part of PBS's second note.
30. Four conspirators of a radical plot to kill the entire Cabinet were
    found out and executed on May 1, 1820.

31.   Dunbar, pp. xv–xvi.
32.   Herbert Read, "Shelley" in *A Coat of Many Colours* (London: George Routledge and Sons, Ltd., 1945), pp. 119–28.
33.   *The Poetical Works*, p. 230.
34.   Ibid., p. 320.
35.   Sylva Norman, *The Flight of the Skylark: The Development of Shelley's Reputation* (Norman, Oklahoma: University of Oklahoma Press, 1954), pp. 144–45.
36.   *The Poetical Works*, p. 37.
37.   Ibid., p. 39.
38.   Ibid., p. 37. As mentioned, PBS was probably a year to a year and a half older than Shelley states here.
39.   Ibid., pp. 38–39.
40.   Ibid., p. 40.
41.   Ibid., p. 47.
42.   Ibid.
43.   Trelawny, p. 81
44.   *The Poetical Works*, p. 96.
45.   Ibid.
46.   Ibid.
47.   Ibid., p. 126.
48.   Ibid.
49.   Ibid., p. 127.
50.   Ibid.
51.   Ibid.
52.   Raben accuses Shelley of "suppressing" certain political poems by not including them in *Posthumous Poems*. He claims that "Similes (for Two Political Characters of 1819)", "Lines Written During the Castlereagh Administration", "Invocation to Misery" and some of the Jane Williams poems were only included in 1839 because Medwin had already published them with his earlier articles.
53.   *The Poetical Works*, pp. 127–28.
54.   Jones, *The Letters of PBS*, Vol. II, p. 102.
55.   Ibid., Vol. II, p. 372.
56.   *The Poetical Works*, p. 158.
57.   Ibid., p. 160.
58.   PBS did express some doubts. Presenting *Prometheus Unbound* to Medwin, and refering to *The Cenci* and dramatic writing in general he wrote, "I do not know if it be wise to affect variety in compositions, or whether the attempt to excel in many ways does not debar from excellence in one particular kind" (July 20, 1820). Jones, *Letters*, Vol. II, p. 219.
59.   *The Poetical Works*, pp. 278–79.
60.   Ibid., p. 279.
61.   Ibid., p. vi.
62.   Ibid,, p. 179.
63.   Ibid., p. 191.
64.   *Essays*, p. iii.
65.   Ibid., p. iv.

66. Ibid., p. vi.
67. Ibid., p. ix.
68. Ibid., p. iii.
69. Bennett, *Letters*, Vol. 2, p. xvii.

APPENDIX A: "A HISTORY OF THE JEWS"

1. (Shelley's footnote, appearing under dividing line at bottom of page 3): "fruit of this tree infused the knowledge of all evil into the hearts of our first parents which through them descended to the whole human race."
2. PBS read aloud the description of the Siege of Jerusalem in Tacitus's *History* on August 24, 1814.

APPENDIX C: BYRON'S DRAFTS AND MARY SHELLEY'S
FAIR COPIES

1. *The original (LB's)*:
   And stains it with a lifeless red
   Which clings to it like stiffened gore

   The fair copy (corrections by LB):
   Discoloured
   And stains it with a lifeless red
   stains it then
   Which clings fast like stiffened gore
   stands thereon

2. McGann, *Lord Byron, The Complete Poetical Works*, Vol. V, p. 716.

APPENDIX D: THE LATE NOVELS:
PERKIN WARBECK, LODORE and *FALKNER*

1. Muriel Spark, *Mary Shelley* (London: Constable,1987), pp. 200–201.
2. Mary Shelley, *The Fortunes of Perkin Warbeck: A Romance* (London: G. Routledge & Co., 1857), pp. 194–95.
3. Ibid., pp. 409–11.
4. Mary Shelley, *Lodore* (London: Richard Bentley, 1835), Vol. I, p. 42.
5. Ibid., Vol. I., pp. 30, 33.
6. Ibid., Vol. III, pp. 10–11.
7. Ibid., Vol. III, p. 21.
8. Ibid.
9. Ibid., Vol. III, p. 164.
10. Ibid., Vol. III, pp. 310–11.

11. Mary Shelley, *Falkner* (London: Saunders and Otley, 1837), Vol. III, pp. 56–57.
12. Ibid., Vol. II, p. 227.
13. *Perkin Warbeck*, pp. 188–89.
14. *Falkner*, Vol. I, p. 116.
15. Ibid.
16. Ibid., Vol. III, p. 305.

Bibliography

MANUSCRIPT MATERIAL

Byron, George Gordon

Draft of *Don Juan*, Canto 6. The Ashley Collection, The British Library.
Draft of *Don Juan*, Canto 7. The Ashley Collection, The British Library.
Draft of *Don Juan*, Canto 8. Harry Ransom Humanities Research Center, University of Texas at Austin.
Drafts of the *Hebrew Melodies*. The Byron-Lovelace Collection. The Bodleian Library.
Draft of *Mazeppa*. The Morgan Library, New York.
Draft of "Ode to Venice". The Morgan Library, New York.
Draft of "To the Po". The Morgan Library, New York.
Fair copy of "To the Po". The Berg Collection, New York Public Library.
Draft of *Werner*. The Morgan Library, New York.

Byron, Anne Isabella Milbanke

Fair copies of the *Hebrew Melodies*. John Murray Publishers, Ltd., London.

Shelley, Mary

Fair copy of *Don Juan*, Canto 6. John Murray Publishers, Ltd., London.
Fair copy of *Don Juan*, Canto 7. John Murray Publishers, Ltd., London.
Fair copy of *Don Juan*, Canto 8. John Murray Publishers, Ltd., London.
Draft, "History of the Jews". The Abinger Deposit, The Bodleian Library.
Fair copy of *Mazeppa*. The Brotherton Library, University of Leeds.
Fair copy of "Ode on Venice". John Murray Publishers, Ltd., London.
Notebook with research notes for *Valperga*. The Abinger Deposit, The Bodleian Library.
Fair copy of *Werner*. John Murray Publishers, Ltd., London.

PRINTED MATERIAL

Allott, Miriam. "Attitudes to Shelley: the Vagaries of a Critical Reputation". In *Essays on Shelley*. Ed., Miriam Allott. Liverpool: University of Liverpool Press, 1982.
Anastaplo, George. *The Artist as Thinker From Shakespeare to Joyce*. Athens, Ohio: Swallow Press, 1983.
Anonymous. *The Last Man, or, Omegarus and Syderia, A Romance in Futurity*. London: R. Dutton, 1806.

Bage, Robert. *Hermsprong, or Man As He Is Not*. Oxford: Oxford University Press, 1985. (First published 1796).

Baldick, Chris. *In Frankenstein's Shadow*. Oxford: Oxford University Press, 1987.

Barcus, James E. *Shelley: The Critical Heritage*. London: Routledge and Kegan Paul, 1975.

Beckford, William. *Vathek*. 1970; rpt, Oxford: Oxford University Press, 1983. (First published 1786).

Beddoes, Thomas L. *Plays and Poems of Thomas Lovell Beddoes*. Ed., H. W. Donner. London: Routledge and Kegan Paul, 1950.

Bennett, Betty T. "The Political Philosophy of Mary Shelley's Historical Novels: *Valperga* and *Perkin Warbeck*". In *The Evidence of the Imagination: Studies of Interactions Between Life and Art in English Romantic Literature*. Eds., Betty T. Bennett, Michael Jaye, Donald Reiman. New York: New York University Press, 1978.

Bigland, Eileen. *Mary Shelley*. New York: Appleton, Century, Crofts, 1959.

Birkhead, Edith. *The Tale of Terror: A Study of Gothic Romance*. London: Constable and Co., 1921.

Blackwood's Edinburgh Magazine. II (March 1818), 613–620. Review of *Frankenstein* by Walter Scott.

Bold, Alan, ed. *Byron: Wrath and Rhyme*. London: Vision, 1983.

Brown, Nathaniel. *Sexuality and Feminism in Shelley*. Cambridge, Massachusetts: Harvard University Press, 1979.

Burke, Edmund. *Reflections on the Revolution in France and on the Proceedings in Certain Societies in London Relative to That Event*. 1969; rpt, Harmondsworth, Middlesex: Penguin, 1984. (First published 1790).

Burnett, T. A. J. *The Rise and Fall of a Regency Dandy: The Life and Times of Scrope Berdmore Davies*. Oxford: Oxford University Press, 1981.

Burney, Fanny. *Evelina, or the History of a Young Lady's Entrance Into the World*. 1968; rpt, Oxford: Oxford University Press, 1985. (First published 1778).

Butler, Marilyn, ed. *Burke, Paine, Godwin and the Revolution Controversy*. Cambridge: Cambridge University Press, 1984.

——. "Druids, Bards and Twice-Born Bacchus: Peacock's Engagement With Primitive Mythology". *Keats-Shelley Memorial Bulletin*, 36 (1985), 57–76.

——. "Godwin, Burke and *Caleb Williams*". *Essays In Criticism*, 32 (1982), 237–257.

——. "Myth and Mythmaking in the Shelley Circle". *Journal of English Literary History*, 49 (1982), 50–72.

——. *Peacock Displayed: A Satirist in his Context*. London: Routledge and Kegan Paul, 1979.

——. *Romantics, Rebels and Reactionaries: English Literature and its Background 1760–1830*. Oxford: Oxford University Press, 1981.

Byron, George Gordon. *The Complete Poetical Works*. 5 vols. Ed., Jerome J. McGann. Oxford: Clarendon Press, 1980–1986.

——. *Byron's Letters and Journals*. 11 vols. Ed., Leslie Marchand. London: John Murray, 1973–1980.

——. *Poetical Works*. Ed., John Jump. 1970; rpt, Oxford: Oxford University Press, 1979. (First published 1904, ed., Frederick Page).

Cameron, Kenneth Neill. *Shelley: the Golden Years*. Cambridge: Harvard University Press, 1974.

——, ed. *Shelley and His Circle*. Vol. III. London: Oxford University Press, 1970.

Cantor, Paul. *Creature and Creator: Myth-Making and English Romanticism*. Cambridge: C.U.P., 1984.

Clairmont, Claire. *The Journals of Claire Clairmont*. Ed., Marion Stocking. Cambridge: Harvard University Press, 1968.

Claridge, Laura P. "Parent-Child Tensions in *Frankenstein*: The Search for Communion". *Studies in the Novel*, 17 (1985), 14–26.

Crawford, Iain. "Wading Through Slaughter: John Hampden, Thomas Gray, and Mary Shelley's *Frankenstein*". *Studies in the Novel*, 20 (1988), 249–261.

Defoe, Daniel. *A Journal of the Plague Year*. London: J. M. Dent and Co., 1953. (First published 1722).

Disraeli, Benjamin. *Venetia*. London: David Bryce, 1853.

Dunbar, Clement. *A Bibliography of Shelley Studies: 1823–1950*. New York: Garland Publishing, 1976.

Dunn, Jane. *Moon in Eclipse: A Life of Mary Shelley*. London: Weidenfeld and Nicolson, 1978.

Edgeworth, Maria. *The Absentee*. London: Baldwin and Craddock, 1833. (First published 1812).

——. *Belinda*. London: Pandora Press, 1986. (First published 1811).

——. *Castle Rackrent*. 1964; rpt, Oxford: Oxford University Press, 1981. (First published 1800).

——. *Harrington*. London: Baldwin and Craddock, 1833. (First published 1817).

——. *Ormond. A Tale*. London: Blackie and Son, 1904. (First published 1817).

Eliot, George. *Romola*. Philadelphia: Porter and Coates, n.d. (First published 1862–3).

Everest, Kelvin, ed. *Shelley Revalued: Essays From the Gregynog Conference*. Leicester: Leicester University Press, 1983.

Ferrier, Susan. *Marriage*. 1971; rpt, Oxford: Oxford University Press, 1986. (First published 1818).

Fleck, P. D. "Mary Shelley's Notes to Shelley's Poems and *Frankenstein*". *Studies in Romanticism*, 6 (1967), 226–254.

Gates, Eleanor M. "Leigh Hunt, Lord Byron and Mary Shelley: The Long Goodbye". *Keats-Shelley Journal*, 35 (1986), 149–167.

Geddes, Alexander, ed. *The Holy Bible, or the Books Accounted Sacred by Jews and Christians; Otherwise Called the Books of the Old and New Covenants*. 2 vols. London: R. Faulder and J. Johnson, 1792 and 1796.

Gilbert, Sandra M. and Gubar, Susan. *The Madwoman in the Attic. The Woman Writer and the Nineteenth-Century Literary Imagination*. New Haven: Yale University Press, 1979.

Godwin, William. *Caleb Williams*. 1970; rpt, Oxford: Oxford University Press, 1982. (First published 1794).

——. *Enquiry Concerning Political Justice*. 3 vols. Ed. F. E. L. Priestley. Toronto: University of Toronto Press, 1946.

——. *Fleetwood: or, The New Man of Feeling*. 3 Vols. London: Richard Phillips, 1805.
Goethe, Johann Wolfgang von. *The Sorrows of Werther*. London: John K. Chapman and Co., 1851. (First published 1774).
Grylls, Glynn. *Mary Shelley, A Biography*. London: Oxford University Press, 1938.
Hatlin, Burton. "Milton, Mary Shelley and Patriarchy". *Bucknell Review*, 28 (1983), 19–47.
Harvey, A. D. "*Frankenstein* and *Caleb Williams*". *Keats-Shelley Journal*, 29 (1980), 21–27.
Hays, Mary. *Memoirs of Emma Courtney*. London: Pandora Press, 1987. (First published 1796).
Hodges, Devon. "*Frankenstein* and the Feminine Subversion of the Novel". *Tulsa Studies in Women's Literature*, 2 (1983), 155–164.
Hood, Thomas. *The Complete Poetical Works of Thomas Hood*. Ed., Walter Jerrold. London: Henry Frowde, 1906.
Hunt, Leigh. *Lord Byron and Some of His Contemporaries With Recollections of the Author's Life, and of His Visit to Italy*. London: Henry Colburn, 1828.
Inchbald, Elizabeth. *A Simple Story*. London: Pandora Press, 1987. (First published 1791).
Joannides, Paul. "Colin, Delacroix, Byron and the Greek War of Independence". *Burlington Magazine*, 125 (1983), 495–500.
Kelly, Gary. *The English Jacobin Novel 1780–1805*. Oxford: Clarendon Press, 1976.
Ketterer, David. *Frankenstein's Creation: The Book, The Monster and Human Reality*. Victoria, Canada: University of Victoria Press, 1979.
Kiely, Robert. *The Romantic Novel in England*. Cambridge: Harvard University Press, 1972.
King-Hele, Desmond. *Shelley: His Thought and Work*. London: Macmillan, 1984.
Leighton, Angela. *Elizabeth Barrett Browning*. Brighton: The Harvester Press, 1986.
Levine, George and Knoepflmacher, U. C., eds. *The Endurance of Frankenstein*. London: University of California Press, 1979.
Lewis, Matthew. *The Monk*. 1973; rpt, Oxford: Oxford University Press, 1986. (First published 1796).
Locke, Don. *A Fantasy of Reason. The Life and Thought of William Godwin*. London: Routledge and Kegan Paul, 1980.
Lovell, Ernest J. "Byron and Mary Shelley". *Keats-Shelley Journal*, 2 (1953), 35–49.
Lyles, W. H. *Mary Shelley: An Annotated Bibliography*. London: Garland Publishing, 1975.
Marchand, Leslie. *Byron: A Portrait*. London: Futura Publications, 1976.
Massey, Irving. "The First Editions of Shelley's *Poetical Works* (1839): Some Manuscript Sources". *Keats-Shelley Journal*, 16 (1967), 29–38.
——. "Shelley's "Music, When Soft Voices Die": Text and Meaning". *Journal of English and German Philology*, 59 (1960), 430–438.
——. *Posthumous Poems of Shelley, Mary Shelley's Fair Copy Book. Bodleian MS. Shelley adds. d. 9*. Montreal: McGill-Queen's University Press, 1969.

Maurois, Andre. *Ariel, A Shelley Romance.* Trans. Ella D'Arcy. 1924; rpt, London: Bodley Head, 1950. (First published 1923).

Mayne, Ethel Colburn. *The Life and Letters of Anne Isabella, Lady Noel Byron.* New York; Charles Scribner's Sons, 1929.

McGann, Jerome J. "The Idea of an Indeterminate Text: Blake's Bible of Hell and Dr. Alexander Geddes". *Studies in Romanticism,* 25 (1986), 303–324.

———. *The Romantic Ideology: a Critical Investigation.* London: University of Chicago Press, 1983.

Mellor, Anne. *Mary Shelley: Her Life, Her Fiction, Her Monsters.* London: Routledge, 1988.

Milner, M. H. *Frankenstein: or the Man and the Monster.* In *Lacy's Acting Editions of Plays.* Vol. 75. London: Thomas Hailes Lacy, 1850.

Moers, Ellen. *Literary Women.* London: The Women's Press, 1978.

Moore, Helen. *Mary Wollstonecraft Shelley.* Philadelphia: Lippincott, 1886.

Moore, Thomas. *Lalla Rookh.* London: George Routledge and Sons, 1891. (First published 1817).

Moretti, Franco. "Dialectic of Fear". In *Signs Taken for Wonders, Essays in the Sociology of Literary Forms.* London: Verso Editions and NLB, 1983.

Nitchie, Elizabeth. *Mary Shelley, Author of Frankenstein.* New Jersey: Rutgers University Press, 1953.

Neumann, Bonnie Rayford. *The Lonely Muse: A Critical Biography of Mary W. Shelley.* Salzburg Studies in English Literature/Romantic Reassessment. Ed., James Hogg. Vol. 85. Institut für Englische Sprache und Literatur Universität Salzburg, 1979.

Norman, Sylva. *Flight of the Skylark: The Development of Shelley's Reputation.* Oklahoma: University of Oklahoma Press, 1954.

———. "Mary Shelley: Novelist and Dramatist". In *On Shelley.* Oxford: Oxford University Press, 1938.

Oates, Joyce Carol. "Frankenstein's Fallen Angel". *Critical Inquiry,* 10 (1984), 543–554.

Origo, Iris. "The Innocent Miss Francis and the Truly Noble Lord Byron". *Keats-Shelley Journal,* I (1952), 1–9.

———. *The Last Attachment.* 1949; rpt, London: John Murray, 1971.

Paine, Thomas. *The Age of Reason.* In *The Theological Works of Thomas Paine.* London: R. Carlile, 1818. (First published 1794).

———. *The Rights of Man.* London: J. M. Dent and Sons, 1954. (First published 1791–2).

Palacio, Jean de. *Mary Shelley dans son oeuvre.* Paris: Editions Klincksieck, 1969.

Palmer, David. *Shelley: His Reputation and Influence.* Sheffield University Thesis, 1982.

Paulson, Ronald. "Gothic Fiction and the French Revolution". *Journal of English Literary History,* 48 (1981), 532–553.

Peacock, Thomas Love. *Nightmare Abbey and Crotchet Castle.* 1969; rpt, Harmondsworth, Middlesex: Penguin, 1986. (First published 1818 and 1831).

Pollin, Burton R. "Philosophical and Literary Sources of Frankenstein". *Comparative Literature,* 17 (1965), 97–108.

Poovey, Mary. *The Proper Lady and the Woman Writer. Ideology as Style in the Works of Mary Wollstonecraft, Mary Shelley and Jane Austen*. Chicago: University of Chicago Press, 1984.

Powers, Catherine R. *The Influence of William Godwin on the Novels of Mary Shelley*. New York: Arno Press, 1980.

Raben, Joseph. "Shelley's "Invocation to Misery": An Expanded Text". *Journal of English and German Philology*, 65 (1966), 65–74.

Radcliffe, Ann. *The Mysteries of Udolpho*. 1966; rpt, Oxford: Oxford University Press, 1984. (First published 1794).

Railo, Eino. *The Haunted Castle: A Study of the Elements of English Romanticism*. London: Routledge, 1927.

Randel, Fred V. "*Frankenstein*, Feminism, and the Intertextuality of Mountains". *Studies in Romanticism*, 23 (1984), 515–532.

Read, Herbert. "Shelley". In *A Coat of Many Colours*. London: George Routledge and Sons, 1945.

Reiman, Donald R, ed. *The Romantics Reviewed: Shelley, Keats and London Radical Writers. Contemporary Reviews of British Romantic Writers*. Part C. London: Garland, 1972.

Rieger, James. "Shelley's Paterin Beatrice". *Studies in Romanticism*, 4 (1965), 169–184.

Rigney, Barbara Hill. *Madness and Sexual Politics in the Feminist Novel*. Madison: University of Wisconsin Press, 1978.

Robinson, Charles E. *Shelley and Byron: the Snake and the Eagle Wreathed in Flight*. London: Johns Hopkins University Press, 1976.

de Sade, Donatien Alphonse, Comte. *Justine, or the Misfortunes of Virtue*. Trans. Alan Hull Walton. London: Corgi, 1965. (First published 1791).

Schenk, Hans George. *The Mind of the European Romantics*. Oxford: Oxford University Press, 1979.

Scott, Walter. *Waverley*. 1972; rpt, Harmondsworth, Middlesex: Penguin, 1985. (First published 1814).

el-Shatar, Safaa. *The Novels of Mary Shelley*. Salzburg Studies in English Literature/ Romantic Reassessment. Ed., James Hogg. Vol. 59. Institut für Englische Sprache und Literatur Universität Salzburg, 1977.

Shelley, Lady Jane, ed. *Shelley and Mary*. 4 vols. London: privately printed, 1882.

Shelley, Mary Wollstonecraft. *Collected Tales and Stories*. Ed., Charles E. Robinson. London: Johns Hopkins University Press, 1976.

——. *Falkner*. London: Saunders and Otley, 1837.

——. *Frankenstein*. Ed., M. K. Joseph. 1969; rpt, Oxford: Oxford University Press, 1984. (First published 1818).

——. *Frankenstein*. Ed., James Rieger. New York: Bobbs-Merrill, 1974.

——. *History of a Six Weeks' Tour Through a part of France, Switzerland, Germany and Holland; with Letters Descriptive of a Sail Round the Lake of Geneva, and of the Glaciers of Chamouni*. London: T. Hookham, Jun. and C. and J. Ollier, 1817.

——. *The Journals of Mary Shelley 1814–1844*. 2 vols. Eds., Paula R. Feldman and Diana Scott-Kilvert. Oxford: Clarendon Press, 1987.

——. *Mary Shelley's Journals*. Ed., Frederick L. Jones. Norman: University of Oklahoma Press, 1947.

——. *The Last Man*. London: Henry Colburn, 1826.

——. *The Last Man*. Ed., Brian Aldiss. London: Hogarth, 1985.

——. *The Last Man*. Ed., Hugh J. Luke, Jr. Lincoln: University of Nebraska Press, 1965.

——. *The Letters of Mary Wollstonecraft Shelley*. 3 vols. Ed., Betty T. Bennett. London: Johns Hopkins University Press, 1980–1988.

——. *The Letters of Mary Wollstonecraft Shelley*. Ed., Frederick L. Jones. Norman: University of Oklahoma Press, 1954.

——. *Lives of the Most Eminent Literary and Scientific Men of Italy, Spain and Portugal*. Vols 86, 87 and 88 of The Cabinet of Biography. Ed., the Rev. Dionysius Lardner (*Lardner's Cabinet Cyclopaedia*) . London: Longman, Orme, Brown, Green and Longman; and John Taylor, 1835, 1837.

——. *Lives of the Most Eminent Literary and Scientific Men of France*. Vols 102 and 103 of *The Cabinet Biography*. Ed., the Rev. Dionysius Lardner (*Lardner's Cabinet Cyclopaedia*). London: Longman, Orme, Brown, Green and Longman; and John Taylor, 1838–1839.

——. *Lodore*. London: Richard Bentley, 1835.

——. "Madame D'Houtetôt". *The Liberal: Verse and Prose from the South*. 2 (1823), 67–83.

——. *Mathilda*. Ed., Elizabeth Nitchie. Chapel Hill: University of North Carolina Press, 1959.

——. "On Ghosts". *The London Magazin*, 9 (1824), 253–256.

——. *Perkin Warbeck*. London: George Routledge, 1857. (First published 1830).

——. *Proserpine and Midas: Two Unpublished Mythological Dramas*. Ed., A. Koszul. London: Humphrey Milford, 1922.

——. *Rambles in Germany and Italy in 1840, 1842 and 1843*. London: Edward Moxon, 1844.

——. "A Tale of the Passions". *The Liberal: Verse and Prose From the South* 2 (1823), 289–325.

——. *Valperga, or the Life and Adventures of Castruccio, Prince of Lucca*. London: G. and W. B. Whittaker, 1823.

Shelley, Percy Bysshe. *The Poems of Shelley*. Eds., Geoffrey Matthews and Kelvin Everest. Vol. 1. London: Longman, 1989.

——. *Essay on Christianity*. In *Shelley's Prose or the Trumpet of a Prophecy*. Ed., David Lee Clark. 1954; rpt London: Fourth Estate, 1988.

——. *A Philosophical View of Reform*. Ed., T. W. Rolleston. London: Humphrey Milford, Oxford University Press, 1920.

——. *Posthumous Poems of Percy Bysshe Shelley*. Ed. Mary Shelley. London: John and Henry L. Hunt, 1824.

——. *The Letters of Percy Bysshe Shelley*. Ed., Frederick L. Jones. Oxford: Clarendon Press, 1964.

——. *Shelley's Poetry and Prose*. Eds., Donald H. Reiman and Sharon B. Powers. New York: W. W. Norton, 1977.

——. *The Works of Percy Bysshe Shelley*. Ed., Mary Shelley. 1839; rpt, London: Moxon, 1854.

——. *Zastrozzi and St. Irvyne*. Oxford: Oxford University Press, 1986. (First published 1810 and 1811).

Simpson, David the Rev. *Essay on the Authenticity of the New Testament:*

Designed as an Answer to Evanson's Dissonance and Volney's Ruins. Macclesfield: n.pub., 1793.

Small, Christopher. *Ariel Like a Harpy.* London: Victor Gollancz, 1972.

Smith, Robert *et al. The Shelley Legend.* New York: Charles Scribner's Sons, 1945.

Snyder, Robert Lance. "Apocalypse and Indeterminacy in Mary Shelley's *The Last Man*". *Studies in Romanticism,* 17 (1978), 435–452.

Solomon, Barbara H. and Berggren, Paula S. *A Mary Wollstonecraft Reader.* New York: Mentor Books, 1983.

Southey, Robert. *Poems of Robert Southey.* Ed., Maurice Fitzgerald. Oxford: Oxford University Press, 1909.

Spacks, Patricia Meyer. *The Female Imagination.* London: George Allen and Unwin, 1976.

Spark, Muriel. *Child of Light: a Reassessment of Mary Wollstonecraft Shelley.* Hadleigh, Essex: Tower Bridge, 1951.

——. *Mary Shelley.* London: Constable, 1988.

——. "Mary Shelley: A Prophetic Novelist". *The Listener,* 45 (1951), 305–306.

—— and Stanford, Derek. *My Best Mary.* London: Allan Wingate, 1953.

Spender, Dale. *Mothers of the Novel.* London: Pandora, 1986.

Sterrenburg, Lee. "*The Last Man*: Anatomy of Failed Revolutions". *Nineteenth Century Fiction,* 33 (1978), 324–347.

St. Clair, William. *The Godwins and the Shelleys.* London: Faber and Faber, 1989.

——. *Trelawny, The Incurable Romancer.* London: John Murray, 1977.

Strout, A. L. "*Maga,* Champion of Shelley". *Studies in Philology,* 24 (1932), 95–119.

——. "Lockhart, Champion of Shelley". *Times Literary Supplement,* 12 August (1955), 468.

Sunstein, Emily. "Shelley's Answer to Leslie's *Short and Easy Method with the Deists* and Mary Shelley's answer, 'The Necessity of a Belief in the Heathen Mythology to a Christian'". *Keats-Shelley Memorial Bulletin,* 32 (1981), 49–54.

——. *Mary Shelley: Romance and Reality.* Boston: Little, Brown and Co., 1989.

Taylor, Charles H. *The Early Collected Editions of Shelley's Poems: A Study in the History and Transmission of the Printed Text.* London: Oxford University Press, 1958.

——. "The Errata Leaf to Shelley's *Posthumous Poems* and Some Surprising Relationships Between the Earliest Collected Editions". *PMLA,* 70 (1955), 408–416.

Thomas, Gordon. "Wordsworth, Byron and 'Our Friend the Storyteller'" *Dutch Quarterly Review of Anglo-American Letters,* 13 (1983), 200–212.

Trelawny, Edward John. *Records of Shelley, Byron and the Author.* 1973; rpt. Harmondsworth, Middlesex: Penguin, 1982. (First published 1858).

Twain, Mark. "In Defence of Harriett Shelley". In *In Defence of Harriett Shelley and Other Essays.* New York: Harper and Bros, 1918.

——. *Letters From the Earth.* Ed., Bernard Devoto. New York: Harper and Row, 1962.

Veeder, William. *Mary Shelley and Frankenstein*. London: University of Chicago Press, 1986.

Volney, Constantin Francois de Chasseboeuf, comte de. *The Ruins, or a Survey of the Revolutions of Empires*. London: J. Johnson, 1796.

Voltaire. *La Bible enfin expliquée par Plusiers Aumoniers [de Sa Majeste Le Roi de Prusse]* Londres [Geneva]: n.pub., 1777, 76.

——. *Zadig and Other Tales*. Trans. Robert Bruce Boswell. London: George Bell and Sons, 1891.

Walling, William. *Mary Shelley*. New York: Twayne, 1972.

Walpole, Horace, *The Castle of Otranto*. 1964; rpt, Oxford: Oxford University Press, 1986. (First published 1764).

Watkins, Daniel P. "Politics and Religion in Byron's Heaven and Earth". *The Byron Journal*, 11 (1983), 30–39.

Webb, Timothy. *Shelley: A Voice Not Understood*. Manchester: Manchester University Press, 1977.

——. *The Violet in the Crucible: Shelley and Translation*. Oxford: Clarendon Press, 1976.

White, Newman Ivey. *The Unextinguished Hearth: Shelley and His Contemporary Critics*. New York: Octagon Books, 1966.

—— et al., eds. *An Examination of the Shelley Legend*. Philadelphia: University of Pennsylvania Press, 1951.

Wordsworth, Jonathan. *William Wordsworth: the Borders of Vision*. 1982; rpt, Oxford: Clarendon Press, 1984.

Index

Notes: (1) Mary Shelley's works are entered under their titles. Significant works by other authors are entered under their names. (2) Most references are to Mary Shelley, unless otherwise stated. (3) The following abbreviations are used: MS – Mary Shelley; PBS – Percy Bysshe Shelley; LB – Lord Byron.

myth, Bible as, 11–12, 14, 22–6,
    45–6

Naples, 79
Napoleon, 49–50, 52, 77
nationalism *see* patriotism and
    nationalism
nature
    unaffected by man's demise,
        121–2, 144
    see also sublime
Neumann, Bonnie, 82, 90
Nitchie, Elizabeth, 2, 84, 97, 119
noble savage idea rejected, 51, 97
Norman, Sylva, 171

Ollier, Charles, 156, 164, 178
optimism
    of Godwin, 36–7, 48
    MS's lack of *see* pessimism
Origo, Iris, 69
Ovid, 16, 41, 44

paganism and Christianity in
    Valperga, 102–3
Paine, Thomas, 7, 16, 22, 25–6, 28,
    79, 111
    Age of Reason, 23, 165
    Rights of Man, 42
Palacio, Jean de, 3, 19
Palmer, David, 165
Paracelsus, 96
patriotism and nationalism
    in *Valperga*, 87–8, 91–2
    and violence, 17–18
Peacock, Thomas Love, 15, 70, 81,
    156, 160, 164, 177–9
peasantry degraded, 94
Peel, Sir Robert, 167
perfectibility, 31, 36, 48–9, 106, 140
    parodied *see Frankenstein*
Perkin Warbeck (MS), 1, 117, 216–19
pessimism, 4–5, 54–5, 56, 186
    see also Frankenstein; grief; *Last
        Man*; *Valperga*
Peterloo, 165, 166
philosophy, 172–3, 175–6
Pitt, William, 34
plague *see Last Man*

Plutarch, 21, 51
Polidori, John, 62
politics and government, 77–8, 182
    attacked by Godwin *see Political
        Justice under* Godwin
    Frankenstein as political novel, 32
    Last Man as political novel, 114,
        134–6, 139, 153, 183
    and *Posthumous Poems*, 164–5,
        166–7, 177
    Valperga as political novel,
        76–7, 82
    see also revolution
Pollin, Burton, 37, 41
Poovey, Mary, 3, 31
Posthumous Poems (of PBS by MS),
    1, 15, 117, 156–85, 186
    suppression attempts by Sir
        William Shelley 138, 156,
        160, 161
power, 40, 84, 89
Prometheus, 5, 44–7
    see also Prometheus Unbound under
        Shelley, Percy Bysshe
prophetic book *see Last Man*
pursuit as theme, 38–40

Raben, Joseph, 163–4, 169
Radcliffe, Ann, 13, 41, 105
radicalism criticised, 12, 188
    see also Frankenstein; Last Man
rationality/rationalism, 31
    parodied *see Frankenstein*
Read, Herbert, 167
reading *see* learning and reading
religion
    and cruelty, 14, 18, 28–9, 44
    other than Judæo-Christian,
        13–14, 22, 203–5
    Satan and God, 43–4, 47
    see also Christianity; "His-
        tory of the Jews";
        Jews
republicanism, 6, 87, 140–3
responsibility for writing denied *see*
    visions
revolution, 137, 188
    France, 6, 19, 32–3, 42–3, 51–2,
        136–7, 188